A New Herodotos

Supplements to the
Dumbarton Oaks Medieval Library

A New Herodotos:
Laonikos Chalkokondyles on the Ottoman Empire,
the Fall of Byzantium, and the Emergence of the West
Anthony Kaldellis

Supplement to DOML 33–34

The Histories
Laonikos Chalkokondyles
Translated by Anthony Kaldellis
published by Harvard University Press

SUPPLEMENTS TO THE
DUMBARTON OAKS MEDIEVAL LIBRARY

A New Herodotos

LAONIKOS CHALKOKONDYLES
on the Ottoman Empire,
the Fall of Byzantium,
and the Emergence of the West

ANTHONY KALDELLIS

DUMBARTON OAKS RESEARCH LIBRARY AND COLLECTION
WASHINGTON, D.C.

19   18   17   16   15   14   1   2   3   4   5   6

Library of Congress Cataloging-in-Publication Data

Kaldellis, Anthony.
   A new Herodotos : Laonikos Chalkokondyles on the Ottoman Empire,
the fall of Byzantium, and the emergence of the West / Anthony Kaldellis.
   —First edition.
      pages cm.—(Supplements to the Dumbarton Oaks medieval library)
      Includes bibliographical references.
         ISBN 978-0-88402-401-9
1. Byzantine Empire—History—1081–1453.
2. Chalkokondyles, Laonikos, approximately 1430–approximately 1490.
3. Greece—History—323–1453.
4. Turkey—History—1288–1453.
5. Civilization, Western—History.
6. Christianity and other religions—Islam.
7. Islam—Relations—Christianity.
I. Title.
      DF601.K35 2014
      949.5'04–dc23
                        2014014253

Text composition: Melissa Tandysh

www.doaks.org/publications

To Carolina, Alfonso, Rafael, Ana Laura, and Jose Antonio,
for the experience of new worlds, and their patience

Contents

Preface and Acknowledgments

This is a not another book on Herodotos, but a book on another Herodotos: Laonikos (né Nikolaos) Chalkokondyles, an Athenian born in ca. 1430 who studied under the Platonist philosopher Plethon at Mistra and who wrote a monumental history in classical Greek of the fall of Byzantium and the rise of the Ottoman Empire. He knew Latin, probably Italian, and possibly Turkish, and his *Histories* combines Byzantine, Ottoman, and western European historical traditions. Simply put, Laonikos is one of the most fascinating historians of all time, with a unique outlook on history and the world around him, but he is also one of the least known. Due to an error made a century ago, his work was dated to ca. 1490, making him the last of the Greek historians of the Fall. It is now clear, however, that he was writing his *Histories* in the 1450s and finished in the mid-1460s,[1] which puts him in a different relationship with his Italian, Greek, and Turkish peers and also much closer to the events he recounts.

Laonikos can and should be claimed by many fields, not just Byzantium. After all, he shows no attachment to the history, leadership, political ideology, or religion of Byzantium and dedicated

---

1   H. Wurm, and E. Gamillscheg, "Bemerkungen zu Laonikos Chalkokondyles," *JÖB* 42 (1992): 213–19, brought the date down to 1469–70; A. Kaldellis, "The Date of Laonikos Chalkokondyles' *Histories*," *GRBS* 52 (2012): 111–36, down to the mid-1460s, no later than 1468 (the problem involves events in Bohemia, and is now definitively solved).

himself to producing an impartial and sober history of the past, even though it included the ruin of his own people, whom he calls the Greeks, and the rise of their conquerors, the Ottoman Turks. He has no discernable religious bias, an amazing feat for the fifteenth century, but one that makes better sense when we understand his intellectual formation. I list here some of the features of the *Histories* that should prove attractive to scholars and students in various fields.

- *Classical studies*: Laonikos self-consciously set out to write a new Herodotos for his world, using predominantly oral sources, but he recast them through a Thucydidean style of writing and severity of expression. His *Histories* is accordingly modeled structurally and in its digressions on Herodotos, but stylistically on Thucydides. He also revived some of the ways by which his two predecessors viewed the world and presented themselves as authors.
- *Early Ottoman history*: The main theme of the *Histories* is the expansion of the early Ottoman Empire, not the collapse of Byzantium, which is treated incidentally. This book will argue that Laonikos used authentic Turkish sources and should be treated as a primary source both for the events themselves and also for how they were viewed by mid-fifteenth-century Turks, his informants. Because of his recently established earlier date, Laonikos emerges as one of the first sources to discuss important aspects of the organization of the Ottoman imperial system.
- *Western perceptions of Islam*: Laonikos stands to make a crucial contribution to this timely topic. Part of his Herodotean project entailed discussing the history and ethnography of all peoples from an objective point of view. He is the first Greek author to describe Islam as a living culture, rather than a theological error, and to view Muslims on their own terms, not in relation

to the Christian world, as does most Byzantine and western medieval literature. Laonikos does not reflect a Christian outlook, nor does he view Muslims through a Christian lens.

- *Renaissance and early modern Europe*: The *Histories* offers ethnographic digressions and historical interludes that cover most of Europe. These do not offer new information, but make him the first Greek author to try to make sense of emerging Europe in the early modern period. Moreover, in using Herodotos as his template, Laonikos was far ahead of the western humanists in developing new ways of representing otherness. His work, which was quickly disseminated, translated, and absorbed in the west, became a major source for views of the Turks and a model for the revival of classical historiography and ethnography.

- *Modern Greek Studies*: Laonikos was a student of Plethon, a Platonist who had advocated a return to Greek identity and paganism (the Byzantines, by contrast, had been Romans and Christians). The *Histories* codifies Plethon's vision on the historical level, by arguing that the Byzantines had been Greeks all along. The two thinkers launched a project of positive (rather than defensive) Neohellenism that ultimately shaped modern Greek identity, especially in its diasporic forms before the Revolution of 1821, when it came "home" to roost.

These strands are all interconnected, and when we pull on one the rest begin to unravel as well. To take the most striking, Laonikos's neutral and even positive discussion of Islam and recognition that Muslims have to be seen on their own terms and not in relation to Christianity was a function of his Herodotean project of ethnography and respect for the customs of others. It was also a function of his break from the Byzantine tradition, including its Roman imperial and Christian past, and his hope that a new Greek nation defined by its own national culture would one day emerge. Laonikos self-consciously set out to model himself on his ancient predecessor Herodotos and to interview native informants about the history of their own people. This, in turn, required him to set aside many of the prejudices of his native culture. He was assisted in this by Plethon, who had previously conjured a "new Hellenic" way of looking at the world.

There is nothing quite like the *Histories* in either Byzantine, humanist, or Ottoman literature. Laonikos should be situated at the intersection of all those traditions, engaged in his own, distinctive project. His neglect in recent times stems from his difficult Greek style, which is sometimes almost impossible to penetrate, and the lack of any complete or reliable translation into any of the major languages of historical research. This monograph accompanies a translation of the *Histories* in the Dumbarton Oaks Medieval Library (2014). I will quote the *Histories* here from that translation and cite the text by the book and chapter numbers that I have devised for the DOML edition. The corresponding volume and page numbers of the Darkó edition, which is inaccessible but used by scholars as a standard for citing the text, are given in the concordance at the back of this volume.

While this study stands alone, it functions also as a joint sequel to two other books, my *Hellenism in Byzantium* (2007) and *Ethnography after Antiquity* (2013). This trilogy explores interlinked facets of Byzantine identity and the representation of both internal and external "others." The present book was essentially completed in 2011 and its publication postponed to coincide with the release of the translation. I have generally not cited works that appeared later. Special mention must be made of Aslihan Akışık's stimulating dissertation, "Self and Other in the Renaissance: Laonikos Chalkokondyles and Late Byzantine Intellectuals" (Harvard University, 2013), which offers, among other things, a distinctive view of Laonikos's context and audience. Two other dissertations are said to be in progress, all of which promise a Renaissance in the study of Laonikos.

The fifteenth century is not a period in which I normally publish. There has been a steep learning curve, and I have incurred many debts. For help with the most difficult passages of the Greek, I thank Charis Messis as well as the expert team of careful reviewers assigned this onerous task by DOML: Richard Greenfield, John Duffy, Niels Gaul, and of course Alice-Mary Talbot. All made important corrections and valuable suggestions for improving the translation. My collaborator on the commentary that will accompany the full translation is Ian Mladjov, who knows all people, places, events, and spelling systems. I have benefited from an extraordinarily useful set of corrections and suggestions by Marios Philippides, who knows this period like no other. I have also pestered many colleagues with questions that stem from the wide range of information in Laonikos. I thank, for their patience, advice, and references to obscure texts and publications: Aslihan Akışık, Patrick Baker, Daniele Bianconi, Stephanos Efthymiades, Bruce Fudge, Thierry Ganchou, Tim Greenwood, Walter Hanak, Jane Hathaway, Han Lamers, Scott Levi, Tim Miller, David Nirenberg, Inmaculada Pérez Martín, Parvaneh Pourshariati, Steve Rapp, Dean Sakel, Stefan Stantchev, Rudolf Stefec, Niketas Siniossoglou, Vasileios Syros, Julia Verkholantsev, and Diana Wright. Finally, I thank my daughter Sarah, whose fantastic sleeping habits made possible the translation of Laonikos, as well as this book.

From Nikolaos to Laonikos

The Life of Nikolaos Chalkokondyles

There are only a handful of events in the life of Nikolaos Chalkokondyles that we can date securely, and those relate mostly to his early life, before he was twenty. After 1447, we have to make inferences. First, a note on his names. It is clear from Kyriacus's testimony (see below) that our author's given name was Nikolaos.[1] "Laonikos," which reverses its elements, was an assumed name. I will therefore call the historical person Nikolaos and the author Laonikos (but only here). It was not uncommon in this period to take on stylized names. Nikolaos's teacher, the great philosopher Georgios Gemistos, took on the name Plethon to evoke Platon

---

1   The family's last name is spelled in a wide variety of ways: D. Kampouroglous, *Οἱ Χαλκοκονδύλαι* (Athens, 1926), 21. When referring to his father (see below), Laonikos spells it *Chalkondyles*, which he may have thought more classical than *Chalkokondyles*, the form preferred by modern convention. In sum, Laonikos Chalkokandyles was the classical version of his name (and his *nom de plume*), while Nikolaos Chalkokondyles was the "real life" version, though we mix and match. Also, "Kyriacus" was how that traveler and antiquarian preferred to spell his name, so I will use it rather than any of the variants scholars have concocted.

while preserving the basic meaning of Gemistos.[2] The governor of Imbros and later historian of Mehmed, Michael Kritopoulos, wrote as the more classical Kritoboulos. Andronikos of Kerkyra, Laonikos's reader in the next century, also reversed his name and wrote as Nikandros. The taking on of classical names was a new feature of the late Byzantine scene, but had some precedent. Satires had been written under the guise of assumed personae ("Timarion" and "Mazaris"), an ancient convention. There were also monastic name-changes. Plethon's opponent Georgios Scholarios, for example, became Gennadios. There was great scope for assumed identities in the fifteenth century and, as we will see, Laonikos had an even broader field from which to choose and craft his own.

Toward the beginning of the *Histories*, Laonikos lists the territories still held by the "Greeks" at the time of his birth. These were "Byzantion and the coast below Byzantion as far as the city of Herakleia; the coast above by the Black Sea as far as the city of Mesembria; the entire Peloponnese except only for three or four cities of the Venetians; and Lemnos, Imbros, and other inhabited islands of the Aegean in that area" (1.8). The omission of Thessalonike puts us after 1423, when it was transferred to the Venetians (the city was then taken by the Turks in 1430). Mesembria was held by the Byzantines until 1452 and Herakleia (i.e., Perinthos), Lemnos, and Imbros until 1453, so they are no help. That leaves the Peloponnese. The situation Laonikos defines came about in 1432, when Centurione Zaccaria, the last Latin to hold effective power over any part of the former principality of Achaea, died. We do not know how precise Laonikos means to be here, and Centurione had been brought to heel by the Palaiologoi

---

2   C. M. Woodhouse, *Gemistos Plethon: The Last of the Hellenes* (Oxford, 1986), 186–88, 264 (for Gennadios's reaction).

already in 1429. On a loose reading, we may assume a *terminus post quem* for Laonikos's birth of ca. 1430. He was born into the most prominent Greek family of Athens, and his father's name was Georgios (as we know from Kyriacus's testimony).

In 1435, the duke of Athens Antonio I died. He was an illegitimate son of the enterprising Florentine Nerio I Acciaiuoli (d. 1394), who had bequeathed Thebes to him. In 1402–3, Antonio had retaken Athens from the Venetians, who had finagled it for themselves out of the terms of Nerio's will in 1394. According to Laonikos, Antonio was a good ruler and maneuvered skillfully among the many powers that were eyeing his desirable patrimony. He "administered the principality in a way that best benefited those who lived in it as well as others" (4.58). Laonikos himself reports that when Antonio died, his widow Maria

sent to the sultan [Murad II] asking that the principality be entrusted to her and to a worthy man of the city, who was a relative of hers and, in fact, my father [Georgios]. She sent this man to the sultan to sound him out, and gave him large sums of money so that he would be able to secure for them the principality of Attica and Boiotia. He set out from the city and journeyed to the sultan, but the leading men of the populace tricked Antonio's wife out of the acropolis because of their hatred for Chalkokandyles. They then installed Antonio's relatives as tyrants and, by driving my family out, prevailed in the city. They made a marriage alliance with Antonio's wife, through a well-born adopted son of hers,[3] and occupied the acropolis. Shortly afterward,

---

3   This convoluted phrase has been taken to mean that Antonio's widow, Maria, was married to Nerio II. This is supported by a Venetian document, but disputed by some historians.

having expelled his wife from the acropolis and driven my family out, they took charge of the affairs of the city. [6.50]

Unfortunately, we do not know enough about the politics of the duchy to make sense of the political alignments here. It is not clear how Maria was related to Georgios Chalkokondyles, who his opponents were, or why they hated him. If the plan was for Georgios to marry Maria so that they could jointly rule over the principality, then they could not have been too closely related. It would also imply that Nikolaos's mother had died by 1435, before he was five.

Georgios traveled to the Ottoman court but was arrested by the sultan, who wanted to appropriate the entire principality (his armies quickly seized Thebes). Georgios somehow managed to flee to Constantinople and from there to the Peloponnese, but he was intercepted at sea by the Acciaiuoli. They returned him to Murad, who released him. All this was told by his son (6.51). The family, at any rate, left Athens when Nikolaos was at most five years old, and possibly a newborn, so we cannot meaningfully say that he was raised in Athens.

We next meet Georgios Chalkokondyles in the service of Konstantinos Dragaš Palaiologos, despot of the Morea (and soon to be the last emperor of Byzantium). In 1444, Konstantinos had initiated a broad offensive against the territories of the sultan in Greece, conquering western Greece, Boiotia, and the duchy of Athens, which, under Nerio II, had previously accepted Ottoman suzerainty. Murad counterattacked in 1446, bringing his armies down to the Isthmos by November; at Thebes, he was joined by Nerio, who did not want to be on the Byzantine side. Georgios was again sent to the sultan:

It so happened that Konstantinos had sent an envoy to sultan Murad, but the requests that he made through him were not moderate, for he demanded that the Isthmos be allowed to stand as it was for him and that he get to keep all the sultan's lands beyond it that he had subjected. Konstantinos thereby incurred the sultan's punishment, and the latter imprisoned his envoy at Serres and held him under guard while he marched against the Peloponnese, even though it was the middle of winter. And that envoy was Chalkokandyles, the Athenian. He imprisoned him at Serres along with his servants, while he marched out. [7.19]

This is the last that we hear of Georgios Chalkokondyles, though there is no reason to believe that he came to harm during this imprisonment (his third) by Murad. Murad quickly overpowered the defenders of the Hexamilion wall and forced the despots to recognize his authority; henceforth, they would be his tributaries. The vivid account that Laonikos gives of the Isthmos battle suggests that he may have been present (7.20–25). If he had been born in ca. 1430, he would by then have been sixteen. Laonikos does say in the opening statement of his preface that the *Histories* includes events that he himself witnessed (1.1), and this is the closest that we can place him to one in time and space (given that he was at Mistra one year later: see below). We infer also from the account of his father's adventures that his family had moved to Mistra and taken service with Konstantinos Palaiologos. We cannot account for the missing decade (1435–46), but the leading Greek family of Athens would have been an asset to the despot, especially when he trained his sights on Nerio II and Athens in 1444.

The family's relocation and high standing at the court is confirmed by a diary entry of the merchant, diplomat, spy, and antiquarian Kyriacus of Ancona, who visited Mistra in the summer of 1447. At the court of the despot Konstantinos, Kyriacus met

Plethon, then about eighty, and Nikolaos. He claims that Plethon was his reason for returning to Mistra, and calls him

> that eminent personage, the most learned of the Greeks in our time, and, if I may say so, [a man who] in his life, character and teaching [is] a brilliant and highly influential philosopher in the Platonic tradition. Also, I saw rushing to meet me in the palace itself the gifted young Athenian, Nicolaus Χαλκοκανδύλης, the son of my good friend, the learned Georgius, in no way unworthy of his father, and furthermore, remarkably learned in both Latin and Greek literature.[4]

Kyriacus does not imply that his friend Georgios was dead; he may have been absent or still in Murad's custody (Kyriacus visited Mistra seven months after the Isthmos battle). Moreover, he does not explicitly say that Nikolaos was Plethon's student, though that is likely to have been the case, and we will see throughout this book the influence that Plethon had on him. Plethon, moreover, seems to have given Laonikos a manuscript of Herodotos to which he had made some corrections, and Laonikos added his own autograph subscription to the manuscript.[5]

Kyriacus was hosted and taken on tours by local notables wherever he traveled in the Greek world. On Imbros in 1444, he had been shown the ruins of the island by none other than Kritoboulos, the future historian of Mehmet.[6] Three years later, when he visited Mistra, he was received by the despot, by Plethon, and by Nikolaos, and on 2 August he records that the "dearly

4   Kyriacus of Ancona, *Later Travels*, 298–301 (slightly modified).

5   See the final section of chap. 2.

6   Kyriacus of Ancona, *Later Travels*, 92.

beloved Athenian youth" gave him a tour of Sparta's ruins. The fascination with Greek antiquity would deeply shape Laonikos's vision of his own world. At any rate, based on Kyriacus's evidence, Nikolaos was roughly between fourteen and eighteen in 1447, which confirms that he was born in ca. 1430. He was an intimate of a despot (and future emperor of Byzantium), of the greatest philosopher of the age, and of the most traveled, well-connected man of the Italo-Greek world. Through Kyriacus and Plethon we can link him, via one or two steps of separation, to just about anyone else in that part of the world (though Kyriacus would return to the east only once more, in 1449, and died in the same year as Plethon, 1452). Mistra was a cosmopolitan place, through which all manner of travelers, diplomats, and scholars passed.[7] Nikolaos met some of the characters whose history Laonikos would later tell, but, more importantly, he made contacts that would serve him as informants when he turned to his vast Herodotean project.

We note also Kyriacus's emphatic claim that Nikolaos knew Latin, which means that he probably also spoke Italian. That would later enable him to gather material on western European history, lore, and ethnography. As we will see, he possibly learned Turkish as well, though we cannot know when.

One person in whose company Nikolaos probably lived at Mistra was his relative Demetrios, possibly his cousin, who would have an illustrious career in Italy as a teacher of Greek and editor of the classics, including Homer. We do not know exactly how the two were related—they may even have been brothers—but I will call them cousins for the sake of convention. Demetrios was between seven and ten years older than Nikolaos, and his life so far probably had the same trajectory, from Florentine Athens to

---

7   Woodhouse, *Pletho*, 4, 84.

Byzantine Mistra.[8] We will keep him in sight, for his career illustrates the opportunities that had opened up to learned Greeks with western connections. Some historians believe that Nikolaos likewise moved to Italy in his cousin's footsteps, but I will argue that he took an alternative path into the Ottoman sphere. At any rate, Demetrios left Mistra and the east for Italy in ca. 1448.

We have no direct or definite information about Nikolaos's whereabouts after 1447 and we know nothing about his activities other than what we can infer from the *Histories*. But that indirect evidence is not insignificant. Moreover, it is now certain that Laonikos finished working on the *Histories* in the mid-1460s, not in the late 1480s as scholars previously believed.[9] There is, then, much less time for which we have to account. It also means that the *Histories* was the work of a man in his late twenties and early thirties, not his fifties and sixties.

With few exceptions, Laonikos's digressions on the history of foreign nations reach to the early or mid-1450s, and this is as true for the west (e.g., the Hundred Years War; the conflicts in Spain) as the east (the wars of the Timurid succession; the White and Black Sheep federations).[10] For example, he says that Belgorod (Akkerman) was the royal capital of Moldavia (3.30), but this was case only in 1448–55. Yet his narrative of Ottoman expansion extends to 1464, when it peters out. Moreover, most of the foreign digressions occur in the first five books, just as they do in Herodotos. This project of collecting ethnographic and geographic information to work up into a narrative modeled closely on Herodotos

8   For his career, see D. J. Geanakoplos, *Interaction of the "Sibling" Byzantine and Western Cultures in the Middles Ages and Italian Renaissance (330–1600)* (New Haven, 1976), chap. 13, and below.

9   Wurm and Gamillscheg, "Bemerkungen"; Kaldellis, "Date."

10   Kaldellis, "Date," citing previous scholarship.

was unprecedented, and suggests that Laonikos had definite goals already in the 1450s. It is likely that the fall of Constantinople in 1453 inspired him to write this history. Its theme, as he puts it in the preface, was "the fall of the Greeks and the events surrounding the end of their realm, and the rise of the Turks to great power" (1.1). The fall of Constantinople occurs at the beginning of Book 8, but already by the mid- to late 1450s it would have been apparent to Laonikos that the Peloponnese would soon fall too, and this he recounts mostly in Book 9. It is likely, then, that Laonikos conceived the project of writing a new Herodotos in nine books in the 1450s. In Book 9, after the fall of Trebizond, we find a statement that closes the account opened at the beginning of Book 1: "so that in a short amount of time the Greeks and the rulers of the Greeks had been overturned by this sultan, starting with the city of Byzantion, after that the Peloponnese, and finally the king and land of Trebizond" (9.78). But Ottoman expansion did not end, and Laonikos was still writing in the mid-1460s, when he left the work lacking a definite conclusion. As far as he knew, he was the first and only person to be writing such a history in Greek (he probably did not know that Doukas was writing his own at the same time).

Meanwhile, Nikolaos's cousin Demetrios had been teaching Greek in Italy and, in 1463, just as Laonikos was finishing the *Histories*, was appointed to the first chair of Greek at Padua, advertised by the Venetian senate.[11] As it happens, the longest foreign digression in the *Histories* is about Venice, a city presented as a rich, dynamic, powerful, and beautiful republic (4.21–40). Many

11   D. J. Geanakoplos, *Greek Scholars in Venice: Studies in the Dissemination of Greek Learning from Byzantium to Western Europe* (Cambridge, MA, 1962), 38; idem, "The Discourse of Demetrius Chalcondyles on the Inauguration of Greek Studies at the University of Padua in 1463," *Studies in the Renaissance* 21 (1974): 116–44; and idem, *Interaction*, 241–64, for a summary of his Inaugural and a translation.

scholars have suspected based on this passage that Nikolaos may have lived there, or at least visited. To extend the parallel between the two cousins' careers, Demetrios had been promoted by Bessarion, a student of Plethon from two generations before. Demetrios was involved in the controversy over Plato, Aristotle, and Plethon that raged around Bessarion in the 1460s, though his role was tangential.[12] Laonikos, we should note, also includes a brief panegyric of Bessarion in the *Histories* (6.14), in connection with the Council of Florence (1437–39). Laonikos begins the *Histories* with a plea for the continued relevance of the Greek language, and the major argument made by Demetrios in his inaugural address was that Greek was essential for all scholars in the west.[13] Moreover, in that address Demetrios also issued calls for a crusade against the Turk.[14] This was not mere rhetoric. It was exactly in 1463 that Venice first declared war on the Ottoman Empire, the very war with whose opening the *Histories* ends. A large part of Book 10 (10.37–43) consists of the fiery speech of the senator Vettore Capello in favor of war, a speech that, according to Laonikos, decided the issue in 1463. This was the same year as Demetrios's appointment and call for crusade, and Bessarion was also backing the Venetian war effort in that year.[15] Parallel lives indeed: the *Histories* seems to mirror the politics and western interests of Demetrios and his cardinal patron.

12   Geanakoplos, *Greek Scholars*, 91–92; Woodhouse, *Pletho*, 371–72. For the context, see J. Hankins, *Plato in the Italian Renaissance* (Leiden, 1991), 236–63.

13   For this parallel, see pp. 204–5 below.

14   Geanakoplos, "Discourse of Demetrius Chalcondyles," 138–39; idem, *Interaction*, 260; for the intellectual context, see N. Bisaha, *Creating East and West: Renaissance Humanists and the Ottoman Turks* (Philadelphia, 2004), 114–15.

15   L. Mohler, "Bessarions Instruktion für die Kreuzzugspredigt in Venedig (1463)," *RQ* 35 (1927): 337–50; Bisaha, *Creating East and West*, 109–14.

Yet we will see that the parallel does not run deep to fundamentals. Laonikos certainly had connections to the west, but he was part of a broader world and immersed in its eastern half too. His "barbarian" politics, like those of Herodotos, are hard to pin down. The *Histories* is hardly crusading material: there is enough praise, blame, and irony to go around for everyone. The first Greek writer to present Islam as a decent culture rather than a religious error, who took a neutral stance in the battle between Christianity and Islam, who seems to mock the papacy, and who admired the "virtue" and resilience of the Turks, should not be confused with his cousin and made into an anti-Turkish Christian crusader. There were points of contact with Demetrios and Bessarion, of course, but not all roads led from Athens to Venice; some led to the Ottoman world.

Scholars have proposed Venice, Venetian Crete, and Athens as settings for the composition of the *Histories*—guesses all. None can be proven and none ruled out (and I am not persuaded that our Laonikos was a correspondent of Michael Apostoles).[16] There are only two traces of psychogeography in the *Histories*: northern Europe is seen from a southern point of view (2.14)[17] and the Aegean is once called "our sea" (9.39). But this proves little. In explaining that Germany is free of plagues, he says that the latter tend to break out more "among us" in the east (2.16). This detail situates him in the east, where a major plague broke out in 1464,

---

16 Summaries of these views in H. Ditten, *Der Russland-Exkurs des Laonikos Chalkokondyles interpretiert und mit Erläuterungen versehen* (Berlin, 1968), 5, 78–79; N. Nicoloudis, *Laonikos Chalkokondyles: A Translation and Commentary of the Demonstrations of Histories* (Athens, 1996), 45–57; K. Zographopoulos, *Ο Λαόνικος Χαλκοκονδύλης και οι απόψεις του για τους Οθωμανούς Τούρκους* (Xanthi, 2002), 41–45. For Apostoles's Laonikos, see Appendix 1. Akışık, "Self and Other," offers an original argument for a Renaissance context.

17 H. Ditten, "Bemerkungen zu Laonikos Chalkokondyles's Deutschland-Exkurs," *ByzF* 1 (1966): 56.

including in the Peloponnese. For a number of additional reasons that I will list below, I believe that an eastern context for the composition of the work, possibly Constantinople, is most likely. I will argue that it was written for a Byzantine, not western, readership.[18] Also, it circulated almost immediately in Constantinople, and this was the only line of the text's transmission that survived.[19] If Laonikos meant to disseminate it among western readers, he failed: that would not happen for decades to come. The only specific informants he ever mentions are the accountants in the Ottoman budget office from whom he obtained the detailed information about the sultan's income that rounds off Book 8 (8.78; cf. 9.90 for some military contractors he may have spoken to). Laonikos makes it clear there that the current sultan is Mehmed II (8.75), and he places this digression in the late 1450s. His information about the budget is mostly accurate[20] and could most easily be obtained in Adrianople or Constantinople. The same is true about the Turkish informants from whom he obtained his knowledge of early Ottoman history, as there was no text available at that time that recorded what he knew, certainly no text available in the west.[21]

While the praise of Bessarion does point to Italy and humanism, it could just as easily have been tribute paid to a former student of the same teacher. Meanwhile, Laonikos's so far unnoticed equivalent praise of al-Bistami, the Persian scholar and jurist also known as Musannifak ("the little writer"), points to the east and

18   See chap. 5.

19   See the end of this chapter.

20   S. Vryonis, "Laonikos Chalkokondyles and the Ottoman Budget," *International Journal of Middle Eastern Studies* 7 (1976): 423–32.

21   See chap. 4; also S. Baştav, "Die türkischen Quellen des Laonikos Chalkondylas," in *Akten des XI. internationalen Byzantinistenkongresses, München, 1958*, ed. F. Dölger and H.-G. Beck (Munich, 1960), 35–42.

the court of Mehmed (10.12). Laonikos says that Bistami had "an excellent reputation for justice at the sultan's Porte, especially as a judge among those who serve at the Porte," and that he "pronounced the most just verdicts of all that we know, and could find exactly how to award justice to those who were on trial." Laonikos writes this when Bistami's son was made governor of Lesbos in 1462. His description of the father implies a personal connection: among all the learned men at the sultan's court, why single out only this man for praise? Bistami was a legal scholar writing in Persian. Moreover, he seems to have joined Mehmed's court only after 1453 and was not the type of man who would have been known in the west or even in the western-occupied lands of the Aegean.[22] There must have been some connection between him and Laonikos to elicit such praise.[23]

Caution is necessary in inferring Laonikos's whereabouts from the "vividness" of his accounts (I have already suggested on that basis that he may have been present at the Isthmos battle of 1446). The one place he certainly knew well, Mistra, does not have a vivid presence in the *Histories* at all. He may well have visited Venice, but there is nothing in his account of it that he could not have obtained from Venetians abroad, other travelers, or written accounts.[24] He calls the Arsenal "very beautiful to behold and very elegant" (4.37), but this is a formulaic phrase. For example, he describes the hero of one of his dark romantic tales, Esau Buondelmonti, despot of Ioannina (d. 1411), in the same terms (4.54). His description

22   J. T. P. de Bruijn, "Musannifak," *EI*[2] 7:663.

23   One possibility for a meeting was at Adrianople in 1457, at the ceremony for the circumcision of Mehmed II's sons (see pp. 146–47 below). Bistami's attendance is attested by Aşıkpaşazade (in R. F. Kreutel, *Vom Hirtenzelt zur hohen Pforte* [Graz, 1959], 208); F. Babinger, *Mehmed the Conqueror and his Time*, ed. W. C. Hickman and R. Manheim (Princeton, 1992), 149.

24   For Venice, see the end of chap. 3. Nor was he limited to Greek sources.

of Turkish tightrope walkers and other performers in Adrianople or, more likely, Constantinople,[25] has no equal in the *Histories* as a personalized witness to folk customs. The following account seems to be based on autopsy (note the tongue-in-cheek comment at the end):

> I will pass by the tightrope walkers, an art at which the Turks excel above all other peoples, so much so that they can advance along the ropes when they are shackled or run along them at full speed with their eyes blindfolded. They perform countless other amazing tricks on them, such as passing through swords or twirling about. One can see these things being done every day in the marketplace called Tahtakale,[26] where the tightrope walkers practice their art (they call this group *cambaz*).[27] One can also see others doing similar things in this marketplace, where the city's exercise grounds are. When they bury a child beneath the earth, converse with him from there, and get him to answer any question that they may have, how could you see this and not be amazed? But these other things, accomplished through some higher power, are less impressive than the men who run around on the ropes. [8.70]

This follows Laonikos's account of the circumcision ceremony for the sons of Mehmed II (in Adrianople, in 1457), which is also

---

25   So, too, D. R. Reinsch, "Η θεώρηση της πολιτικής και πολιτιστικής φυσιο-γνωμίας των Ελλήνων στους ιστορικούς της Ἅλωσης," *Études balkaniques* 6 (*Byzance et l'hellénisme: L'identité grecque au Moyen-Âge*) (1991): 80.

26   Derived from Persian, this meant "the area below the castle." In both Edirne and Istanbul, it was associated with, and came to stand for, the market areas.

27   Derived from Persian, this means an acrobat.

described vividly; he may have attended.[28] For all these reasons, then, and because of his intimate knowledge of the Ottoman system of governance and war, I believe that the *Histories* was researched and written close to the centers of Ottoman power, most likely in Constantinople. As we will see, that was where the *Histories* appears in our manuscript record, no more than a decade after it was finished. And as early as 1476, a certain Andreas Chalkokondyles ("Andriya son of Halkokondil") is listed among other ex-Byzantine aristocrats (including two Palaiologoi) as a tax-farmer working for the Ottoman government in the region of Constantinople. He apparently had huge amounts of capital to invest in this business.[29] This suggests that branches of the family pursued alternative careers under the sultans, which did not take them to Italy.

Laonikos the Athenian

By the 1450s, Nikolaos's world presented him with a broad range of options for fashioning an authorial identity. He could highlight his Athenian origin and create a neoclassical profile for himself; or play up his court connections from Mistra; or take on a "service identity," as a loyal spokesman for the sultans (cf. Kritoboulos), possible Latin employers (cf. Doukas), or the former despots and emperors (cf. Sphrantzes). He could have written in Latin and assimilated to prevailing western norms, as did his cousin Demetrios, other students of Plethon (e.g., Bessarion), and another possible contact, Nikolaos Sekoundinos from Euboia.[30] He could have remained loyal to Byzantine tradition, like most who fit his

---

28   See pp. 146–47 below.

29   N. Necipoğlu, *Byzantium between the Ottomans and the Latins: Politics and Society in the Late Empire* (Cambridge, 2009), 229.

30   For Sekoundinos, see chap. 4.

cultural profile, and been a *Romaios*, identifying with the now lost society of Romanía that we misleadingly call "Byzantium" and that was now adjusting to life under the sultans. Or he might be a Greek, in the way defined by Plethon and other intellectuals of the late Palaiologan Empire. In fact, he could have avoided national labels and joined the transnational culture of the Orthodox Church and monasticism, drifting into the orbit of Scholarios, who saw himself as a Christian above all. In sum, the Aegean world, what he called "our sea," was experiencing tremendous changes. Nikolaos could also have tapped his Florentine connections—we have seen how he praised Antonio I Acciaiuoli—and become a hybrid colonial subject, seeking patronage in Italy or from Italians in the Aegean.

Nikolaos opted for Athens and for Hellenism, and so became Laonikos. The very first words of the *Histories* are "Laonikos the Athenian," though they are in the dative, with greater (nominative) importance going to the events that the *Histories* will record. I will examine his Hellenism—the matrix of his *Histories*—below. Here I will note two ways by which Laonikos emerges as a proud Athenian. In different ways, he manages to subordinate both the sultan and all the powers of mainland Greece, especially the western ones, to his native city.[31]

The end of Book 4 contains a seemingly disorganized miscellany on the western powers in Greece in the late fourteenth and early fifteenth century. It jumps around in time and place with no regard for chronology, but a close look reveals that this section does contain an organizing principle, which is the history of Nerio I and Antonio I Acciaiuoli, the rulers of Athens. Laonikos manages this through mastery of the Herodotean "fluid link" that creates multiple enframed digressions. Specifically, Laonikos

---

31   For a problem in his knowledge of recent Athenian history, see Appendix 2.

is listing the sons of Manuel II Palaiologos, which brings him to Theodoros II, despot of the Peloponnese, who succeeded Theodoros I, Manuel's brother. By mentioning Theodoros I's marriages, one of which was to a daughter of Nerio I, he is now able to go back to 1204 and give a brief history of the Latin presence in Greece (4.49). He discusses Euboia first and how it came under Venetian control, but brings the discussion back to Nerio through a marriage connection (otherwise unknown) that he made with Euboia (4.50). He then says that Nerio gave another daughter to Carlo Tocco, which enables him to digress on the Tocco of Kephallonia, the Albanians of Epeiros, and the rule of Ioannina (4.51–56). This digression-within-a-digression closes with a return to the marriage alliance between Carlo and Nerio. Starting again from Nerio, Laonikos moves in a new direction, to his illegitimate son and heir Antonio, specifically to his defeat of the Venetians of Euboia (which links up with the earlier discussion of Euboia) and his capture of Athens (4.57). Two sections are now devoted to his rule in Athens (4.58–59), after which we return to Theodoros II and the Peloponnese (4.60), the starting-point. The circle has closed, and we see that Athens was the connecting thread, the center of focus, and the climax of the digression. Overall, it is well done.

Mehmed II also comes under the spell of Athens in the *Histories* on two occasions. Returning from his incursion into the Peloponnese in 1458, Mehmed "turned to Attica and toured the city of Athens, observing the Peiraieus and its harbor, and approved Ömer's noble deed [he had secured Athens in 1456]. I have learned that the sultan thought more highly of this city and its acropolis than any other in his territory, and that he greatly admired its ancient magnificence and its buildings" (9.14). This four-day visit was recounted also by Kritoboulos,[32] whose goal was to somehow

32   Kritoboulos, *History* 3.9.7.

"normalize" the Conqueror according to Byzantine norms and whose account has contributed to the image of his "Philhellenism" in modern scholarship. At this point, Laonikos seizes the opportunity to update his history of Athens from the death of Nerio II in 1451 to the expulsion of Franco by Ömer in 1456 (9.15–18), which then brings us back full-circle to the sultan, who "beheld the acropolis and was amazed by it" (9.18). This is Laonikos's version of Horace's *Graecia capta ferum victorem cepit.* Mehmed tours Athens a second time in 1460 (at 9.59), after the conquest of the Peloponnese, but Laonikos's description there is subdued. Still, according to our historian, Athens was the only place that caught the sultan's attention for "its ancient magnificence and buildings." Constantinople, by contrast, fails to have such an effect on him. Laonikos here again reveals himself as the Athenian he boasts to be in the first words of his *Histories.*

A Note on the History of the Text of the *Histories*

Laonikos has left so few traces of the process by which he composed the *Histories* that we cannot reconstruct the history of the text in gestation and revision, before it was released to its audience and fate. I noted above that most of Laonikos's foreign digressions, both east and west, point to a date in the mid- to late 1450s, which suggests that he was already collecting information by then. He may then have been planning to write a multi-book narrative of the fall of the Greeks, loaded toward the front with ethnography and geography, as in Herodotos.

Nor can we be entirely certain of the state of the text at the point when he did stop working on it, at some point between 1464–68, and more likely closer to the beginning of that period. The work is unfinished, breaking off in an unsatisfying tangle of confusing sentences regarding Venetian activities on Lemnos and the Peloponnese in early 1464.[33] These are not the only signs that the work is incomplete. There are a number of lacunae in the text, many of a word or two where Laonikos did not know a name or a distance and so left a blank to fill in later. But there are also cases where part of a sentence seems to be missing, assuming that these are not ambiguities created by faulty grammar or errors created in the transmission. Not all these lacunae are marked in the Darkó edition, so I have tried to indicate them in the DOML edition. There are twenty such possible lacunae, but not about two per book: there are six in Book 3, the book with the most ethnography, and many of those gaps are names and facts that Laonikos had not yet found.[34]

The text, in other words, may be not only unfinished but unrevised too. This is confirmed by the appearance of stylistic singularities: Laonikos always calls the Byzantine capital "Byzantion," except once when he calls it the City of Constantine (in his own voice; there is another in a speech).[35] He always writes numbers out, except once when he uses a Greek numeral (4.57). He scrupulously avoids Byzantine offices and technical terms, except once when he mentions the office of *mesazon* (7.61). He uses a Thucydidean dating formula only once—it is the very last line of the text (10.60). I suspect that all these (except the last)[36] are slips that would probably not have made it past a final round of revisions.

---

33   So noted already by K. Güterbock, "Laonikos Chalkondyles," *Zeitschrift für Völkerrecht und Bundesstaatsrecht* 4 (1909): 81, 96; E. Darkó, "Zum Leben Laonikos Chalkondyles," *BZ* 24 (1923–24): 37.

34   Names, distances, etc.: *Hist.* 1.28, 3.13 (two), 3.20, 3.41, 5.40, 7.34, 7.65, 9.72, 9.92; parts of sentences: 2.19, 2.31, 3.27, 3.56, 5.33, 5.37, 7.69, 8.70, (9.36, in an interpolation), 9.38, 10.40.

35   *Hist.* 6.4; speech: 10.41; 9.36 is in an interpolation (see below). I exclude the speech because Laonikos allowed his speakers to use forms that he himself did not: see Vlad's reference to Vlachia at 9.96.

36   For the Thucydidean dating formula, see p. 38 below.

The text also seems to have contained many grammatical mistakes, almost on every page. These appear in all the surviving manuscripts, one of which dates to very soon after Laonikos ceased to work on the text (see below). I am referring to minor errors in the grammar, not to obscure or poorly written, garbled sentences, of which the text also has its share. The modern editors, especially Tafel and Darkó, corrected most of these errors, restoring sense to otherwise incomprehensible passages. But it is likely that these go back to the original text that Laonikos left behind or allowed to circulate, as it is highly unlikely that they would have been introduced by copyists, and in such a short amount of time no less. In other words, when it appears to scholars that the text at any point is "corrupt," it may simply just be sloppily written or unrevised to begin with. This is a problem that future editors of the text will have to face.

There are, moreover, three and possibly four interpolated passages in the *Histories*, identified mostly on stylistic but also on thematic grounds. The first recounts episodes from the history of Trebizond in the fifteenth century (9.28–33); the second is the digression on the regions, religion, and neighbors of Georgia (9.35–36); the third describes the fate of the population and imperial family of Trebizond under Ottoman rule (9.71–81); and the fourth tells the fate of Anna Komnene, daughter of the executed emperor David of Trebizond (in 10.13). I have argued elsewhere that these passages were possibly added by Georgios Amiroutzes, a philosopher and high official of the empire of Trebizond who was present at the fall of his city (in 1461), was involved in the arrest and execution of the imperial family (in 1463), and gained the favor of Mehmed in the 1460s; he disappears from the historical record in 1469.[37]

---

37 For a study of these passages, see A. Kaldellis, "The Interpolations in the *Histories* of Laonikos Chalkokondyles," *GRBS* 52 (2012): 259–83. For Amiroutzes, see B. Janssens

Amiroutzes fits exactly the profile of the interpolator, and in one of the interpolations he seeks to explain his own role in the arrest of the Komnenoi. If this argument is correct, then these interpolations must have been added very soon after Laonikos stopped writing, within five years at the most. It also suggests that Laonikos was writing in Constantinople.

This thesis is supported by the manuscript tradition of the *Histories*. The earliest manuscript, Parisinus graecus 1780, is now known to have been copied by Demetrios Angelos, a student of medicine and scribe active in Constantinople between the 1440s and 1470s, the last date to which we can fix him.[38] Possibly he was active after that, but a watermark ties the manuscript closer to the middle of the century than later (though obviously not before 1464). As it happens, Angelos also copied a short philosophical work by Amiroutzes, meaning that they were acquainted, and both appear to have been on close terms with Kritoboulos, who was finishing his *History* in the 1460s and may have relied in part on the *Histories* of Laonikos.[39] All the interpolations

---

and P. Van Deun, "George Amiroutzes and his Poetical Oeuvre," in *Philomathestatos: Studies in Greek and Byzantine Texts Presented to Jacques Noret for his Sixty-Fifth Birthday,"* ed. B. Janssens, P. Van Deun, and B. Roosen (Leuven, 2004), 297–324; J. Monfasani, *George Amiroutzes: The Philosopher and his Tractates* (Leuven, 2011), esp. 5–12.

38 For a general study of the mss. tradition, see H. Wurm, "Die handschriftliche Überlieferung der ΑΠΟΔΕΙΞΕΙΣ ΙΣΤΟΡΙΩΝ des Laonikos Chalkokondyles," *JÖB* 45 (1995): 223–32. For Par. gr. 1780 in particular, E. Gamillscheg, "Der Kopist des Par. gr. 428 und der Grosskomnenen," *JÖB* 36 (1986): 287–300, previously identified its copyist as Amiroutzes, but it was reattributed to Angelos by B. Mondrain, "Jean Argyropoulos professeur à Constantinople et ses auditeurs médicins, d'Andronic Éparque à Démétrios Angelos," in *ΠΟΛΥΠΛΕΥΡΟΣ ΝΟΥΣ: Miscellanea für Peter Schreiner zu seinem 60. Geburtstag,* ed. C. Scholz and G. Makris (Munich, 2000), 223–50; see also eadem, "Démétrios Angelos et la médecine: contribution nouvelle au dossier," in *Storia della tradizione e edizione dei medici greci (Atti del VI Colloquio Internazionale Paris 12–14 Aprile 2008),* ed. V. Boudon-Millot et al. (Naples, 2010), 293–322.

39 Kaldellis, "Date."

in question appear in the manuscript copied by Angelos and in another one that appears to be independent and was copied later in the century.[40] This means that the interpolation existed already in the manuscript on which Parisinus graecus 1780 was based. Unfortunately, we cannot see into the narrow time-gap between the end of Laonikos's work on the *Histories* and the addition of the interpolations (between a few months and a few years in the mid- to late 1460s), but those added passages were almost certainly the work of Amiroutzes or of his circle (which included Angelos, the copyist).[41] There were no other intellectuals active in Constantinople who fit the requisite profile better, and we can tie them to the manuscript tradition of the work. This also means that we can tie Laonikos to Constantinople with greater confidence than before. It is less clear that we can situate him personally in those literary and intellectual circles. Amiroutzes, for example, had clashed with Plethon at the Council of Ferrara-Florence, but that was a long time ago and we should not assume that their relations led to rigidly hostile factions. It was among these intellectuals that the *Histories* began to circulate, unfinished though it was.

40   Namely, Par. gr. 1781; see the stemma in Wurm, "Handschriftliche Überlieferung," 232. For the copyist of that manuscript, Georgios Moschos, a Corfiot, see B. Mondrain, "Les Éparque, une famille de médecins collectionneurs de manuscrits aux XVe–XVIe siècles," in *Η ελληνική γραφή κατά τους 15° και 16° αιώνες*, ed. S. Patoura (Athens, 2000), 15–159.

41   In a personal communication, Thierry Ganchou has argued that they were the work of Angelos himself, not Amiroutzes. His arguments concern the first interpolated passage only, which is not good history and so, he argues, it could not have been written by Amiroutzes, who would have known better; cf. T. Ganchou, "Théodôra Kantakouzènè Komnènè de Trébizonde (°~1382/ †1426), ou la vertu calomniée," in *Geschehenes und Geschriebenes: Studien zu Ehren von Günther S. Heinrich und Klaus-Peter Matschke*, ed. S. Kolditz and R. C. Muller (Leipzig, 2005), 337–50. But Byzantine history (and not only) provides many examples of bad histories written by people who would have known better. More than what he might have known, what matters is what point he was trying to make at a later time. Both are difficult to recover.

CHAPTER 2

The Marriage of Herodotos and Thucydides

Laonikos's *Histories* is a hybrid fusion of Herodotos and Thucydides. It is easy to see that the overall conception of the project and its structure is Herodotean (as it features the expansion of an Asian monarchy punctuated by ethnographic digressions and leading to climactic battles with the Greeks), while the style and austere approach are largely Thucydidean.[1] But most scholarship does not go beyond this in its analysis, simply noting a few borrowings and parallels. This chapter will deepen our understanding of Laonikos as an author by revealing how he modeled the style and structure of the *Histories* on his classical predecessors, in effect creating his own authorial persona. I will first uncover the overall patterns that structure the work by breaking down the distribution and density of the narrative material and digressions. I will then examine how Laonikos combined Herodotean and Thucydidean modes to shape his narrative of Turkish, Byzantine, and western history.

---

1 Darkó, "Zum Leben," 36–37; A. Markopoulos, "Das Bild des Anderen bei Laonikos Chakokondyles und das Vorbild Herodot," *JÖB* 50 (2000): 210–11.

The Structure and Contents of the *Histories*

Laonikos's *Histories* is about half the length of Herodotos's, with 107,000 words (rounding up) to Herodotos's 190,000 (and Thucydides's 154,000). It is divided into ten books, roughly equal in length. Their approximate lengths, measured in the pages of the Darkó edition, are as follows: 51, 50, 54, 47, 56, 42, 45, 54, 67, and 40. Book 10 is short because it is most likely unfinished. Book 9 is long because it contains interpolations on the history of Trebizond, the fate of its ruling family, and the geography and religion of Georgia. Without those it would be closer to 59 pages long. The last event recorded in the work is the opening phase of the Venetian-Turkish war of 1463–79. This is important because it means that Laonikos was writing Book 10 while the war was ongoing: he did not know how it would end and so could not structure the end of the *Histories* as Herodotos could. He did not know whether he was writing toward an Ottoman or a Venetian victory. In the mid- to late 1450s he may have decided to write the history of the rise of the Turks and the fall of the Greeks with some definite terminus in mind, but by the early 1460s the project had become open-ended. We do not know why he stopped writing in mid-stride (mid-sentence even).

Scholars conventionally say that the *Histories* covers the years 1298–1464, but this is inaccurate in two respects. First, Laonikos gives no dates: events are loosely coordinated in relation to each other. Therefore, it was impossible for him to designate the year 1298. In fact, he does not even begin with what we call 1298, but rather with the pre-history of the Greeks (from Dionysos onward), their conquest by the Romans, the establishment of what we call Byzantium (which Laonikos calls the kingdom of the Greeks), and the relations between the popes and the Greeks down to the Council of Ferrara-Florence in 1439 (1.1–8). He then turns to the Turks and, in the style of Herodotean ethnography, traces their origins in relation to the Mongols and Oğuz before turning to Ertoğrul and his son Osman (1.9–13). No date can be fixed to such an introduction. The *Histories* is not a chronicle, at least not its first seven books, which are more like a nebula of loosely interconnected information about the known world, through which winds an intermittent narrative core of Ottoman expansion that is increasingly well defined as we reach the later books. The work is not defined by dates, but by links, whether tight or loose, that move us from one constellation of events, geography, or ethnography to the next.

The structure of the *Histories* is fully and deliberately Herodotean. The backbone and main narrative axis of Herodotos's *Histories* is the expansion of Persia, including both its triumphs and reverses. The main geographic and ethnographic digressions are placed at that point in the narrative where the people or place in question is encountered by the Persians or, through what we may call secondary linkage, where they are necessary to explain the background of that people or place. Most of the digressions are in the first six books, while the remaining three contain the narrative climax of the work. Laonikos's *Histories* is structured in exactly the same way, only with the Ottoman Turks taking the place of the Achaemenid Persians, and victory going to them in the end. Herodotos recounts the victory of Greece over Asia; Laonikos the victory of Asia over Greece and Europe.

Laonikos was not the first Byzantine writer to make the decline of the Empire his chief theme. In ca. 500, the last pagan historian Zosimos recounted the decline of Rome by evoking and reversing Polybios, the historian of the rapid growth of Roman power (Zosimos's first words are "Polybios of Megalopolis").[2] Michael

2   F. Paschoud, "Influences et échos des conceptions historiographiques de Polybe dans l'antiquité tardive," in *Polybe*, ed. F. W. Walbank, Fondation Hardt pour l'étude de l'antiquité classique, Entretiens 20 (Geneva, 1974), 305–44.

Attaleiates did the same in the eleventh century, comparing the men of his age unfavorably to the heroes of the Roman Republic.[3] Laonikos has turned to Greek models instead of Roman (or Biblical) ones, producing a Hellenocentric version of previous Byzantine narratives of decline, which were Romanocentric (as the Byzantines were Romans).

The narrative axis is punctuated, then, by digressions that make up the nebula of the known world, the *oikoumene*. Let us consider the narrative pace schematically, per book:

I:	over 100 years (?–1389)
II:	11 years (1389–1400)
III:	2 years (1400–1402), but also 69 years of the life of Timur
IV:	19 years (1402–21)
V:	ca. 20 years (1421–episodes in the 1420s, 30s, and 40s)
VI:	ca. 10 years (from the 1430s to 1444)
VII:	8 years (1444–52)
VIII:	5 years (1452–57)
IX:	4–5 years (1457–62)
X:	2–3 years (1462–64)

This is messy, but we can see that the temporal parameters become more defined in the last five books, as the narrative becomes fuller and as increasingly more pages are devoted to each segment of time. Book 1 is an introduction with a long running start, and almost the whole of Book 3 is a digression on the life and conquests of Timur. But there is a major problem with these statistics, which

---

3   D. Krallis, *Michael Attaleiates and the Politics of Imperial Decline in Eleventh-Century Byzantium* (Tempe, 2012).

is that they do not account for the distribution of digressions and so do not tell us how much space Laonikos really devotes to each segment of time as opposed to other matters that interested him along the way. As the backbone of the *Histories* is the sequence of Ottoman rulers, it would be more useful to exclude digressions and calculate how many narrative pages are devoted to each sultan. We cannot do this with absolute precision, of course, for it is impossible to exactly define a digression (some are more and some less relevant to the main narrative). I have included as part of each reign information about the politics of the states with which each sultan was at war (including Byzantium, though not the entire life of Timur in Book 3). The rough count and ratio of pages per year illuminates the distribution of material (names in italics are not historical reigns):

SULTAN	NO. OF PAGES	NO. OF YEARS	PAGES PER YEAR
BOOK 1			
Gündüz-Alp	0.5	unknown	–
Oğuz-Alp	< 0.25	unknown	–
Ertoğrul	2	unknown	–
Osman	5	ca. 44	ca. 0.12
Orhan	4	ca. 34	ca. 0.12
Süleyman	4	ca. 15	ca. 0.27
Murad I	20	29	0.69
BOOKS 2–3			
Bayezid	46	13	3.54
BOOK 4			
civil wars	13	11	1.18
Mehmed I	10	9	1.11
BOOKS 5–7			
Murad II	93	30	3.10
BOOKS 8–10			
Mehmed II	139	13	10.69

The balance is heavily in favor of Mehmed II, just as it is for Xerxes in Herodotos: both benefit from being closer to the time of writing, of course, but also all the ethnography is placed in the earlier books, which further diminishes the page-per-year ratio of the earlier sultans. Murad II and Mehmed II have less interrupted narratives. The anomaly is Bayezid, who has an unusually high page count and ratio, even when we remove, as I have, the account of the life of Timur (barring the Asia Minor campaign). This is, in part, due to the long speeches that punctuate his reign and the detail in which the Ankara disaster is recounted.

According to these calculations, then, roughly 33 percent of the *Histories* consists of ethnographies and other digressions— that is, material that is not directly part of the political-military narrative. The number of pages that such digressions take up in each book is as follows (excluding the interpolations in Book 9): 6, 16, 36, 23, 25, 21, 1, 7, 0, and 3. The relatively small number in Book 1 goes up, if we reckon the prehistories of the Greeks and Ottomans as ethnographies analogous to those that other people receive in later books.

Laonikos does not offer a single absolute date in the entire work, not even for the fall of Constantinople. In this, he imitates Herodotos, but to an extreme. Herodotos did not have a chronological scheme available to him, but he did try to provide a relative and coordinating chronology in some cases.[4] Laonikos gives the reign-length of most of the sultans when he reports their deaths (all these lengths are wrong);[5] also of the prophet Muhammad,

---

4   D. Lateiner, *The Historical Method of Herodotus* (Toronto, 1989), 114–25; D. Feeney, *Caesar's Calendar: Ancient Time and the Beginnings of History* (Berkeley, 2007), 72–80.

5   *Hist.* 1.28 Orhan (number missing); 1.58 Murad (31 years); 3.65 Bayezid (25 years); 4.2 İsa (4 years); 5.1 Mehmed (12 years); 5.9 the rebel Mustafa (3 years in Europe); 7.63 Murad II (32 years).

who "reigned" for ten years (3.18); Konstantinos IX Palaiologos (8.24: wrong again); and, inexplicably, the rule of René the Good over Naples (5.67: wrong again). In only three cases does he say how long other types of events lasted (counting only those lasting for more than a year), and only one of them is correct.[6] In the vast majority of cases, Laonikos simply says that an event happened "afterwards," or "not long afterwards." Either marker can refer to a few days or a few decades.[7] In very few cases in the first seven books, he does say exactly how long afterward an event took place.[8] In the last three books, which cover the reign of Mehmed, and as the number of years covered in each book gradually diminishes, Laonikos becomes explicitly annalistic. The structure of the narrative here is year-by-year, clearly labeled but still not correct in every instance.[9] It is not a coincidence that these were the years, after 1453, when Laonikos was probably already gathering the material for the *Histories*.

Later chapters will examine separately how the digressions are structured and integrated into the main narrative. The remainder of this chapter will examine how Laonikos fashioned himself as a historian by combining elements from Herodotos and

---

6   *Hist.* 2.6 (Andronikos IV kept his father and brother imprisoned for over three years); 2.27 (Bayezid's siege of Constantinople lasted ten years; actually eight); 4.10 (Manuel, son of Manuel II, was imprisoned for seventeen years, which appears to be fictitious). For events lasting one year, see 5.29 (Konstantinos's siege of Patras); 8.63 (the papal expedition to the Aegean); 9.61 (Graitzas's resistance to the Turks).

7   See, for example, Appendix 2.

8   *Hist.* 2.27 (the following year); 3.35 (the following summer); 3.37 (three years later); 5.35 (a year after that); 7.29 (the following summer); 7.34 (Murad II spent a year in peace).

9   *Hist.* 8.1 (the following summer); 8.2 (the following winter); 8.3 (the following summer); 8.44 (the second year after the capture of Constantinople); 8.46 (the following year); 8.65 (the following summer); 8.69 (the following summer); 9.26 (the following year); 9.63 (the following summer); 10.16 (the following summer).

Thucydides. We have seen some aspects of this already in the over-all structure of his narrative.

Style and Approach: Thucydides

There are times when Laonikos dons a Herodotean persona and times when he dons a Thucydidean one. A striking example of the latter is when he first refers to his own father. It is a dry and dis-passionate account of his father's failure at politics leading to the exile of his family, which dislocated the author himself, though he is too detached to mention himself directly. He recounts his father's failure as if he were talking about a stranger, and it is only toward the end that he parenthetically adds the crucial words, "my father" (6.50). He mentions his father, moreover, only because his actions were part of the political story at hand, and mentions only those actions of his that were relevant to that story. In this way, he does not treat his father any differently from anyone else in the *Histories*. All this, of course, is directly modeled on Thucydides's brief appearance in his own *History*, as an Athenian general posted to the north who fails in his mission (like Georgios) and is, accord-ingly, exiled from his city (4.104–7, 5.26).[10] More like Thucydides and utterly unlike Herodotos, Laonikos never mentions himself as a historian engaged in the process of collecting information. He never reveals his movements or his sources, with the exception of the Ottoman budget officials (8.78; cf. 9.90).

Laonikos's prose, like Thucydides's, is austere and lacks sensa-tionalism, and he copies many phrases and expressions directly

---

10   According to the *Souda* (s.v.), Herodotos's life was also marked by exile from Halikarnassos, first at the hands of the tyrant Lygdamis and then, after the historian allegedly overthrew him, by fear of the murderous populace.

from him.[11] He also maintains an emotional distance from events. There are no laments in his account of the fall of Constantinople, which is reported matter-of-factly and not given climactic narrative prominence, being placed at the start of Book 8. He does say that "this calamity seems to be the greatest that ever took place throughout the world in its excess of suffering" (8.30), but that is the extent of his commentary, and he quickly moves on to internal Ottoman developments. He says the same thing, contradicting himself (if we press the point), about the fall of Sebasteia (Sivas) to Timur in 1400: "It is said that the misfortune suffered by this city surpassed any misfortune that any city has ever experienced" (3.46; other sources report horrific things there). Sebasteia was not even a Greek city by that point.

Thucydidean austerity dampens humor. I have found only one pun that is perhaps meant to be funny. Laonikos feigns sexual propriety at the end of the story of the pretty Florentine girl who managed to poison King Ladislao of Naples (he had agreed to lift his siege of her city if she had sex with him). Laonikos explains in detail how she applied the poison to his genitals after their intercourse and, in Herodotean fashion, notes that there were different theories as to who put her up to it and made her "most decorous" for the king's pleasure (ὡς εὐπρεπεστέραν φανῆναι τῷ βασιλεῖ). He then ends the matter by saying that "it is not decorous to speak more of it [οὐκ εὐπρεπῆ]" (5.66). The word's repetition with different uses undermines the propriety: what more could Laonikos have possibly said? He has already told all the juicy parts. The same section contains what might be one of only two tongue-in-cheek

---

11   A list is in F. Rödel, "Zur Sprache des Laonikos Chalkondyles und des Kritobulos aus Imbros," *Programm des königlichen humanistischen Gymnasiums Ingolstadt 1904–1905* (Munich, 1905): 12–34; for Herodotos, see Appendix 3.

comments in the work. Florence, he says, "has the most surpass-
ingly beautiful women in Italy, and among them are virgins too"
(5.66). The second, regarding Turkish popular entertainers, we
quoted in the previous chapter. That is the extent of his humor.

There are also only two passages that might be openly sarcas-
tic, albeit still dry. That is how I read his statement that the popes
"change their names on the assumption that they become more
holy than their previous selves and undergo a total transformation"
(6.28). This jibe acquires its force from the nasty sexual polemic
that characterizes Laonikos's presentation of the papacy and is
best appreciated in connection with it.[12] Likewise Murad II's
human sacrifice after his capture of the Hexamilion wall in 1446,
where Laonikos may have been present: "he bought about six
hundred slaves and sacrificed them to his father [Mehmed I], performing an act of piety through the murder of these men" (7.26).
Otherwise, Laonikos keeps a distance from events. There is only
one Thucydidean aphorism. During the Hundred Years' War, "the
French now turned to religion—indeed, people generally turn to
religion at such a time" (2.37)—enter Joan of Arc.

Like Thucydides, but unlike most previous Byzantine historians,
there are no mythological allusions or comparisons; no extended
metaphors, images, or similes; and almost no scenes from everyday
life. There are no *ekphraseis*, that is, vivid rhetorical descriptions of
places, monuments, works of art, or individual people, excepting a
brief physical description of Venice (4.37). Thucydides did authorize the use of speeches, which Laonikos uses, in some cases skillfully (the best are by İbrahim at 3.52; Uzun Hasan's mother at 9.72;
and Vettore Capello at 10.37–42). The absences I have noted are the
result of choice, not an inability to use rhetoric; Laonikos avoided
mere ornament. Most striking is the absence of pointed allusions

12   See chap. 5.

to the poets, especially Homer. If he uses poetic language at all, he does not draw attention to it, as did other Byzantine writers.

Desiccated is a better term for the prose. There are virtually no sayings, proverbs, or aphorisms (with the exception noted above); no incredible stories,[13] dreams or visions (not even the words for them), weird tales, strange creatures, extraordinary coincidences, direct divine interventions, or inexplicable human acts, such as we find in Herodotos. The edges of his *oikoumene* are not occupied by dog-headed, headless, or man-eating people, not even through unconfirmed report. He explicitly notes that India and Khatai (possibly China) are so far that incredible tales are inevitably told about them, but they should not be believed (3.68).[14] Excepting a few sex-tales (almost all Italian), human motivation in the *Histories* is strictly Thucydidean, i.e., the desire to conquer or the fear of being conquered.[15] In Herodotos, by contrast, the motivation of kings and cities spans the range of thoughts and feelings known from both history and fairy tales: they can go to war for any kind of reason (say, to test a hypothesis) and with any kind of opponent (e.g., the wind).[16] Laonikos does not even hint at such possibilities.

Like Thucycides, Laonikos avoids biography, by which I mean narrative accounts of the childhood or private life of his protagonists. As with his father Georgios, all his characters enter at the point where they impact history and disappear when they become irrelevant. A partial exception is the background of

13   Except the story of the bull and the corpses at 10.57, introduced by the distancing λέγεται.

14   For the decline of the belief in monsters in the west, in part due to travelers to Mongolia, see R. Bartlett, *The Natural and the Supernatural in the Middle Ages* (Cambridge, 2008), 102–6.

15   Cf. Thucydides, *History* 1.23.

16   Cf. F. Baragwanath, *Motivation and Narrative in Herodotus* (Oxford, 2008).

Janko Hunyadi, which even includes anecdotes (5.49–50; see 7.57–60 for his dramatic escape from Varna). The second half of Book 5 is the most biographical, being loosely structured around the colorful career of Alfonso V of Aragon and, to a lesser degree, of Álvaro de Luna. But these are strictly political biographies, and partial ones at that. They are subordinated to the geographical logic of Laonikos's digresssions, and their chronology is broken up to the point of being incomprehensible.[17] Laonikos avoids personal anecdotes. He likes sex-stories involving Italians,[18] but they are not normally about his protagonists. He reveals his attitude toward tall tales when recounting the Ottoman invasion of Wallachia in 1462: "It is even said that Vlad himself entered as a spy into the sultan's camp and went around to observe its condition. But I cannot believe that Vlad would willingly expose himself to such a danger, as he would have been able to use many spies of his own, but this tale, I believe, was made up to give a sense of his daring" (9.98). Little of Herodotos would have survived this standard.

We have so far considered Laonikos's Thucydidean traits as a historian. I turn now to an evaluation of his Greek prose style, which also reflects an effort to imitate his fellow Athenian.

The chief reason why Laonikos has been so little studied is his prose style, which is not easy to read, to put it mildly. With a few exceptions, it is a complex form of Attic Greek, replete with duals, optatives, and other classicizing elements. Though he was writing two thousand years after Thucydides, in an age when the European languages, including modern Greek, were well established, he still managed a passable imitation. Unsuspecting classicists may be taken in by some passages. Laonikos reveals

17   See p. 57 below.
18   See p. 168 n. 131 below.

his awareness of internal Greek diglossia when he says that "those those who understand the better sort of Greek [οἱ ἄμεινον Ἑλληνικῆς ἐπαΐοντες φωνῆς] call Bulgaria lower Mysia" (1.39), i.e., they use a classicizing ancient term instead of a contemporary colloquial one, which is what Laonikos himself does throughout.

While no one in the fifteenth century spoke the way that Laonikos wrote, we should refrain from labeling his prose as "artificial," as so many philologists of Byzantine prose have done. For one thing, all literature is artificial—no one ever spoke in the language of Homer, Pindar, or Thucydides either. Also, we should not assume that elevated forms of classical Greek in Byzantium were reserved exclusively for writing. While the style of Laonikos is too convoluted and obscure to have ever served as a vehicle of oral communication, the same is not true of that of his teacher Plethon, which was a more lucid and direct version of roughly the same Attic standard. We have one report, by the humanist Filelfo, that Attic Greek was, in fact, spoken at the court of the late Palaiologoi,[19] and scholars of Byzantine Greek are only now looking into the question of the linguistic performativity of rhetorical texts.[20] While previous Byzantine historians in the high style wrote (in part) for oral presentation,[21] there are no signs that Laonikos had anything like that in mind, even though some of his battle narratives or digressions might have served the purpose.

Laonikos's quest for purity entailed the exclusion of Christian terms (bishops are "archpriests") and Byzantine offices (despots

19   Quoted in N. Wilson, *Scholars of Byzantium* (London, 1983), 5; cf. I. Ševčenko, "Levels of Style in Byzantine Prose," *JÖB* 31 (1981): 289–312.

20   E. C. Bourbouhakis, "Rhetoric and Performance," in *The Byzantine World*, ed. P. Stephenson (London and New York, 2010), 175–87.

21   B. Croke, "Uncovering Byzantium's Historiographical Audience," in *History as Literature in Byzantium*, ed. R. Macrides (Ashgate, 2010), 25–53.

are *hegemones* or the like). We will discuss below how this affects his picture of fifteenth-century politics.[22] Exceptions to his Atticism are the Ionic case endings that he uses for some barbarian names, which draw him into the ambit of Herodotos but make him look more archaic, and his use of some Turkish terms for offices and ranks at the Ottoman Porte (especially at 5.12–13, which explains them and authorizes their subsequent use). In this regard he is not consistent, for he classicizes the sultans (as *basileis*), viziers (as *prytaneis*), and *beylerbeys* (as *strategoi*), but not the lesser ranks treated in Book 5. He includes some Hungarian military terms (e.g., 7.5). I will discuss his use of classical ethnonyms in the chapter on digressions and ethnography.

Laonikos's vocabulary is minimalist, with the same words and phrases occurring over and over again with brutal and predictable regularity. Compare, for example, the almost identical way in which he records two separate raids by Bayezid.[23] The most common noun is probably χώρα ("land," "territory"); after that, "army" or "king." Among the verbs, "marching" and "plundering" appear most often. He uses words in their classical and not contemporary sense, so, for example, a *perioikos* is a neighbor, not a dependent farmer; also, a *tyrannos* is not an oppressive ruler but someone who has established personal rule outside of a formal constitutional mechanism. Laonikos likes rare words and compound verbs from Herodotos and Thucydides, especially compounds of ἵημι and ἵστημι, which are a pain to translate, and one sometimes has to dig

---

22   See the fourth section of chap. 3.

23   Cf. *Hist.* 2.3: ἐπέδραμε μὲν οὖν καὶ τὴν Ἰλλυριῶν χώραν, καὶ πολίσματα ἄττα ἑλὼν ἠνδραποδίσατο, καὶ τήν τε Ἀλβανῶν χώραν ἐπιπέμψας στράτευμα ἐληΐζετο, with 2.10: τὴν χώραν ἐδῄου, καὶ πολίσματα ἄττα ἑλὼν τῆς Ἀλβανῶν χώρας ἐπὶ Ἰλλυριοὺς ἤλαυνέ τε καὶ ἐδῄου τὴν χώραν, λείαν τὰ ἐκείνων ποιούμενος.

into LSJ entries to find the sense intended.[24] The LSJ will suffice for translating him; one does not need to consult dictionaries of Byzantine Greek.

Laonikos tried deliberately to write in a "difficult" Thucydidean manner and he succeeded, but at great cost. His sense is often obscure, and syntactical connections sometimes have to be inferred from context or through intuition. For example, there are many abrupt and unsignalled changes of subject, often in the middle of a sentence, and an excessive use of reflexive pronouns, sometimes in repetitive and confusing combinations. He does not always specify whom he is talking about, or the subject of the sentence, which creates confusion. Laonikos often uses indirect speech, and confuses the accusative modifiers, so that it is not clear whether they go with the subject or object. He sometimes turns a genitive absolute into the subject of the main verb. Conversely, he can be needlessly repetitive. For example, he starts many sentences by repeating or summarizing what he said in the previous one, and he can repeat the same word many times in just a few lines.[25]

The prose is not all bad, of course; if it were not comprehensible, Laonikos would not be a source for anything and could not be translated. His unfortunate difficulties arose from his attempt to imitate the style of Thucydides, which had long been criticized in antiquity and Byzantium for some of the same vices. But Laonikos did manage to produce some lucid and gripping narratives, among the best being his account of the siege of Belgrade in 1456 (in

24   E.g., ἀναγιγνώσκω as "induce someone" (on a few occasions) and a rare sense of ἐπιλεξάμενος (at 7.43). Zographopoulos, Λαόνικος, 56–57, provides a handy list of Laonikos's stylistic borrowings and idiosyncrasies.

25   See, e.g., "not long afterwards" in 6.24; "imprisoned" in 6.42; and "Boiotia" in 6.46.

Book 8). His account of the siege of Constantinople in the same book is also quite good.

I close this section with the most inexplicable imitation of Thucydides in the *Histories*. I mean its ending, the very last words, for only here did Laonikos use a Thucydidean dating formula: ταῦτα μὲν τοῦ χειμῶνος ἐς τὴν Πελοπόννησον ἐγένετο (10.60), referring to the winter of 1463/64. I cannot explain it, but I want to repeat the suggestion of Diana Wright (pers. comm.), who brooded on it and decided: "If I were writing a novel here, I would have him—aware that he had contracted plague & that it went fast [there was a bad outbreak that year]—writing that last line, all he could manage, to identify himself at the end with his master."

Modalities and Templates: Herodotos

Laonikos emulated the rigor, austerity, and literary register of Thucydides, but that filter did not exclude Herodotean historio-graphical modalities or language from his text. The very conception of his project, as we saw, is Herodotean, and this is reflected, to begin with, in the title. Ἀποδείξεις ἱστοριῶν can be translated, inelegantly perhaps, as "Demonstrations of Inquiries" and alludes to Herodotos's opening words: "this is the demonstration of the inquiries [ἱστορίης ἀπόδεξις ἥδε] made by Herodotos" (1.1). This is not just an archaizing affectation. As we will see, Laonikos compiled the information in his *Histories* largely from oral sources, not through books. His was the most fully Herodotean research project that anyone had ever undertaken since antiquity. Laonikos does not lose sight of this after the title. The verbs that he typically uses for his research are the Herodotean πυνθάνομαι and ἀναπυνθάνομαι,[26]

---

26   See the list in Appendix 3 for this and other parallels. See Akışık, "Self and Other," for a parallel and independent study of Herodotean elements.

used even in the expression ἀναπυνθανόμενος εὗρον (5.54). At the end of Book 5, when he rounds off his digression on the geography and kingdoms of Spain, he returns to his title: "These things, then, have been here recorded at such a length as a presentation of research [ἀναγέγραπται ἐς ἀπόδειξιν] that contributes to the overall theme of the work" (5.79).

Laonikos's opening statement combines Herodotean and Thucydidean elements with his own comment on the role of the historian. The intention of preventing events from becoming unknown to future generations is Herodotean (cf. Hdt. 1.1 μήτε ἀκλεᾶ γένηται with *Hist.* 1.1 μηδὲν αὐτῶν ἀκλεῶς ἔχειν), while he took from Thucydides the boast that the events in his history would be more worthy of remembrance than any before. The notion that historiography is a debt repaid to Nature is Laonikos's own. Of course, Laonikos was not the first to imitate the opening statements of Herodotos and Thucydides. It is precisely in this imitation that he reveals himself as a historian in the Byzantine tradition, an affinity that he otherwise did his best to disguise. While the rest of his work has little to do with Byzantine historiography in either form or approach, nor ever refers to a previous Byzantine writer, the opening words resonate with a long tradition of such imitation.[27]

Laonikos borrows much vocabulary and many expressions directly from Herodotos in both his narrative and ethnographic passages. I will discuss the latter in a separate chapter below. As for the narrative, much of it concerns wars, and the concise way in which Laonikos recounts them relies on Herodotos's narrative

---

27 For discussions of the prefaces of the Byzantine historians, see the second volume of H. Lieberich, *Studien zu den Proömien der griechischen und byzantinischen Geschichtsschreibung*, 2 vols. (Munich, 1898–1900); R. Maisano, "Il problema della forma letteraria nei proemi storiografici bizantini," *BZ* 78 (1985): 329–43; A. Kaldellis, "The Historical and Religious Views of Agathias: A Reinterpretation," *Byzantion* 69 (1999): 206–36.

style. A ruler will first learn what his enemy has been doing, gather his own army, and send envoys to "make trial" of their intentions. The enemy will usually not "come to terms," whereupon he will "set out and march forth" to conquer a region or city, and "enslave" it, all in about so many words. If there is a battle, the two sides will come to blows, one will be routed, and the other will pursue. With a few predictable exceptions,[28] most battles are reported in this dry way and are over quickly. Laonikos's vocabulary for such events is Herodotean. I have quoted sample "template" passages in Appendix 3, which the reader can compare to any number of similar ones in Laonikos. In that Appendix, I have also provided a sampling of Herodotean expressions lifted by Laonikos. Rather than lay them out here, I prefer to discuss how Laonikos presented himself as a Herodotean *type* of historian.

More important than occasional parallels and borrowings in the narrative are expository comments that reveal the image that Laonikos wanted to project of himself as a historian. Like Herodotos, and using the same language, he often acknowledges his inability to ascertain the truth in some matter or to be precise about it, for example, the origin of the Turks (1.10), Albanians (1.29), Slavs (1.38, 3.31), and Hungarians (2.17); where Bayezid settled some captives (2.46); where artillery was first invented (5.15); whether Hunyadi ever served Ali, the son of Evrenos (5.50); and the origin of the feud between Guelphs and Ghibellines (6.18).[29] On two occasions he refuses to divulge information,[30] a practice more common in Herodotos. It is possible that in the first of these

28   The exceptions are Ankara, Varna, Constantinople (1453), Kosovo (II), and Belgrade.

29   For the language of these declarations, see Appendix 3. For a study of these modalities in Herodotos, see Lateiner, *Historical Method.*

30   *Hist.* 5.54: the names of some men killed by Vlad III; 10.43: the reason why the pope was at war with Malatesta.

two passages Laonikos hides the names of Vlad's victims less because of discretion than his desire to imitate Herodotos. He occasionally offers contrasting opinions, for example, regarding the origin of the Turks and Slavs (both in Book 1), but not nearly as frequently as Herodotos does. Like Thucydides, he never names sources, though on one occasion he attributes contrasting opinions to collective national sources in the notorious manner of Herodotos ("the Phoenicians say . . . but the Persians say . . ."). This concerns the death of Murad I at Kosovo, where the two national viewpoints are those of the Turks and the Greeks (1.56–57, 2.2).[31] Here and only here does Laonikos explicitly allow his reader to make up his own mind about the matter, but his phrasing is not similar to Herodotos's equivalent statements, being more like that of Prokopios.[32] We may here be catching a rare glimpse into Laonikos's elusive Byzantine reading. Later "national citations" are not placed in constraring pairs.[33] Therefore, most of the Herodotean modes (i.e., conflicting opinions; national viewpoints; and allowing the reader to decide) cluster in the first and early second books, suggesting that Laonikos may have begun writing the *Histories* with the intention of imitating Herodotos more thoroughly than he did when it actually came down to it.

Herodotos often disagrees with what his sources tell him, or disbelieves them and takes sides in controversies. Laonikos rarely does this. He disagrees with those who believe the Albanians are

---

31   See the third section of chap. 4.

32   Cf. *Hist.* 2.2: ἀλλὰ ταῦτα μὲν ἴτω, ὅπῃ ἑκάστῳ προσφιλὲς ἡγεῖσθαι περὶ αὐτῶν with Hdt. 3.122 πάρεστι δὲ πείθεσθαι ὁκοτέρῃ τις βούλεται αὐτέων (also 5.45) and Prokopios, *Secret History* 4.45 ἀλλὰ ταῦτα μὲν ὥς πη ἑκάστῳ φίλον, ταύτῃ δοκείτω; cf. *Wars* 3.11, 31, 7.27.20, 8.12.35.

33   *Hist.* 7.15 cites Turkish claims about the number of Turks that fell at Varna; 8.22 cites "the Greeks" regarding the capture of Notaras and the death of Orhan.

Illyrians (1.29; i.e., Slavs)[34] and finds it unlikely that Muhammad's tomb floats in mid-air in a temple (3.20).[35]

In terms of narrative signposting, he once uses a Herodotean phrase to indicate that he has said enough about a topic, but frequently uses his phrases for returning to the main narrative after a digression. Only in one instance does he deploy Herodotos's famous fatalism: "But these things had to end in this way, propelled as they were by an evil fortune..." (8.43).[36] *They*, in this instance, were the Byzantine despots of the Peloponnese, under whose rule Laonikos's himself had come of age. We will examine below what he thought of them (not much).

Moving now from the historiographical modalities that Laonikos lifted from Herodotos to the actual narrative content of the *Histories*, we find that he modeled many of his episodes on corresponding passages in Herodotos. This is especially pronounced in Book 1, possibly because Laonikos had less primary material and filled the gap with more of what was driving him at the outset, an enthusiasm to create a Herodotean "inquiry." After summarizing the history of the Greeks, he lays out different views on the origins of the Turks in the form of a Herodotean exchange of opinions ("some say... but others say"), though these opinions are unattributed.[37] A few of the episodes of early Turkish history that he recounts parallel episodes in Herodotos too closely to be credible. The story of Günduz-Alp who was chosen as a leader because of his ability to render just verdicts is built on that of Deiokes the Mede, though it lacks the subtle reflections on the emergence and consolidation of tyranny with which Herodotos infused it. But

34 See the fifth section of chap. 3.

35 See the second section of chap. 4.

36 See Appendix 3 for these phrases.

37 Markopoulos, "Bild des Anderen," 213–14.

structurally it stands at the same point in the narrative of Asiatic monarchy, namely, the origin of oriental leadership.[38]

Likewise, Laonikos's pre-Ottoman kings (e.g., 1.12: Ertoğrul) make war on the Greek cities of western Asia Minor, just as Herodotos's pre-Persian barbarian kings (the Lydians) do. The way in which the Ottomans capture Adrianople in Laonikos is almost certainly not historical but comes straight out of the world of Herodotos, most likely the capture of Sardis by the Persians. A Turkish soldier saw a young man coming out of the city to harvest grain in secret and followed him back in; he then reported to his commander and led the army into the city.[39] Book 1 of Laonikos ends with the death of Murad I at the battle of Kosovo (1389), whom Laonikos presents in his ensuing obituary as the founder of the Ottoman Empire, just as Book 1 of Herodotos ends with the death of Cyrus in battle,[40] and Book 2 in both historians begins with the succession. Timur's organization of his army expands on what Herodotos says about Spartan orders.[41] The exhaustion of Timur's army in pursuit of the Skythians (i.e., Mongols) was not historical but replayed the experience of Darius in pursuit of the Skythians, to which Laonikos himself had just alluded.[42] Murad II's council of war before the battle of the Zlatica pass (1443) evokes the council of Xerxes, who was debating whether to invade Greece;

---

38 Cf. *Hist.* 1.11 with Hdt. 1.96–100; cf. G. Moravcsik, *Byzantinoturcica*, vol. 1, *Die byzantinischen Quellen der Geschichte der Türkvölker* (Berlin, 1958), 393. For the story in Herodotus, see T. Harrison, *Writing Ancient Persia* (Bristol, 2011), 34.

39 Cf. *Hist.* 1.35 with Hdt. 1.84. The date and manner of the capture of Adrianople continues to elude historians: H. İnalcık, "The Conquest of Edirne," *ArchOtt* 3 (1971): 185–210; E. A. Zachariadou, "The Conquest of Adrianople," *StVen* 12 (1970): 211–17.

40 Cf. Markopoulos, "Bild des Anderen," 214.

41 Cf. *Hist.* 3.5 with Hdt. 1.65 (note both the συσσίτια and the ἐνωμοτίας).

42 Cf. *Hist.* 3.35 (cf. 3.22) with Hdt. 4.124–42; see the fifth section of chap. 4.

both feature a lone, but eloquent, advisor who pleads for caution.[43] These are all invented speeches. Laonikos's account of the
Ottoman budget does not reproduce the content of Herodotos's
equivalent passage for the Achaemenid Empire, but was certainly
included in the *Histories* in emulation and evocation of it.[44]

In a later chapter we will examine separately what is probably
the most important way in which Laonikos imitates Herodotos,
namely, in his geographic and ethnographic digressions. His sys-
temic use of these templates also creates, in the classically educated reader, a pervasive resonance between the worlds of the
two authors, even beyond those specific passages where we can
posit deliberate, targeted modeling. Given Laonikos's classical
ethnonyms, the same agents seem to be involved in recurring
relationships. For example, when Laonikos says that a "king of
Egypt" (here a Mamluk sultan) conquered Cyprus and subjected
it to tributary status (in 1426), we may be reminded of a "king of
Egypt" in Herodotos (the Pharaoh Amasis) who likewise "conquered Cyprus and subjected it to tributary status." Herodotos's
language here is not exactly the same as that used by Laonikos,
but is language that he uses regularly elsewhere.[45] This resonance
cuts both ways. It is not only that readers of Laonikos might be
reminded of Herodotean episodes, but that they will be reminded
of fifteenth-century history *when they go back to read Herodotos.*
No one who has struggled with Laonikos's long accounts of war
between the Turks and the "Paionians" (i.e., the Hungarians)
will fail to recall them when he rereads Herodotos's account of

43 Cf. *Hist.* 6.34–39 with Hdt. 7.8–13 (see also Bayezid's war council before the
battle of Ankara at 3.52–54); cf. Moravcsik, *Byzantinoturcica,* 1:393.

44 Cf. *Hist.* 8.73–78 with Hdt. 3.89–97.

45 Cf. *Hist.* 3.42 with Hdt. 2.182 (εἷλε δὲ Κύπρον ... καὶ κατεστρέψατο ἐς φόρου
ἀπαγωγήν).

the Persian attempt to conquer . . . the Paionians.⁴⁶ Laonikos's is a
world made up of the same elements meeting once again, replaying the conflict between east and west.⁴⁷

Laonikos's Manuscript of Herodotos

By a stroke of fortune we possess Laonikos's copy of Herodotos.
This manuscript, which contains Herodotos from start to finish,
and only that, was copied in 1318 by Nikolaos Triklines, probably
in Thessalonike. It is Laurentius 70.6 (i.e., it is in Florence). The
whole can be conveniently accessed online.⁴⁸ At 340v., at the bot-
tom of the last page of text, after the subscription of Nikolaos the
copyist, we find a second subscription:

λαονίκου τοῦ ἀθηναίου δοκοῦσι δὲ ἔμοιγε οἱ ἕλληνες χρη-
σάμενοι ἀρετῆ(ι) μείζονι ἢ κατὰ ἄν(θρωπ)ον ἀποδείξασθαι
μὲν ἔργα οἷα ἡμᾶς πυνθανομένους ἐκπλήττεσθαι, τυχεῖν
δὲ κήρυκος οὐ πολλῷ(ι) τινι τῶν ἔργων αὐτῶν ἀποδέοντος·
ἡροδότου ἁλικαρνασέως, τούτων ἢ ἔκαστα ἐγένετο θεία(ι)
πομπῆ(ι) ἐπεξιόντος.

[Belonging to] Laonikos the Athenian. It seems to me that
the Greeks displayed a virtue greater than what is merely
human, and that they made a demonstration of deeds such
as to amaze us when we learn about them in our inquiries.
They [the Greeks] were also fortunate to have a herald who

---

46   Hdt. 5.12–17.

47   See the fifth section of chap. 4.

48   At http://teca.bmlonline.it/TecaRicerca/index.jsp. Search for Plut.70.07
(no spaces; accessed 25 November 2013). Editors of Herodotos designate it as either
T or N.

himself did not fall far short in worth of the deeds themselves, I mean Herodotos of Halikarnassos, who recounted
these events in the way in which each happened, in a manner
akin to a divine procession [i.e., of events].[49]

I will return to the contents of this subscription. First, a note on
the history of this manuscript.

Laur. 70.6 had a complicated and itinerant history between 1318
and 1480, when it was used in Rome by Demetrios Raoul Kabakes
to make his own copy. Unfortunately, there has been no systematic effort to review all the facts and hypotheses about it that
would enable us to contextualize Laonikos's place in its history.
I provide a basic, comprehensive outline in Appendix 4, though
there is clearly need for an expert paleographer to take a close
look. For example, there are a number of corrections, notations,
and restorations in this manuscript, all of which were attributed to
Laonikos by Hemmerdinger. But this cannot be correct, for some
of these corrections passed into Marc. gr. 365, which Bessarion
himself wrote on the basis of Laur. 70.6, in 1436 at Mistra.[50]
Laonikos was probably no more than six years old at that time.
Moreover, Bianconi has shown that folios 164r–165v were restored
by Plethon himself (though he then confused Laonikos with his
cousin Demetrios; there is, in fact, no evidence that Demetrios
ever possessed this book).[51] We need a comprehensive study of

49 For the text, see A. Turyn, *The Byzantine Manuscript Tradition of the Tragedies
of Euripides* (Urbana, 1957), 230 n. 212a (slightly modified). I thank Aslihan Akışık
for kindly bringing this to my attention; see her "Self and Other," 8–10, 213–14, for
additional aspects.

50 B. Hemmerdinger, *Les manuscrits d'Hérodote et la critique verbale* (Genoa,
1981), 119.

51 D. Bianconi, *Tessalonica nell'età dei Paleologi: Le pratiche intellettuali nel riflesso
della cultura scritta* (Paris, 2005), 138–39.

the authorship of all the corrections and marginal notes in the manuscript. It is possible that some were made by Laonikos.

At any rate, Laur. 70.6 was located at Mistra by 1436 and it was probably given by Plethon to Laonikos. But for how long did the latter have it? A problem is posed here by Alberti's hypothesis that Lorenzo Valla used Laur. 70.6, along with other manuscripts, to make his translation of Herodotos in Rome during the 1450s. This would allow only a narrow timeframe in the late 1440s and perhaps early 1450s for a young Laonikos to read it and make his subscription—a possibility that cannot be ruled out. But, fascinating though it is to contemplate that this book was used by Plethon, Bessarion, Laonikos, and Valla, the hypothesis of Valla's use does not seem secure (see Appendix 4). He may have used a different manuscript in the same line of transmission. If this is the case, then Laonikos may have owned it until the end of his life, whenever that was, but not beyond 1480, when it was used in Rome by Kabakes.

Laonikos's subscription points to a more mature reader than the seventeen-year-old whom Plethon was teaching in 1447. In its imitation of Herodotos, the vocabulary, style, and themes of the subscription are strikingly similar to those of Laonikos's *Histories*. Both begin with the same words ("Laonikos the Athenian") and suggest that when he wrote the former Laonikos was already contemplating, or even currently writing, the latter. In the preface of his *Histories*, Laonikos refers to the Greeks ἀποδεικνύμενοι ἔργα μεγάλα (1.3), just as they do here in the subscription: ἀποδείξασθαι μὲν ἔργα οἷα ἡμᾶς πυνθανομένους ἐκπλήττεσθαι (we saw also that πυνθάνομαι is a verb that Laonikos uses to the same Herodotean effect in his *Histories*). Both texts are explicitly concerned with the "virtue" and "fortune" of the Greeks, though they take roughly opposite stands on the matter.[52] More generally, Laonikos's concern

52 See chap. 5.

47

in the subscription with ἀπόδειξις and "inquiries" suggests that he was thinking of his own ἀποδείξεις ἰστοριῶν. This may have been as early as 1450, but we know that he was gathering materials by the mid- to late 1450s. It is more likely that this is the voice of Laonikos the historian, rather than the young student of Plethon. In this case, we can rule out that Valla had this manuscript in the 1450s.

Moreover, the panegyrical surface of the subscription seems to contain an undercurrent of dissatisfaction at the performance of more recent Greeks, and this, I will argue below, also points to a later date for the subscription. Laonikos was amazed at what the Greeks had performed in Herodotos precisely because he was so disappointed by their recent failures.

Geography and Ethnography

The ethnographic digressions, dispassionate presentation of Islam, and inclusion of authentic Turkish traditions set Laonikos's *Histories* apart from his predecessors in Byzantine tradition and also from contemporary western writers striving to imitate classical models. Laonikos does not refer to any author in either tradition, and gives the impression of being a lonely historian, reviving Herodotos's project after a gap of almost two thousand years. It is these digressions, more than the main narrative itself, that have attracted attention to the *Histories*. They make up one third of the text.

Rather than provide a historical commentary on the foreign material, which was done in a series of important articles in the 1960s by Hans Ditten,[1] this chapter will examine their literary structure and basic modes of representing otherness, especially Laonikos's debt to Herodotos and the voice that he created in order to talk about foreign peoples. I will then consider aspects

---

1   Beyond Ditten, I will be citing what little scholarship exists on these digressions, much of which tends to summarize them. The analysis that I offer is my own, except for points specifically referenced.

of the politics of these digressions, including Laonikos's homogenizing political vocabulary; his pan-Slavic theory, one of the first to be articulated in modern times; and his sources and attitudes to the Italian republics, especially Venice. His view of Islam and Muslims will be discussed in the next chapter.

Narrative Structures

Before entering a more detailed analysis, I will give an overview of the context and distribution of the major foreign digressions in the *Histories*. I omit the Greeks and the Turks, whose prehistories kick off Book 1, because they are treated differently in the work from anyone else (and from each other). Turkish material is scattered throughout, and the Greeks never receive any explanatory digressions; they are taken for granted. These two peoples will therefore be discussed in separate chapters. The following list, which aims at a broad overview, also omits minor references, as well as reports on the recent political history of foreign peoples that is directly relevant to the narrative theme of the *Histories*, namely, Turkish expansion.

BOOK 1: the main digression here is on the origin of the "Illyrians" (1.29, 1.38), which is Laonikos's collective term for what we call Slavs.

BOOK 2: Sigismund's crusade allows Laonikos to digress on Germany (2.14–16) and Hungary (2.17). The aftermath of Nikopolis triggers an account of the Wallachians (2.22–23). Manuel II's journey to the west leads to a discussion of the French (2.30–37), which includes the Hundred Years' War, and the British (2.38–43), which includes the causes of the tides (of the Thames and in general).

BOOK 3: the career and conquests of Timur permit a general survey of Asia: the Caspian Sea (3.10–11); Arabia and Islam (3.13–20); the Mongols (3.24–25, 32–33); Russia and its surrounding peoples, e.g., Lithuanians and Poles (3.26–31); Mamluk Egypt (3.39–42); and India-Khatai (China) (3.66–68).

BOOK 4: a brief conflict between the Ottomans and Venice leads to a long account of Venice's origins, history, constitution, economy, and buildings (4.21–40), including a brief discussion of Milan. There is also a complex, "enframed" description of the colonial powers of mainland Greece (4.49–60) that is more an account of current politics than ethnography, though it does divulge origins.[2]

BOOK 5: the first half includes brief accounts of Bosnia (5.39–40) and Ardeal (5.45), while the second half takes leave of the main narrative to discuss Genoa (5.57–60), the war between Genoa and Aragon (5.61–63), the kingdom of Naples and its conquest by Alfonso V (5.64–70), and the kingdoms of Spain (5.71–79).

BOOK 6: the account of the Council of Ferrara-Florence is actually taken up mostly by an account of the other cities and powers of Italy, including Ferrara and Florence themselves, the papacy, and the rise of Sforza at Milan (6.8–10, 6.12, 6.17–30).

BOOK 10: Laonikos revisits the Illyrian debate (10.16–17).

What triggers the digressions? Many of them are fairly brief and synoptic notes on a single people introduced at the point in the narrative when they are first mentioned or become important to the military narrative. The exception to this class of single-people digressions is that on Venice in book 4, which is huge by comparison to the others, although it is still focused on one place. There are also complex digressions that include more than one people. That on France and Britain is prompted by Manuel's journey to the west,[3] but Laonikos strangely never mentions Manuel's visit

---

2 See the second section of chap. 1.

3 A. Ducellier, "La France et les Îles Britanniques vues par un byzantin du XVe siècle: Laonikos Chalkokondylis," in *Économies et sociétés au Moyen Âge: Mélanges*

to Britain, only his stay at the court of Charles VI the Mad in Paris. Here, the digression seems to supersede the main narrative: we arrive at Britain not in the company of the emperor but because the digression on France leads to a discussion of the Hundred Years' War, which, in turn, prompts Laonikos to discuss Britain.[4] Meanwhile, he seems to forget the emperor.

All the Asian and Muslim digressions are placed in Book 3. If we consider the career of Timur as part of the main narrative, rather than as a digression itself from the sequence of the Ottoman sultans, we find that a large part of that book consists of such passages. If we exclude the account of the Ankara campaign too, which is presented mostly from Bayezid's narrative point of view, and focus on Timur's career to that point, we find that there is barely enough material on the rise and reign of Timur to fill up a few pages, and it is vague at that. Timur rose to power from humble beginnings (a notion that he himself may have spread);[5] he campaigned around the Caspian Sea; he had some kind of relationship with the Chaghadai; he fought for years against the Mongols of the Horde; he attacked the Syrian territories of the Mamluks; and there was some conflict with the king of India-China. Laonikos has taken a small amount of vague information about Timur with few names (we hear instead about "the city," "the king," etc.) and padded it with speeches, generic military narrative, classical templates, and digressions so that it takes up a whole book. It is likely that his sources for Timur were Turkish, which is why all aspects of Timur's life that involve Turks, both diplomatic and military,

---

offerts à Edouard Perroy (Paris, 1973), 439–45; idem, "L'Europe occidentale vue par les historiens grecs des XIVème et XVème siècles," ByzF 22 (1996): 119–59.

4   S. Moraitis, "Sur un passage de Chalcondyle relative aux Anglais," REG 1 (1888): 94–98; A. A. Vasiliev, "La Guerre de Cent Ans et Jeanne d'Arc dans la tradition byzantine," Byzantion 3 (1927): 241–50.

5   B. F. Manz, The Rise and Rule of Tamerlane (Cambridge, 1989), 15.

are vastly more circumstantial and reliable.[6] If we look closely at what Laonikos has done, it is actually impressive, if disappointing to the historian. He does much the same with the Council of Ferrara-Florence (see below). This is not different from what Herodotos did with the careers of Cyrus and Cambyses, which are mostly taken up by ethnography. The protagonist here hovers in the background and makes brief appearances.

The digressions in Book 3 range from Russia to Egypt and from a certain kingdom of Arabia to a conflation of India and China. They are normally single-topic digressions prompted by Timur's campaign against the place in question. There are two exceptions to this rule. First, there was no kingdom of Arabia in the fifteenth century and Timur did not campaign there. The source of the error is unknown, but Laonikos uses this imaginary "Arabia" to situate his general discussion of Islam.[7] Second, the digression on the Mongol-controlled north includes a secondary digression on the Russians, Permians, Prussians (Teutonic Order), Samogitians, Bohemians, Poles, Lithuanians, and Moldavians.[8] This secondary discussion is a digression from the account of the Mongols, prompted by the fact that the Russians paid tribute and were

6   N. Nicoloudis, Μεσαιωνική Μακεδονία, Θράκη και Μικρά Ασία: Προσεγγίσεις και αντιπαραθέσεις Βυζαντινών, Σλάβων και Τούρκων (Thessalonike, 2006), 219; idem, "Byzantine Historians on the Wars of Timur," Journal of Oriental and African Studies 8 (1996): 83–94 For his Turkish sources, see the third section of chap. 4.

7   See the second section of chap. 4.

8   H. Ditten, "Ἡ περὶ Ῥωσίας παρέκβασις τοῦ Λαονίκου Χαλκοκονδύλου," Παρνασσός 3 (1961): 89–99; idem, "Bemerkungen zu Laonikos Chalkokondyles's Nachrichten über die Länder und Völker an den europäischen Küsten des Schwarzen Meeres (15. Jahrhundert u. Z.)," Klio 43–45 (1965): 185–246; idem, "Die Korruptel Χωρόβιον und die Unechtheit der Trapezunt und Georgien betreffenden Partien in Laonikos Chalkokondyles's Geschichtwerk," in Studia Byzantina: Beiträge aus der byzantinischen Forschung der Deutschen Demokratischen Republik zum XII. Internationalen Byzantinistenkongress in Oxford, ed. J. Irmscher (Halle, 1966), 57–70; and idem, Russland-Exkurs.

subject to the Mongols. But most of the other peoples he then goes on to discuss had never been under Mongol control, so the digression here exceeds its bounds and becomes basically an account of eastern Europe.

The western digressions in Books 4, 5, and 6 have a different structure altogether. Setting aside that on Venice in Book 4, which is really a longer and more complex single-topic digression, these three books each contain a single manifold digression in which different kinds of information are stitched together in a seemingly meandering way. But the rambling appearance is deceptive, as these digressions are quite artfully put together. Two of them contain a narrative axis onto which secondary digressions are knotted, like an Inca Quipu. We have already examined the deliberate way in which Laonikos structures his account of the (mostly Latin) powers of mainland Greece around the career and diplomacy of Nerio I, the lord of Athens.[9] His account of the Council serves the same purpose in Book 6. He actually says almost nothing about the Council itself and seems to have been utterly uninterested in the religious issues at stake. But when the emperor reaches Ferrara, Laonikos devotes a full two and a half pages to the adulterous relationship between Parisina Malatesta, the wife of Nicolò III d'Este, lord of Ferrara, and his illegitimate son Ugo, which ended with Nicolò executing both wife and son and "devoting himself to frivolous fun in order to find some consolation for his fate" (6.8–10). Laonikos devotes more space to this piece of Italian opera than he does to the Council itself, and infuses it with Herodotean language.[10] Why? Does the story point somehow to

9   See the second section of chap. 1.

10   W. J. Aerts. "*Imitatio* and *Aemulatio* in Byzantium with Classical Literature, Especially in Historical Writing," in *Constructions of Greek Past: Identity and Historical Consciousness from Antiquity to the Present*, ed. H. Hokwerda (Groningen, 2003), 97. Laonikos could not possibly have known the works of Bandello, who died

the Council? Is it a joke about unholy unions, such as was about to happen at the Council on a religious level? Is it some kind of blasphemy about the "Father and the Son"? Or does Laonikos merely mean to imply that the Council, hosted initially by Nicolò, was precisely the kind of "frivolous fun" an Italian lord could have?

The Council then moves to Florence, which prompts an account of its republican constitution (6.12).[11] When the Greeks return home, they repudiate their agreement with the pope (6.16), so Laonikos returns to Italy to explain what was keeping the pope busy in Italy. He explains the wars raging there, especially the war between Venice and Milan, the strife between Guelphs and Ghibellines, and the rise of Sforza to the rule of Milan (6.17–24). The point of all this is to set the stage for the pope's refusal to hold up his end of the bargain (6.25):

> When the Greeks returned home, the pontiff Eugenius sent no help to them worthy of note. Then the Greeks immediately changed their minds and regretted having broken their agreement with the pontiff. But he was not sending aid for the following reason. He was involved in a war that had broken out in Italy between him and the Tuscans over a territorial dispute, and he had to maintain an army, expenses, and a general who was from his family.

Laonikos concludes with an overview of the powers in Italy, dividing them into tyrannies and republics (6.26, 6.30). This overview is interrupted by a fairly long account of the election of new popes, which counts as Laonikos's ethnography of the papacy, after a

---

in 1562. For this error, see A. Pippidi, *Visions of the Ottoman World in Renaissance Europe* (New York, 2013), 32–33.

11   See the last section of the present chapter.

fashion (6.27–29). This is interesting for two reasons. First, it seems to rank the papacy among the tyrannies of Italy.[12] Second, it is a hilarious piece of sexual polemic directed against the popes, reversing the hostile image that westerners had of the Byzantines by slyly comparing the popes to eunuchs and women.[13]

The digression on the Council is brilliantly structured. Not only does Laonikos use the Council and its aftermath as a thread on which to tie his discussions of Italian politics, he manages to bracket the Council between the image of a lord spying down through a peep-hole in the ceiling on his wife having sex with his own son and, at the other end, the image of a newly elected pope sitting in a throne with a hole in it so that his testicles dangle below, where they are felt up by a man whose job it was to ascertain that the pope was, in fact, a man. What with Italian men being shaven and all, how can you know who is a man and who a woman? I doubt a better way could have been devised to trivialize and delegitimate the Council and its underlying purpose. Scholars have noted that Laonikos does not mention the role that his teacher Plethon played at the Council or the great interest that he sparked among Italian humanists with his lectures.[14] I propose that he may not have wanted to associate him with the comic freak-show of this account and the bad faith that marked both sides involved in the Council.

Structurally the most complex digression in the *Histories* is that on Genoa, Naples, Alfonso V of Aragon, and Spain that takes up almost the whole second half of Book 5.[15] This one does

12 For "tyrant" in Laonikos, see the fourth section of the present chapter.

13 See pp. 187–88 below.

14 E.g., Woodhouse, *Plethon*, 136.

15 H. Ditten, "Spanien und die Spanier im Spiegel der Geschichtsschreibung des byzantinischen Historikers Laonikos Chalkondyles (15. Jahrhundert)," *Helikon* 3 (1963): 170–95; M. Morfakidis, "La península ibérica en la obra de Calcocondilas," *Erytheia* 6 (1985): 69–82; M. Morfakidis and E. Motos Guirao, "Un pasaje de

meander, though in a good Herodotean way. Its exceptional nature is acknowledged by Laonikos himself, who offers at its end the most elaborate statement closing a digression in the *Histories*: "These things, then, have been here recorded at such a length as a presentation of research that contributes to the overall theme of the work. I now return to the point where I began this digression, having been led so far away" (5.79). This digression also has the most tenuous link to the main narrative. It begins when Laonikos notes that Murad II kept peace with Genoa (5.57), which serves as a (meager) prompt for an account of Genoa (5.57–61) and its war with Alfonso V of Aragon (5.62–63). It then melds into an account of Alfonso's effort to take Naples from the French (5.64), which takes us back to Ladislao of Naples and his attack on Florence (5.65–66); to Giovanna II, René the Good, and Alfonso's sieges of the city (5.67–69); Alfonso's brother Juan in Navarre (5.70); the lands of the kingdom of Aragon (5.71); Castile, Portugal, and Granada (5.72–73); and the war between Alfonso and Castile, whose armies were led by Álvaro de Luna (5.74). We now realize that this was a flashback, as Laonikos tells us that it was at this point that Alfonso went to Italy (5.75). We return to Spain and the war between Castile and Granada, waged by Juan II and Álvaro (5.76–77), and close with the dynastic arrangements of Castile, Navarre, and France (5.78–79). Most of this is irrelevant to the theme of the rise of the Turks and the fall of the Greeks, though it does illustrate that Christian powers were expanding at the expense of the Muslims in the western Mediterranean, in contrast to what was happening in the east.

Laonicos Calcocondylas relativo a la batalla de la Higueruela y sus consecuencias inmediatas," in *Relaciones exteriores del Reino de Granada: IV Coloquio de Historia medieval Andaluza*, ed. C. Segura Graiño (Almeria, 1988), 71–82; and A. Ducellier, "La peninsule ibérique d'après Laonikos Chalkokondylis, chroniqueur byzantin du XVème siècle," *Norba* 5 (1984): 163–77.

We might label this as "ethnogeography gone wild," a game of seemingly free association, as we find often in Herodotos. Herodotos prefaces his *Histories* with the theme of conflict between east and west and begins with the Lydians because they were the first to subject Greeks to their power (1.6). When he comes to the Lydian king Alyattes and his war against Miletos, he mentions Periandros's involvement in the conflict, which prompts the story of Arion and the dolphin (1.24), which itself has nothing to do with the Lydians and Miletos. There are many such associative chains of material in Herodotos, some prompting major digressions. But Laonikos's western digression is not unstructured; rather, it has three narrative axes that artfully fade into each other, namely, the Genoese, Alfonso, and Álvaro, each of which brings forth the geography or history of northern Italy, southern Italy, and Spain, respectively. Each figure is the protagonist of his own section, and the move from one to the next is effected by transitional passages that recount their mutual wars, Genoa against Alfonso and Alfonso against Álvaro. It is in this way that they "fade" into each other. It is fitting to place Alfonso in the middle position here, as he was the figure who most linked Italy and Spain in the first half of the fifteenth century. It is also fitting that a digression that begins by noting that a sultan who was expanding his realm in the Balkans and was at peace with a major European power (Genoa) should end with a tale about how Castile was gaining the upper hand against its Muslim neighbor (Granada). The balance of power was shifting differently at opposite ends of the Mediterranean, and Laonikos moves us artfully from one end to the other.

Geography

Laonikos is not primarily a geographical writer. He is more interested in peoples than places. Usually his foreign lands simply "extend" or "reach" from here to there and are bounded mostly by their neighbors or some sea. There might be a city or two and a river to act as a landmark. It would be impossible to draw up a map of the world from his geographical description, even though he touches on most places between Mongolia and Portugal and between Britain and Arabia. It is also hard to form an impression of the overall layout of any particular region from his descriptions, which tend to be linear and one-dimensional, except for Spain. He does manage to convey a sense of the relation of Spain's kingdoms to each other and its overall shape, albeit with errors (5.71–72). Ducellier managed to produce a passable map based on Laonikos's accounts.[16]

His descriptions of other lands are incomplete or confused. He lists most of the regions of France, for example, but not their geographical relation to each other (2.30–31).[17] His account of the geography of Germany is impossibly difficult to follow, especially his effort to distinguish between upper and lower Germany, and may be corrupt or garbled from the start (2.14–16).[18] He correctly notes that Arabia is bounded by Egypt, Syria, and Persia, but then confusingly describes how one might reach it, or Asia Minor, from the Phasis river in Iberia by the Caucasus (3.13). He seems to fuse Britain with the Frisian banks when he says that the tides cause the British Isles to go from three to one and back again (2.38), unless he is copying Diodoros of Sicily on the promontories of Britain that become islands when the tide comes in.[19] His Caucasus, following

16   Ducellier, "Peninsule ibérique," 177; also Ditten, "Spanien und die Spanier"; Morfakidis, "Península ibérica."

17   Ducellier, "France et les Îles Britanniques"; idem, "L'Europe occidentale."

18   Ditten, "Deutschland-Exkurs"; idem, "Zwei verschiedene 'Wien' bei Laonikos Chalkokondyles," *BBulg* 5 (1978): 323–28.

19   Cf. Diodoros of Sicily, *Bibliotheke* 5.22.2–3; noticed by J. Harris, *Greek Emigres in the West, 1450–1520* (Camberley, 1995), 50–51.

some ancient writers, included both the mountains that we call by that name, but also the Hindu Kush (1.3).[20]

Laonikos obviously had oral informants for much of his contemporary geography. His main written source, however, was again Herodotos. Like him he divides the world into three parts (Europe, Asia, and Libya)[21] and calls Asia Minor "lower" Asia (as opposed to "upper" Asia, which is the rest of Asia for us).[22] It has been proposed that Laonikos used his teacher Plethon's *Corrections to Some of the Mistakes in Strabo*, a brief collection of notes that mostly correct Strabo on the basis of Ptolemy and deal only with his theoretical discussion of the shape of the inhabited world.[23] Plethon was working on Strabo after his return from Italy, i.e., in the 1440s, when he became acquainted with Laonikos. I will discuss here the first of the two putative debts.[24]

Plethon corrects Strabo's claim that the Caspian Sea was open to the outer ocean.[25] He adds that Aristotle (*Meteorology* 351a) says that many rivers flow into it and that it is connected to the Black Sea by an underground channel. Neither Plethon nor pseudo-Aristotle

---

20   Cf. Arrian, *Anabasis* 5.3–5.

21   Ditten, "Bemerkungen," 188–89.

22   The distinction is made by Herodotos, *Histories* 1.177; cf. *Hist.* 1.9–10, 3.13, 3.44, etc.

23   I.e., Strabo, *Geographika* 2.5.13–33; for Plethon, see A. Diller, "A Geographical Treatise by Georgius Gemistus Pletho," *Isis* 27 (1937): 441–51; cf. idem, "The Autographs of G. Gemistius Pletho," *Scriptorium* 10 (1956): 32; Woodhouse, *Plethon*, 181–86.

24   Ditten, *Russland-Exkurs*, 45, 91; N. Nicoloudis, "Observations on the Possible Sources of Laonikos Chalkokondyles's *Demonstrations of Histories*," *Byzantina* 17 (1994): 78–79; Zographopoulos, Λαόνικος, 51–52, who gives a long list of information that Laonikos could not, in fact, have derived from Plethon. The following discussion comes from A. Kaldellis, "The Greek Sources of Laonikos Chalkokondyles," *GRBS* 52 (2012): 738–65.

25   Plethon, *Corrections* 1 (p. 442); Strabo, *Geographika* 2.5.18.

name those rivers. Laonikos says that "this sea is large because many rivers flow into it and it stretches over many stades; it is said not to open out into the outer ocean at any point. But I have learned that there is a channel that leads from it and flows out into the Indian Ocean" (3.11). Plethon might be the authority behind the "it is said," but there are no verbal parallels. Moreover, Laonikos names the Indian Ocean, not the Black Sea, as the outlet of the channel, and he names the rivers that pour into the Caspian Sea (the Araxes and Choaspes), while Plethon does not. In fact, both Herodotos and Ptolemy had said that the Caspian was an enclosed sea that did not communicate with the ocean.[26] The debate between them and the proponents of the opposite view had been laid out by Eustathios in the twelfth century.[27] This tradition was probably the basis for Plethon's correction and likely for that of Laonikos too. Laonikos's account of the peoples who live by the Caspian, following immediately upon his description of it, is similar to the account in Herodotos of the peoples living by the Caucasus, likewise following upon his description of the Caspian.[28] Laonikos conjoins the names Hyrkania and Kaspia for this sea in a way that follows Ptolemy and not Plethon. It is not necessary, then, to believe that Laonikos was following Plethon here. The only point that they have in common is that the sea was enclosed, and there was a solid ancient tradition behind that anyway.

The possibility emerges, then, that Laonikos might have used Ptolemy and the pseudo-Aristotelian *Meteorology* independently of Plethon. Interestingly, in 1465–66 Ptolemy was being made

---

26   Hdt. 1.202–3; Ptolemy, *Geography* 7.5.4.

27   Eustathios of Thessalonike, *Commentary on Dionysios Periegetes* 227.

28   Cf. Herodotos's ἔθνεα δὲ ἀνθρώπων πολλὰ καὶ παντοῖα with Laonikos's ἔθνη πολλά τε καὶ ἄλκιμα; cf. also Hdt. 4.90 with *Hist.* 1.12 on the Tearos river and the city of Ainos.

available to Mehmed II himself by Georgios Amiroutzes and his son and then by Georgios of Trebizond; Amiroutzes was just then getting his hands on Laonikos's *Histories*.[29] At roughly that time, Michael Apostoles, possibly also a student of Plethon, claims in his letters from Crete that he too was reading and copying Ptolemy.[30]

So it is not clear that Laonikos had Plethon's *Corrections* when writing the *Histories*.[31] Plethon, following Ptolemy, accepted the theory that the Nile flows down from the mountain of the Moon (*Selenaion*),[32] whereas Laonikos follows the pseudo-Aristotelian *Meteorology* in saying that it flows down from the Silver mountain (*Argyron*).[33] Laonikos seems to have taken the notion that the Tartesos river (the Guadalquivir?) originates in the Pyrenees from the *Meteorology* too—making that text his main source for rivers and seas—though from that text it had passed into the geographical tradition.[34] The error that Germany begins at the Pyrenees is unique to him, though there are possible textual problems here.[35] It may be based on Herodotos's report (2.33) that the Danube originates by "the city of Pyrene,"[36] repeated in the *Meteorology*.

In sum, for his geography Laonikos used oral informants and Herodotos, probably the Aristotelian *Meteorology*, and possibly

29   Babinger, *Mehmed*, 248–50; J. Raby, "Mehmed the Conqueror's Greek Scriptorium," *DOP* 38 (1983): 24; Monfasani, *George Amiroutzes*, 9–10. For Amiroutzes and Laonikos, see the third section of chap. 1.

30   Michael Apostoles, *epp.* 3 (Legrand) and 121 (Noiret).

31   Plethon, *Corrections* 7 (pp. 444–45) knew that the *Sinai* and *Seres*, encompassing what we call the Chinese, lived to the east of the Indians and Skythians, whereas Laonikos seems to confuse Σίνη with India (3.66: the mss. Συήνη was emended by Tafel to Σίνη, but Laonikos may have been using a different spelling).

32   Plethon, *Corrections* 2 (p. 443); Ptolemy, *Geography* 2.5.3.

33   *Hist.* 3.40; pseudo-Aristotle, *Meteorology* 350b.

34   *Hist.* 2.14; pseudo-Aristotle, *Meteorology* 350b.

35   Ditten, "Deutschland-Exkurs," 51–58.

36   Hdt. 2.33.

Ptolemy. He does not seem to have used Plethon's *Corrections*, though he might have read it at Mistra. There is no solid evidence that he used Strabo directly.

Neo-Herodotean Ethnography

Laonikos's synoptic ethnographical digressions in Books 2–3, especially those of the Christian world, are couched in Herodotean terms. Laonikos sometimes lifts statements from Herodotos verbatim and applies them to other people, giving his world a thoroughly Herodotean feel, even though the elements have been rearranged. I provide a sample list in Appendix 3. The most striking examples occur in his discussion of the Germans, who are called the healthiest people of which we know (2.16), following what Herodotos had said of the Libyans (4.187), and who would be the most powerful of all the people in the world if they but united under one ruler, following what Herodotos says about the Thracians (5.3). I will revisit this last statement. Germany, he says, has neither earthquakes nor plagues; curiously, the seventh-century historian Theophylaktos Simokattes, also a hyper-Atticist, has the Turks make the same boast about their own lands.[37] Is this possibly another glimpse into Laonikos's Byzantine reading?

Most nations in Laonikos's *Histories* are given ethnonyms from Herodotos, but this was typical in Byzantine rhetoric and historiography.[38] So the French he calls Celts (and France is "Galatia"); the Bulgarians are Mysians, the Hungarians are Paionians, the Russians Sarmatians, the Wallachians Dacians, the Mongols Skythians, and the Serbs Triballoi. He does the same with some

---

37 *Hist.* 2.16 with Theophylaktos, *History* 7.8.13.

38 A. Kaldellis, *Le discours ethnographique à Byzance: continuités et ruptures* (Paris, 2012), chap. 9.

place names (so Cairo is Memphis, Mistra Sparta, Monemvasia Epidauros, and Thessalonike is Therme) and offices (bishop is archpriest and vizier is *prytanis*). In most cases, this is a simple one-to-one substitution, so his classical names are translatable into whatever name we find more familiar (the way English "Germany" can be translated today into *Deutschland* or *Allemagne*). Like many Byzantine historians before him, Laonikos occasionally translates his own terms, explaining that the Mysians are also known as Bulgarians and the Triballoi as Serbs (1.32); there is also an equivalence between Dacians and Vlachs (6.47; at 9.96 it seems that Dacia is Vlachia). He calls Naples both "Naples" and "Parthenope," after the original Greek name, but this might be both hyper-archaic and hyper-modern: perhaps Laonikos knew that Alfonso V had promoted the cult of the nymph Parthenope at Naples.[39]

Not all of his classical names are neutral, however, or without problems. He calls the Byzantines, who were Romans, "Greeks," but this was a central part of his political agenda, and I will discuss it separately below; it was not a mere classical substitution. Laonikos also makes an inexplicable statement concerning the Hungarians, whom he calls Paionians throughout. Discussing their origins, he alludes to two schools of thought, that they were originally either Getai or Dacians, but takes an agnostic position (2.17). He then adds that "this name is what they use for themselves and what they are called by the Italians, and so it would not really be correct for me to call them by any other name." It is not clear which name he means (presumably "Paionians"), but this is not what they called themselves or what they were called by the Italians (for example, in his *Commentaries*, Aeneas calls them *Hungari*). The term *Oungroi*, moreover, was established in Byzantine usage along with

---

39   K. W. Christian, *Empire without End: Antiquities Collections in Renaissance Rome, c. 1350–1527* (New Haven, 2010), 47.

"Paionian" and other ethnonyms ("Turks"). We may be dealing with an unrevised or obscurely written passage here.

This onomastic classicism is an act of ethnographic translation. Even the types match up on occasion with classical ethnography, for example the "Celts" (i.e., French) are impetuous and rush into battle without much of a plan (2.20), like the Celts of the ancient ethnographic imagination.[40] The role of Herodotos's Persians in Laonikos's *Histories* is played by the Turks, and while they are not called Persians some of their stereotypical qualities adhere to them, for example, traces of oriental despotism and servility (9.88). But it is not primarily in such specific parallels, which are few, that Laonikos's world reveals its debts to Herodotos; it is, rather, in the conceptual framework of Laonikos's ethnographic imagination. The basic template, for both thought and expression, is provided by statements in Herodotos such as that "the Lydians have the same customs as do the Greeks" (1.94: Λυδοὶ δὲ νόμοισι μὲν παραπλησίοισι χρέωνται καὶ Ἕλληνες), and alongside *nomoi* we find "language," "lifestyle," and other such organizing concepts (ἔθιμα, δίαιτα, ἤθη, etc.). These are the main ingredients of Laonikos's synoptic ethnographies.

Like his prose generally, the digressions are minimalist and abstract. There is one people in each place and it has one language,[41] customs, religion, material culture, and a territory bounded by other peoples or natural features. Very little flora is described and almost no fauna. While Laonikos does mention specific cultural idiosyncrasies of each people, his analytical categories are often filled with more abstractions. Specifically, his

---

40   Cf. the French "Celts" in Anna Komnene, *Alexiad* 5.5.5.

41   An exception would appear to be what Laonikos calls Hungarian Wallachia (Transylvania or Ardeal), whose people "speak the language of the Hungarians in part and in part also that of the Wallachians" (5.45).

ethnography is self-referential, or at least relational in a way that is not always grounded. Like the Lydians in Herodotos who have the same customs as the Greeks (except they prostitute their daughters!), the Hungarians "are like the Germans in terms of weaponry and in way of life and customs, and favor a luxurious life as, they say, the French and the Germans do" (2.17). Now, when we turn to the Germans, we find out that "as a political community they are organized in the same way as the Romans, whose customs and way of life they have adopted. They are also like the Romans in most other respects" (2.16). As we will see, however, these "Romans" do not really exist. They are a principle for organizing ethnographic relations in the west, but are otherwise an always-deferred signifier, not, apparently, a real flesh-and-blood people.[42] So except for the specific, idiosyncratic cultural traits that Laonikos attributes to the Hungarians and Germans, we ultimately cannot form a precise idea of their "customs."

As for the French, to whom the Hungarians are also compared, "their way of life is more luxurious than that of the Italians and their dress is similar" (2.34). At least Laonikos is consistent, in that both the Hungarians and French seem to be soft, or softer than the Italians, but nothing in the *Histories* explains in what way the Italians are "hard." This too is deferred. As for the British, "they have the same dress, customs, and way of life as the French" (2.39). The Russians have the customs of the Greeks, but the material culture of the Mongols (3.26). The people of Ardeal (roughly in Transylvania) "have the same customs and lifestyle as the Hungarians" (5.45)—which takes us to the Germans and the French, which takes us to the Romans and the Italians. But as a cultural standard the Romans are a fiction, and while Laonikos says a lot about Italy he does not provide any information that can

42   See the second section of chap. 5.

plug the gap in his discussion of other people. It is like being ushered into a room full of people and being told exactly how they are all related to each other, but not who they are.

I do not mean to imply that these comparisons exhaust Laonikos's ethnography, but they are a curious feature of it. He does still manage to provide a great deal of specific information about each people. The western lands about whose politics and internal configuration he gives the most detailed information are Italy and then Spain (without comparisons to others), with France a distant third. It is an interesting coincidence that this is the order of the rulers of Athens, seen looking back in time from Laonikos's vantage point: Florentines, Catalans, and Burgundians. His breakdown of the regions of France begins with Burgundy and devotes more attention to it than the others (2.31). Can we see this as more Athenocentrism in the *Histories*?

Where Laonikos's comparative approach pays dividends is in his treatment of languages. I will examine below his grasp of the Slavic continuum, which was more accurate than that of some later Slavic theorists. For western Europe he approaches languages through comparison too, but here it works. The language of the French "differs from that of the Italians, but not so much that one might believe theirs is a different language from that of the Italians" (2.34); "The Wallachians speak a language that is similar to that of the Italians, but so corrupted and different from it that it is difficult for the Italians to understand anything they say, unless they recognize words that are spoken distinctly" (2.22).[43]

___

43   See H. Ditten, "Laonikos Chalkokondyles und die Sprache der Rumänen," in *Aus der byzantinistischen Arbeit der Deutschen Demokratischen Republik*, ed. J. Irmscher (Berlin, 1957), 1:93–105, on the textual problems of some passages; also 102–4 for the Herodotean origin of Laonikos's terminology for languages. Cf. Pius II, *Commentaries* 11 (53:737): "The Wallachians speak Italian, but an imperfect, corrupted Italian."

Italy is again the standard, but he never "explains" the Italian language, or the languages of Spain. Other languages are incomparable. Hungarians "speak a language that is like that spoken by no other people and is entirely different from that of the Germans, Bohemians, and Poles" (2.17); also Lithuanian (3.30). The phrase is modeled on that in Herodotos about the cave-dwelling Ethiopians (4.183)—except that Herodotos then compares it to the sound made by bats. The British "speak their own particular language, which does not sound at all like that of the Germans, the French, or any of their neighbors" (2.39). In the early fifteenth century, that must have depended on whom one spoke to.

Interestingly, Laonikos says little about the languages of Muslim peoples, with this exception: certain garments "are produced by Persians called Ajems; for all who speak the language of the Ajems are Persians and can converse in the Persian language" (3.71). Unfortunately, he does not devote a digression to contemporary Persians. I suppose that this is because he did not want them to distract from his transference of their narrative role to the Turks.

Besides its tendency to abstract and compare, Laonikos's ethnography is also generally upbeat. Most cities are prosperous and large and most people are hardy in war. He generally focuses on what each nation is good at, rather than the opposite, and no Christian or Hellenocentric bias inflects his accounts. When he can praise a people for its antiquity, extent, and power he does, even though it creates a crowd at the top of the ladder. For example, we saw above that he lifts what Herodotos says about the Thracians and applies it to the Germans, that if they united they would be the most powerful people in the world (2.16). But he says basically the same thing about the Mongols too (3.32), and in his preface he hopes that the Greeks will, in the future, unite under their own king again and deal with their neighbors from a position of strength (1.2). He might even have been thinking of Aristotle's opinion that the Greeks could rule the world if they united in a single state.[44] The French are great, prosperous, and ancient (2.30), but the Slavs too are "the most ancient and largest among all the peoples in the world" (1.38). Greatness here is probably a function of physical extent, not glory. But we are elsewhere told that the Germans inhabit a larger part of the world than anyone but the Mongols (2.16), and Timur learned that the Mongols "are the most ancient among all the peoples in the world" (3.22). There cannot be two "most" ancient peoples. Now, Laonikos calls the Mongols "Skythians," yet in Herodotos (4.5) the Skythians believe themselves to be "the youngest of all peoples."[45] Germany is the best governed of all the lands to the northwest (2.15), and London is second to none among western cities (2.40). Meanwhile, "the race of the Arabs is populous and wealthy and second to none in its prosperity among all the people of Asia. It is ancient and has spread over a large part of Asia" (3.13). Laonikos likes the phrase "second to none," and uses it to praise at least seven men of different ethnic background, but most were contemporaries of each other![46] Finally, we have a western author whose view of "the Other" is *too* upbeat and positive!

On the negative side, the French perhaps think too highly of themselves (2.30, 2.34), which gets them into trouble at Nikopolis (2.20), and the Wallachians are not well governed (2.22), a mild way of putting it. He thinks the British and the Flemish are naïve for allowing their guests to greet the woman of the house with a

---

44   Aristotle, *Politics* 7.7 (1327b30–33).

45   F. Hartog, *The Mirror of Herodotus: The Representation of the Other in the Writing of History*, trans. J. Lloyd (Berkeley, 1988), 27–28, who notes that Justin, *Epitome of Pompeius Trogus* 2.1 says that they themselves believed the opposite.

46   *Hist.* 1.49, 2.8, 2.26, 3.51, 4.10, 4.56, and 6.14.

kiss, even on the street! (2.39)[47] But that is all. In sum, Laonikos is more discreet and non-judgmental than Herodotos, whose relativism did not prevent him from rejecting or critiquing many of the foreign customs that he described.[48]

Laonikos does not present his geography and ethnography as an "update" or "correction" of Herodotos. Indeed, he never mentions Herodotos or any other classical, Byzantine, or western source. He could easily have highlighted his new information and passed himself off as a great scholar, innovator, discoverer, and even explorer. Instead, his world is inscribed on what appears to be an almost clean slate. He does not engage in textual polemics. It is as though no one had ever written about all this before. This, in fact, might be part of his emulation of Herodotos, who had few "authors" to respond to. Laonikos's world emerges on its own terms, as a kind of parallel universe to that of his model. Its general structure is the same, as are the people who populate it and the narrative that holds them together, though its elements have been rearranged. Laonikos's world is haunted, not predetermined, by that of Herodotos.

The Functions of an Archaic Political Landscape

There is a tension inherent in the classicism of Laonikos's Herodotean project. On the one hand, he wants to recognize cultural

47   This was comically altered by his sixteenth-century adapter Makarios Melissourgos (= *Georgius Phrantzes: Chronicon Maius*, 215), who made the British polygamous, and probably misunderstood (and attributed to the Irish) by Nikandros of Kerkyra, *Journeys* 45.5: Moraitis, "Sur un passage de Chalcondyle." Nikandros's editor doubts that there is a textual relationship here or elsewhere with Laonikos (20 n. 2), but they have the same vocabulary, categories, and some verbal parallels, for example, regarding the English longbow: *Hist.* 2.40 with Nikandros, *Journeys* 43.2.

48   E.g., Hdt. 1.199, 2.63–64, 4.46; cf. Lateiner, *Historical Method*, chap. 7; R. Thomas, *Herodotus in Context: Ethnography, Science and the Art of Persuasion* (Cambridge, 2000), passim.

and religious diversity in a way that no one in the Christian world had yet done, by mapping out different peoples, places, customs, religions, and languages in a relatively non-judgmental way. His outlook is neither Christian nor premised on the superiority of one culture or state. On the other hand, his generic templates tend to strip people and customs of their distinctiveness and subsume them under timeless categories. It is not only the "vernacular" that is sacrificed for its formal or classical equivalent (e.g., Celt for French), but cultural nuance is lost when everyone is pressed into the same mold. I will consider here Laonikos's political categories.

Most of Laonikos's world was ruled by monarchs, but let us first note the exceptions. While Germany has a king (8.59), it also has certain "widely-known and prosperous cities, some of which are governed under their own authority by egalitarian regimes" (2.15: ὑπὸ σφῶν αὐτῶν ἐς τὸ ἰσοδίαιτον εὐθυνομένας). Laonikos lists Nuremberg, Strasbourg, and Hamburg, but says nothing more about them. Italy also has some republics (πολιτεῖαι: 6.30, 8.63), notably Venice and Florence, whose constitutions Laonikos discusses at length. His use of political theory is limited to an observation that Venice went from being a democracy to an aristocracy when the people became too busy with their private affairs (making money in trade) and so entrusted the government to the best men (4.33). This evidently worked out well for them, but Laonikos appears neutral between the two forms.

When it comes to monarchies, Laonikos has four types (which may really be only three). Some nations have kings, *basileis*, for example, those we call Castile, Aragon, France, Britain, Hungary, Byzantium, the Ottoman Turks, the Mongols, Trebizond, and whomever it was Timur ruled. The difference between a sultan, a khan, and a Byzantine *basileus* is obliterated, for Laonikos uses only the term *basileus*. Below them comes a wide range of generic *hegemones* or *archontes*, which we may translate simply as "rulers."

This group includes governors of provinces subordinate to a king, including the Byzantine despots; the rulers of formerly autonomous but now dependent territories, such as Serbia and Wallachia; less powerful rivals, such as Karaman in Asia Minor; and magistrates in any political system, including free cities. It is not, however, clear why the ruler of the Greeks is a *basileus* while the ruler of Wallachia is a *hegemon*, when both were basically vassals of the sultan.

The third type of rule is a tyranny, a polyvalent term. In a minority of instances, it may mean "oppressive despotism," though in this sense it occurs not as a primary designation, but a characterization of someone's behavior (1.11, 4.12, 4.54). The primary meaning of "tyrant" for Laonikos is that which it had in the sixth century B.C., that is, a ruler whose position is more personal or derived from his family than from what we might call a constitutional consensus. But it does not necessarily have negative connotations. Here more than anywhere Laonikos attempts to recapture a pre-classical outlook.[49] He most consistently calls tyrants the rulers of Milan (both the Visconti and Sforza) and the Florentine rulers of his native Athens. This usage is not polemical:

49 J. F. McGlew, *Tyranny and Political Culture in Ancient Greece* (Ithaca, 1993); C. Dewald, "Form and Content: The Question of Tyranny in Herodotus," in *Popular Sovereignty and its Discontents in Ancient Greece*, ed. K. A. Morgan (Austin, 2003), 25–58. In his *Commentaries*, Pius II calls tyrants the Palaiologoi despots of the Peloponnese (3.3.1–2; v. 25, 195; and 8: v. 35, 523, though "despot" on the next page) and the Gattilusi of Lesbos (10: v. 43, 633). It is not clear what sense he was going for here, though it seems not to be the classical negative one. As for Renaissance concepts of tyranny, H. Baron, *The Crisis of the Early Italian Renaissance: Civic Humanism and Republican Liberty in the Age of Classicism and Tyranny* (Princeton, 1966), fails to theorize tyranny (even when he discusses Salutati's treatise *De Tyranno*: 100–103, 146–66; cf. the enigmatic reference at 161); see R. G. Witt, "The *De Tyranno* and Coluccio Salutati's View of Politics and Roman History," *Nuova Rivista Storica* 53 (1969): 434–74. For legal attempts to define tyranny via constitutional theory, see J. Black, *Absolutism in Renaissance Milan: Plenitude of Power under the Visconti and the Sforza 1329–1535* (Oxford, 2009).

as we saw, Laonikos praised Antonio I Acciaiuoli (4.57–58). There are tyrannies in Germany (e.g., Austria) that are to be distinguished from "egalitarian" cities (e.g., Nuremberg) and from episcopal states (2.15). But he generally believes that all Germany is well governed, without regard for these distinctions. Some cities in Russia are tyrannies (3.26) and some too in Italy, besides Milan: Genoa sometimes (5.60) and others (6.26).

In singular cases the label is used for rulers who are otherwise *hegemones*: the rulers of Burgundy (2.19), Wallachia (2.23), Serbia (4.9), and the emirs of Anatolia (6.1). It is not clear why they are called tyrants in these unique instances (in the case of Wallachia and Serbia perhaps because they had seized power). The only place where Laonikos seems to define the term is in the case of the "king of Arabia"—though no such thing existed: "by custom they have a king who is not a tyrant but is appointed by them on a footing of equality and equal rights" (3.13). By this standard, however, the Ottoman sultan could not have been a king, rather than a tyrant. We should not press for more precision or consistency. But when Laonikos says of the prophet Muhammad that "his lawcode bears the mark of a just man, not someone who became a tyrant" (3.18), he means this as praise.

The fourth and final category of monarch in the *Histories* is what we might translate as a "Roman emperor" or, better, "emperor of the Romans." Now, there were two figures called that in the early fifteenth century, a "German" one and a Byzantine one, though they had different titles; those titles meant very different things to their subjects; and they lacked a theoretical framework to accommodate their co-existence. Laonikos calls them both *basileis*. While we may call them both "emperors," they had little in common. In the west, emperor was a title bestowed for a variety of reasons over time that meant different things. One of them, for example, was that the ruler in question exercised some kind of general authority over a number of different peoples or subordinate kingdoms. The sense in which he was Roman or "of the Romans" was also elusive.[50] The Byzantine emperor, by contrast, was simply the ruler of the Roman people, which is who the Byzantines were, despite our reluctance to call them that. It is confusing to call both of these figures "emperors," because they cannot be compared. Our undifferentiated use of the term also blurs important distinctions, such as between *being* and *having* an empire, or between *being an empire* and *having an emperor*. The Roman Republic, for example, had an empire before it had an emperor: Should we classify it as an empire because of its conquests? Byzantium, on the other hand, had an emperor, even when it did not exercise imperial dominion over conquered lands: should we call it an "empire" just because it had a ruler whose title *basileus* we prefer to translate as "emperor" rather than "king"? In my view, modern scholarship has not sufficiently theorized these terms and uses them loosely out of sheer inertia. In this sense, Laonikos is perhaps right to treat the Byzantine ruler as just another *basileus*, the king of a particular people (even if I do not agree with him that they were the *Greek* people).

Since the Principate, the Greek-speaking east had called what we call the Roman emperor "the *basileus* of the Romans." In Laonikos's terms, this would be the king of the Romans. Laonikos, however, believed that those whom we call Byzantines were Greeks, so their ruler was for him a national king, "the king of the Greeks" or "the king of Byzantion." The last ruler in Constantinople whom he regards as the *basileus* of the Romans

---

50   R. Folz, *The Concept of Empire in Western Europe from the Fifth to the Fourteenth Century*, trans. S. A. Ogilvie (London, 1969)—a book with many conceptual problems; B. Arnold, *Medieval Germany, 500–1300: A Political Interpretation* (Toronto, 1997), 75–125; B. S. Bachrach, "Pirenne and Charlemagne," in *After Rome's Fall: Narrators and Sources of Early Medieval History*, ed. A. C. Murray (Toronto, 1998), 219.

is Justinian (4.19). After that (he does not say exactly when), they become Greeks for him, even though he knows perfectly well that in their own eyes they remained Romans.[51]

Laonikos believed that Rome and the Romans were western entities and that the pope typically appointed their king (*basileus*)—whoever exactly these western "Romans" were, which is unclear.[52] I suspect that he would have been content to call these western emperors "*basileis* of the Romans," i.e., kings of the Romans, for he does just that at 1.6 (and he calls Constantine that at 1.5 and Justinian at 4.19). However, a title commonly used by the Palaiologan emperors was not just *basileus* but "*basileus* and *autokrator* of the Romans." We need not now discuss the subtle and changing nuances of the term *autokrator* in Byzantine usage, which some modern scholars take as their justification for "enhancing" *basileus* ("king") to "emperor."[53] But Laonikos's purpose is precisely to strip the Greeks of the delusion that their monarch was the *basileus* and *autokrator* of the Romans (1.5), and so he deliberately transfers that title to the western emperor, calling him *basileus* of the Romans (1.6), or *basileus* and *autokrator* of the Romans (2.13, 2.32), or *autokrator* of the Romans (2.18, 2.20, 2.24, 5.79, and 8.59)—even though, of course, the Greek word *autokrator* was not used in the west. In other words, it is the *Roman* part of the title that interests him, which he provocatively wants to transfer to the west, not the *autokrator* (or the *basileus and autokrator*). He wants his (Greek) readers to know that the titles and rights that they believed belonged to the Byzantine emperor were actually due to the western emperors. *Autokrator* was not a term

---

51   See chap. 6.

52   See the second section of chap. 5.

53   Even the entry in the *Oxford Dictionary of Byzantium* (1:235) shows that the meanings of *autokrator* were too complex to reduce in this way.

used in the west, where its Byzantine nuances were moot (the title of the western emperor was something like *Romanorum imperator semper Augustus*, or *Römischer Kaiser* in German). But Laonikos was not trying to be precise here, any more than when he called the sultan *basileus*. The point he was making to his Greek audience concerned who did and who did not own the Roman legacy in the fifteenth century, and about the Roman pretensions that his readers had to surrender before they embraced the new Greek identity that he and Plethon were offering them.

In sum, Laonikos's rulers are either national kings, subordinate rulers, or "tyrants." We might be tempted to "translate" his *basileis* and *hegemones* into a dozen different local forms, filling his text with sultans, emperors, kings, khans, despots, voivodes, and what not. But this, I believe, would be a mistake. First, it would obliterate his deliberate classicism and minimalism, which folded all positions into a simple schema that does, after all, contain a political ideology of its own. His unconventional terminology (e.g., "king of the Greeks") offers a distinct view of the world, its people, and the nature of their political systems. To introduce an army of ostensibly authentic titles from a dozen languages would distort his text and imbue it with a local specificity that it deliberately lacks; we would also lose the quaintness of his tyrants. We would have to dig into encyclopedias to find the proper titles for a host of Islamic monarchs. Nor could we be consistent about it. At what point, for instance, would we stop calling the Ottoman rulers emirs and start calling them sultans (all the while translating Laonikos's one term *basileus*)?[54] (It is, by contrast, possible to replace his classical ethnonyms with more familiar versions, e.g., Paionians with Hungarians, because this involves a one-to-one correspondence of terms and so is, in fact, an act of simple translation.)

---

54 Cf. H. W. Lowry, *The Nature of the Early Ottoman State* (New York, 2003), 37.

Second, it would be misleading to translate his *"basileus* of the Greeks" as "emperor of the Greeks" (for all that some modern historians use that hybrid polemical term). Laonikos's point was to deny his Greeks *any* Roman claim or association, including the imperial title, and we have no authority to override him when trying to understand him or to understand the Byzantines themselves (whose outlook he did not share). He emphatically did not believe that the king of the Greeks was an emperor. To be truly "authentic," we would have to call the Byzantine ruler "emperor of the Romans," but that effaces Laonikos's entire point.

Third, what one called the sultan was a controversial issue in that age. Doukas called the sultans *rulers, tyrants,* and *barbarians,* because he hated them and wanted them to seem illegitimate; that is why he never called them *basileis.* For him, it was the Byzantine (Roman) ruler who was the *basileus.* By contrast, Kritoboulos calls Mehmed II *basileus* precisely to present him as the legitimate successor of the *basileis* of the Romans whom he supplanted by conquest.[55] But this does not mean that Laonikos was "closer" to Kritoboulos. For one thing, he does not have a theory of legitimacy, certainly not one that is grounded in titles. When he refers to the *basileus* without qualification, he usually means the sultan, but this is only because the sultan is his narrative focus.[56] His world is populated by many kings, and no one of them seems to enjoy any preeminence. In contrast to Kritoboulos's panegyical exercise, then, by placing all monarchs on more or less the same level Laonikos makes them and their subjects seem less different from each other. This was a way of affirming their common humanity.

55   For a survey, see K. Moustakas, "Byzantine 'Visions' of the Ottoman Empire: Theories of Ottoman Legitimacy by Byzantine Scholars after the Fall of Constantinople," in *Images of the Byzantine World: Visions, Messages and Meanings. Studies Presented to Leslie Brubaker,* ed. A. Lymberopoulou (Farnham, 2011), 215–29.

56   *Pace* Moustakas, "Byzantine 'Visions' of the Ottoman Empire," 224.

Laonikos did not believe in incommensurate cultures that could not understand each other. His classical taxonomies cut through the distractions of titles, enabling his world to be compared to that of Herodotos and its members to each other.

The "Illyrian" Question and the Origin of the Slavs

A question that, for unknown reasons, preoccupied Laonikos—he turns to it four times (1.29, 1.38–39, 3.31, 10.16–17)—concerns the origin of the Illyrians.[57] Here we have to be careful with terminology. "Illyrian" means two things for him: all Slavs or Slavic-speakers, on the one hand, and the kingdom of Bosnia, on the other (as part to whole). It is easy to see which of the two he means in each instance, and we would not go wrong if we translated the first as "Slavs" and the second as "Bosnians." Then everything makes sense. Otherwise modern readers can become confused, especially when he categorically denies that Albanians are Illyrians (1.29, 10.16). Other contemporary sources did refer to the Albanians as Illyrians,[58] and there is, of course, a vigorous modern debate about the relation between Albanians and the ancient Illyrians, especially linguistically,[59] but as far as I can tell Laonikos's argument does not involve the ancient Illyrians. He must have known about the ancient Illyrians from ancient sources, but does not draw them into his argument about modern Illyrians. When he says that Albanians are not Illyrians, he means that they are not Slavs. It is not clear what he thought the exact relation between ancient and modern (i.e., Slavic) Illyrians is, and he seems to accept the

---

57   Ditten, *Russland-Exkurs*, 17–19, 63–64.

58   Citations in Ditten, *Russland-Exkurs*, 106–7 n. 128.

59   J. Wilkes, *The Illyrians* (Oxford, 1995), 277–80. See the papers in Ch. Gaparis, ed., *Οι Αλβανοί στον Μεσαίωνα* (Athens, 1998).

Bosnians as the archetypal "Slavs," probably because their territory was the land that he regarded as ancient Illyria.[60] But when he says that "the Albanians should be associated more with the Macedonians than with any other people in the world. For they are like no one else, except the Macedonians" (10.17), I have no idea what he means; Laonikos never explains who these "Macedonians" are.[61] Certainly they were not Slavs, by his definition.

Laonikos is prompted to discuss the "Illyrian question" by his mention of Serbs (1.29), Bulgarians and Serbs (1.38–39), Russians (3.31), and Bosnians (10.16–17). His basic theory is that

> Serbs, Bulgarians, Illyrians [here Bosnians], Croatians, Poles, and Russians speak one and the same language. So if we must draw a conclusion from this evidence, it would be that they are all one and the same people, being of the same race. But over time their customs began to deviate from each other and they settled in the different lands in which they had arrived. But nothing clear is said about them by anyone that we could present as reliable history. [1.38]

Elsewhere (10.17), he admits that the Slavic languages have differentiated:

60   Pius II, *Commentaries* 3.6.2 (25:201) also says that "the Bosnians were originally an Illyrian people," but does not explain what "Illyrian" meant to him. In Book 12 (43:795–96), he says that "the Croatians, Dalmatians, Bosnians, Serbians, Rascians, and Bulgarians (called Mysians by the ancients) speak Slavonic; the Wallachians a corrupt Italian; the Transylvanians German."

61   Pius II, *Commentaries* 6 (35:458) says only that Albania was once a part of Macedonia. At 35:460, he has Skanderbeg respond to a hostile letter by saying that the Albanians are Epirots and if "you" (i.e., the Italians) call them Macedonians, then you are conceding to us a far greater ancestry (he clearly takes this as referring to the ancient Macedonians). Ditten, *Russland-Exkurs*, 106, has proposed that Laonikos was following Pius here, which I doubt: see p. 90 below.

I also agree with those who say that the Illyrian race derives its name from the land, but that it has dispersed into groups that have spoken different languages at different times so that it consists of many races that differ from each other with respect to language but to which this name, Illyrians [Slavs], is given.

It should be noted that Laonikos is refreshingly correct in identifying Slavic languages. Later Slavist and Illyrianist theorists would jumble together a whole bunch of irrelevant languages, usually in an effort to enhance the prestige of their own.[62] We must also remember that he has translated most of the modern names into classicizing equivalents, so the list above actually reads Triballoi, Mysians, Illyrians, Croatians, Poles, and Sarmatians, and he later adds Permians (3.27)[63] and Dalmatians (10.16). "Illyrian" would remain a standard way of referring to Slavs until the eighteenth century.

The "Illyrian question" for Laonikos is whether the original homeland of the Slavs, from which they set out to settle in their present locations, was on this or the other side of the Danube. At 1.29, he suggests that the original homeland of the Slavs was in Bosnia, and that the Serbs moved east and north from there. That is also why he uses the generic "Illyrian" as the particular classicizing ethnonym of the Bosnians: they are the only Slavs who have not moved from the original homeland. At 1.38, he repeats this theory, but adds an alternative, which he thinks less likely, namely that the Illyrians came down from the extreme north and settled south of the Danube. In the next paragraph, however, he seems to

62   J. Fine, *When Ethnicity Did Not Matter in the Balkans: A Study of Identity in Pre-Nationalist Croatia, Dalmatia, and Slavonia in the Medieval and Early-Modern Periods* (Ann Arbor, 2006), 223–33. See also the previous note for Pius II.

63   Of course, the Permic languages are not Slavic or even Indo-European, but by this point many Permians near the Russians might have been speaking Russian.

reverse his position and argue that it makes more sense that they came from the north (1.39). By 3.31, Laonikos claims that he is no longer able to support either position. By 10.16, however, he seems to have reverted to his original position: he presents both theories, but finds the Illyrian homeland hypothesis preferable (this time the alternative has the Slavs chased south by the Skythians).

Anyone who wants to wade into the details of these argu-ments—I will not do so—should be warned that many of Lao-nikos's crucial statements are obscure, possibly contain spelling and other mistakes that he failed to revise, or have been restored by modern editors. It is especially unfortunate when his vague claims fuel nationalist historiography. For example, at 1.38 he seems to imply that the *Serbs* are "the most ancient and largest among all the peoples in the world. They either broke away from the Illyrian tribe and settled in this land or, as some claim, came from beyond the Danube." In context, however, it seems that he is not speaking only of the Serbs. The antecedent of *genos* is "the Bulgarians and the Serbs," but beyond that the statement is really about all Slavs who left the original homeland. They remained Illyrian, even though they "broke away from the Illyrian tribe." This type of confusion is caused by the double use of "Illyrian" to refer both to both Slavs as a whole and to Bosnia as the original homeland, in particular. Compare also the (apparent) absurdity of 10.17: "Based on the fact that the Illyrian race has advanced to great power and dispersed to many locations throughout Thrace, I would draw the conclusion that this race consists of Illyrians [Slavs], not Albanians." The second mention of the Illyrians in that passage refers to "descendants of the original Illyrians," i.e., Bosnians. At 10.16, he says that "this Illyrian race is ancient and lives by the Adriatic Sea, and they are mentioned as flourishing in many places. Today they are called Bosnians." He is saying the same thing here as in the statement above that has been taken to be about Serbs only. He never meant to imply that Serbs were any different from the other Illyrians who "broke off from" the original Illyrians.

Besides, by the "greatest nation" Laonikos almost certainly means "most populous" or "spread over the widest area," which again shows that he is not thinking of the Serbs only. Also, I do not know why he would call the Slavs the most ancient nation (when his Greeks go back to Dionysos). But we have seen how liberal Laonikos can be with compliments, so recipients of his praise should not quote it in their internet ramblings. As it happens, Laonikos elsewhere says that Timur learned about the Skythians (i.e., Mongols) "that this race is the most ancient among all the peoples in the world" (3.22). In his typical minimalist way, Laonikos uses exactly the same words here as for the Serbs/Slavs above.[64]

The question of Slavic origins is still hotly debated today.[65] Laonikos attests to the existence of a vigorous fifteenth-century debate on the identity of the Illyrians. Were they the Albanians or those whom most at the time were calling Slavs?[66] Where had the latter come from? The two issues would seem to be separate, but in the early fifteenth century the Illyrian label was being applied by westerners to both Slavs and Albanians in Dalmatia. There was ample room for confusion. As always, Laonikos does not identify his sources or opponents, which only adds to our confusion. He

64   Cf. 1.38: τὸ δὲ γένος τοῦτο παλαιότατόν τε καὶ μέγιστον τῶν κατὰ τὴν οἰκουμένην ἐθνῶν, with 3.22: ὡς εἴη τε τὸ γένος τοῦτο παλαιότατόν τε τῶν κατὰ τὴν οἰκουμένην ἐθνῶν.

65   Cf. F. Curta, *The Making of the Slavs: History and Archaeology of the Lower Danube Region, c. 500–700* (Cambridge, 2001), with P. Heather, *Empires and Barbarians: Migration, Development, and the Birth of Europe* (London, 2009).

66   For local and international terminology, see Fine, *When Ethnicity Did Not Matter*, esp. 138–39, 163, and chap. 4 for the local, humanist-inspired use of "Illyrian" in place of "Slav."

never uses the term "Slav," which, even in a single instance, would have clarified his argument (on a few occasions, by contast, he does use "Vlach" and "Bulgarian" to explain himself: 1.38–39).

Laonikos is the first Greek writer to express a pan-Slavic "Illyrian" thesis, though he was obviously involved in a contemporary debate over that question. One thinker to whom I believe he was directly responding was Plethon. In 1450, Plethon wrote a brief eulogy for the mother of the emperor Konstantinos IX. To the Byzantines she was known as Helene Palaiologina but she was born Jelena Dragaš, daughter of the Serb lord Konstantin Dragaš (whose genealogy Laonikos mangles in the *Histories*). As per the conventions of eulogies, Plethon begins by praising her ancestry, in this case her people as a whole:

> By race she was a Thracian. The Thracians are an ancient *genos*, ranked among the greatest of the peoples in the world, not so much on this side of the Danube, where it reaches from the Black Sea all the way to Italy, but more so beyond the Danube where they who speak the same language as those do here have settled the lands as far as the outer Ocean, a region almost inhospitable on account of the cold. It is populous, much more so than those on this side of the Danube.[67]

Plethon goes on to cite ancient Thracians known from classical literature to have contributed to religion and the Muses.

Plethon here is using the classical ethnonym "Thracian" for the Slavs where Laonikos would use "Illyrian." I believe that Laonikos used this text, for there are two direct verbal parallels

---

67   Plethon, *Monodia for Helene Palaiologina* 267–68; see Woodhouse, *Plethon*, 309–12, for the context.

in their accounts, namely the greatness of the people in question (i.e., their geographical extent) and the cold that makes the far north almost uninhabitable.[68] More importantly, they share the concept of a single people defined by a common language who have settled in lands both south of the Danube, from the head of the Adriatic to the Black Sea, and north of it, all the way to the extreme north. The identity of their geographical definitions, as well as the two verbal parallels, proves that Laonikos had this text when he was writing the *Histories*. This is not surprising, given that Plethon composed it in 1450, only three years after a young Laonikos is attested at his side at Mistra. This does not mean that Laonikos was uncritically following Plethon. His change of classical ethnonyms from Thracian to Illyrian allows him to locate the Slav homeland differently and more precisely, and it prevents the famous Thracians of antiquity from being seen as proto-Slavs, as Plethon proposed. There were no famous Illyrians in ancient literature who were worth claiming. Unlike Plethon, Laonikos avoids identifying the ancient and modern versions of the people in question.

The more interesting question is where Plethon and Laonikos found the notion of a single people who spoke the same (or closely related) languages and who had settled from the Balkans to the arctic north. To my knowledge, no such notion appears in prior Byzantine literature. Was it derived from Slavic speakers or perhaps from western ethnography? This would be an interesting inquiry into the early history of pan-Slavism.

---

68   Cf. Plethon's παλαιόν τε τὸ γένος καὶ ἐν γενῶν τοῖς μεγίστοις κατὰ τὴν οἰκου-μένην with *Hist.* 1.38: τὸ δὲ γένος τοῦτο παλαιότατόν τε καὶ μέγιστον τῶν κατὰ τὴν οἰκουμένην ἐθνῶν; also ἤπειρον σχεδόν τοι τὴν ἀοίκητον διὰ ψῦχος with 1.38: ἔστε ἐπὶ χώραν τὴν διὰ τὸ ψῦχος ἀοίκητον. Many ancient texts call that zone uninhabitable due to the cold; the most relevant to Plethon and Laonikos is pseudo-Aristotle, *Meteorology* 362b9 (see above for their use of that text) and Strabo, *Geographika* 2.1.13.

Laonikos's Sources for the West

The question of Laonikos's sources is bound to be much discussed when scholars turn their full attention to his *Histories*. I fear, however, that the discussion will be largely inconclusive, as his sources for recent history and foreign places were, for the most part, oral. I am not the first to say this, but what I will do is refrain from speculating at length on the identity of his informants (it is just too easy to point to "merchants," "diplomats," "Venetians," the expatriate Greek community in Italy, his cousin Demetrios, the wide circle of Plethon's students, etc.).[69] Laonikos does not tell us the identity of his sources or anything about his own movements. He does occasionally refer to textual research, but the clearest case concerns ancient writers (3.31: they do not clear up the matter of Illyrian origins). However, there was no library anywhere in the world in the 1450s that could have provided him with even a fraction of the material in the *Histories*. There were probably no Byzantine histories after those of Gregoras and Kantakouzenos (whose narratives end in the 1360s), and there were few Ottoman histories and texts on western European ethnography and recent history. Laonikos's research was mostly oral. It is worth imagining the vastness of this project, which replicated the labors of Herodotos. It entailed interviewing informants, keeping huge amounts of disparate notes, and then transposing their testimony into the Herodotean-Thucydidean style of the *Histories*, all without the use of a chronological framework. For all that the text lies at an extreme of literary elitism, it is basically an oral history.

Laonikos had to translate all his information into the elevated register of his text and format it to his distinctive discursive patterns. As a result, there is no way that we can identify specific sources behind the typecast presentations that he gives for each

---

69   So Nicoloudis, "Observations."

people—his definitions of their location and geography, religion, language, and "lifestyle." But Laonikos's digressions, especially the western ones, operate on two largely unconnected levels: very general background information about a people, on the one hand, and specific narrative episodes, on the other. These are exactly the results that we would expect from oral research, for "oral traditions tend to be episodic, self-contained stories that... often include no specific chronological markers."[70] I will concentrate on Laonikos's material on the west, though I believe that he gathered information about the east in a similar way. I will discuss his Turkish sources in the next chapter.

The western material for which Laonikos might have had a specific source, whether written or oral, includes his account of Charlemagne and the Paladins in Spain (2.32–33), the Hundred Years' War (2.35–37), the constitution and history of Venice (4.21–40), the career of Hunyadi (5.48–50), the complicated digression on Genoa, Alfonso V, and Álvaro de Luna (the second half of Book 5), and the Italian stories that crowd the account of the Council of Ferrara-Florence, including stories about Ferrara, Florence, the papacy, and the rise of Sforza (6.8–10, 6.12, 6.17–30). Identifying exact sources for this material will mostly prove to be impossible, but we can begin to narrow the range.

The digression on Charlemagne in Spain points to one type of source, the French *roman* tradition. Laonikos is correct that those events "are famous and greatly celebrated in song by everyone down to our time throughout Italy, Iberia, and especially France" (2.32). By his time these songs had been written down, as well as translated into other languages and into prose, so we cannot know

---

70   R. Van Dam, *Remembering Constantine at the Milvian Bridge* (Cambridge, 2011), 9; cf. O. Murray, "Herodotus and Oral History," in *Achaemenid History*, vol. 2, *The Greek Sources*, ed. H. Sancisi-Weerdenburg and A. Kuhrt (Leiden, 1997), 93–115.

how or where Laonikos encountered them, given that his homogenizing prose has obliterated the style of the original, except for one
trace: he spells the Paladins' names in their Italian forms (Orlando,
Rinaldo, Oliviero), which means that he had an Italian version, not
the French *Song of Roland* we read today.[71] Besides, in the version
transmitted by Laonikos, the Paladins "subjected most of the land
of Iberia, settled it, and . . . gave the land, namely Castile, Navarre,
and Aragon, over to their followers . . . Rinaldo inherited the war
and bequeathed it to the kings of Castile" (2.33). These claims, and
Rinaldo himself, do not appear in the *Song of Roland*, but they do
resonate in the context of the war against the Muslims in Spain. To
give but one example, the Latin *Poem of Almería*, celebrating the
conquest of Almería in 1147 by Alfonso VII of León and Castile,
compares the "emperor" Alfonso to Charlemagne and one of its
other heroes to Roland and Oliver.[72]

71   Italian: F. Grabler, "Aus dem Geschichtswerk des Laonikos Chalkokondyles,"
in *Europa im XV. Jahrhundert von Byzantinern Gesehen*, ed. F. Grabler and G. Stökl
(Graz, 1954), 89 n. 18; Ditten, "Spanien und die Spanier," 193 n. 164. For vernacular
Italian versions of Roland, see P. Rajna, *Le fonti dell'Orlando furioso: Richerche e studii*, 2nd ed. (Florence, 1900). In his "Contributi alla storia dell' epopea e del romanzo
medievale, VII: L'onomastica italiana e l'epopea carolingia," *Romania* 18 (1889):
1–69, Rajna argues for the diffusion of the tales in Italy based on naming patterns.
Ducellier, "Europe occidental," 128, argues for a Spanish source. For the Renaissance
reception of Charlemagne tales, see Bisaha, *Creating East and West*, 30–42.

72   *Poem of Almería* 17–18, 228–29. For the problems surrounding the Roland-
tradition in Spain, see E. von Richthofen, "Problemas rolandinos, almerienses y cidianos," *Anuario de estudios medievales* 5 (1968): 437–44. For the context of imperial
propaganda behind the comparison to Charlemagne, see Folz, *Concept of Empire*,
57. For French tales about the Paladins in Spain and how they will rule it, see S. C.
Akbari, *Idols in the East: European Representations of Islam and the Orient, 1100–1450*
(Ithaca, 2009), 189. For the imperial prerogatives derived from the Carolingians
and claimed by the counts of Barcelona, at least since the twelfth century, see
M. Innes, "Historical Writing, Ethnicity, and National Identity: Medieval Europe
and Byzantium in Comparison," in *The Oxford History of Historical Writing*, vol. 2,
400–1400, ed. S. Foot and C. F. Robinson (Oxford, 2012), 500.

Laonikos relied on the *roman* tradition to reconstruct the relations between France and the Iberian kingdoms and, as we will see below in our analysis of his view of Islam, he responded to claims made in the *Roman de Mahomet* and related texts. Two scholars who studied his Iberian tales have independently proposed that his account of the battle of Higueruela (1431) between Granada and Castile (under the command of Álvaro de Luna) was based not on written sources but on the "romances fronterizos" that circulated after such events.[73]

A picture is building up of a classicizing history constructed partly out of materials culled from vernacular songs and poems. Future students of Laonikos's sources should ideally command the medieval poetic tradition. They may find, for instance, that his account of the Hundred Years' War is also a Thucydidean transcription of information culled from vernacular versions of its main events, for example the battle of Agincourt (1415).[74] There might be room to make exciting discoveries in this direction.[75] However, we should resist the temptation to link Laonikos to specific texts that circulated in written form, and situate him rather against a background of fluid stories and tales. Those that happened to be written down were only the tip of the iceberg of oral culture.

---

73   Morfakidis and Motos Guirao, "Pasaje de Laonicos," 77, on *Hist.* 5.77.

74   Agincourt in *Hist.* 2.37. For a sample of contemporary accounts, see A. Curry, *The Battle of Agincourt: Sources and Interpretations* (Woodbridge, 2000). Ducellier, "France et les Îles Britanniques," 445, argues that Laonikos had a British source for the Hundred Years' War, given his comments about French arrogance. But these do not occur in his account of the war, and could have been made from a Byzantine perspective just as well. Moreover, he presents the war mostly as a French experience. For other channels by which knowledge of it might have reached Byzantium, see J. Harris, *The End of Byzantium* (New Haven, 2010), 69.

75   I have entertained the odds that Laonikos's account of the casual way that wives in Britain kiss house-guests (2.39) was influenced by the story of *Gawain and the Green Knight* (ca. 1390).

A second type of source is biographical, for which the plausible western candidates in the *Histories* are Álvaro, Alfonso, and Hunyadi, who dominate the second half of Book 5. Hunyadi and Álvaro are among the few individuals in the *Histories* whose early lives are discussed (at 5.49–50 and 5.75). Laonikos seems to be the first author to record two unlikely stories about Hunyadi, namely that he was apprenticed to Ali, the son of Evrenos, and that he chased down a wolf while in the service of the Serbian despot. These stories were later taken up by, or independently reported in, Romanian and Serbian "popular traditions."[76] It would be interesting to know whether these later traditions were actually based on the text of Laonikos. Their anecdotal nature indicates that Laonikos himself had them from oral traditions circulating about Hunyadi's early life, possibly in the same types of poems as those discussed above. But such sources cannot account for Laonikos's rigorous information about Hunyadi's subsequent wars against the Turks.

The final category comprises Laonikos's Italian material, which breaks into two categories: descriptions of the constitutions of Venice (4.21–40), Genoa (5.57–60), and Florence (6.12), including aspects of the history of the two first cities; and isolated episodes from Italian history that are largely disconnected from the main narrative and often relate insignificant events at length. The latter category includes the tale of the ancestor of the Visconti who slew a dragon and rose to rule Milan, a patent attempt to explain the family's coat of arms (4.30); the assassination of King Ladislao of Naples by the girl whom he demanded to sleep with to end his siege of Florence (5.65–66); the affair of the wife of the marquis Nicolò III d'Este of Ferrara with his bastard son Ugo (6.8–10); the botched attempt by Marsilio da Carrara to take back Padua (6.19); Sforza's takeover of Milan (6.20–24); the origin of Joachim

76   C. Mureşanu, *John Hunyadi: Defender of Christendom* (Iaşi, 2001), 48.

of Fiore (6.29); the careers of Bernardino of Siena and Giovanni da Capistrano (8.58); and other, shorter stories.

It is almost certain that Laonikos had these scattered Italian notices from oral sources. Certainly, these events are recounted in Latin and Italian written sources, but we would have to imagine Laonikos having access to a huge library in Italy, selecting only isolated episodes from each work (probably only one from each), and managing in the process to overlook the wealth of information about Italian affairs in those histories that would have either corrected his other errors or given him a better understanding of the context of those episodes. We can safely rule out textual research on Italy. Previous scholars, moreover, believed that Laonikos was writing as late as 1490 in Venice or Venetian Crete. But if we reposition him in the late 1450s and early 60s, as we must, and place him in the Greek-Turkish world, as I suspect we should, then his potential access to western historiography narrows significantly, and there was much less out there for him to consult about events of the early fifteenth century. This effectively eliminates the possibility that he read Pius II's *Commentaries*, for all the similarities between them.[77] Eric Cochrane's survey of humanist historiography covers many texts that refer to the same events, but were either written too late or had better information than Laonikos, and I have been unable to establish positive links with any of them. As for identifying his oral sources more specifically, we should resist the "degrees-of-separation" game. Through

---

77 The *Commentaries* have a similar structure: a main narrative thread (the life of Pius himself) interrupted by digressions of varying length, many of them ethnographic. Those digressions have many structural affinities with Laonikos's, though they are typically longer, uninfluenced by Herodotos, and often give different or incompatible information. Both authors finished writing at around the same time, and the *Commentaries* would not have been available to Laonikos in any case.

Plethon and the Council, or the dukes of his native Athens, we can connect Laonikos to virtually anyone in the west in only two or three steps.[78]

Florence and Venice: Sources and Politics

Let us turn, finally, to the "constitutional" digressions on Venice, Genoa, and Florence. No Byzantine had yet written an account of how Italian republics were governed, though Byzantine statesmen must have had a solid understanding of how Venice operated, at least by the Palaiologan period.[79] It may be that from the viewpoint of Byzantine imperial ideology, Venice was basically an upstart, having once been within the imperial orbit,[80] and there was no convenient model by which to explain how a city could make itself independent from the empire and then rival and conquer it by devoting itself to trade. Byzantine thinkers were committed

78   E.g., Geanakoplos, *Interaction*, 213, notes that Bernardino was at the Council, and so Laonikos might have learned about him that way (217–18); for more speculation, see D. K. Giannakopoulos, "Η θεώρηση του πολιτικού συστήματος των ιταλικών κρατιδίων (α΄ μισό του 15ᵒᵘ αιώνα) από το Λαόνικο Χαλκοκονδύλη," *Έῷα καὶ Ἑσπερία* 5 (2001–2003): 69–88. To give other examples, Ladislao of Naples was the patron of Nerio I of Athens; Alfonso V claimed the duchy of Athens as king of Naples and appointed a Catalan as its nominal title-holder against Antonio I; and the last Acciaiuoli duke, Franco, corresponded with Sforza of Milan. But Laonikos does not mention any of these links. For the possible connection to Alfonso through Sekoundinos (Sagundino), see the third section of chap. 4.

79   For the silence of Byzantine sources on the constitutions of the Italian cities, see Kaldellis, *Le discours ethnographique*; for the later period, see A. E. Laiou, "Italy and the Italians in the Political Geography of the Byzantines (14th Century)," *DOP* 49 (1995): 74–98; V. Syros, "Between Chimera and Charybdis: Byzantine and Post-Byzantine Views on the Political Organization of the Italian City-States," *Journal of Early Modern History* 14 (2010): 451–504.

80   Ioannes Kinnamos, *History* 6.10, is revealing of Byzantine attitudes.

to monarchy and saw other types of regime as too unstable.[81] In this, as in so many other matters, however, Laonikos had no such preconceptions. He knew, of course, that Genoa *was* unstable: factions would bring in foreign powers and so the city went through phases of outside domination (5.57–60). But the attention that he devotes to the constitutional arrangements of these Italian republics, more detailed than his reports on any other political system except the Ottoman Empire, reflects not only his greater interest but also perhaps a subtly expressed preference for republican regimes. As always, he hides his own views.

His account of the constitution of Florence is short and neutral (6.12). He says little about its history elsewhere, other than to praise the beauty of its girls in recounting Ladislao's siege (5.66). As for his description of its constitution, an intriguing possibility presents itself.[82] Leonardo Bruni, the humanist chancellor of Florence, wrote a five-page treatise in Greek on the *Constitution of Florence* in connection with the Council of Ferrara-Florence, which moved to Florence in January 1439. It seems that he dedicated it to Amiroutzes, the intellectual from Trebizond and supporter of Union (who clashed at the Council with Plethon).[83] This was the same Amiroutzes, who, I argued, may have been responsible for placing the interpolations into Laonikos's *Histories* at some point in the late 1460s. Plethon, Laonikos's teacher, was also among the original (intended?) readers of Bruni's treatise, for we have his copy of it with corrections to Bruni's prose.[84] It is

---

81   T. Shawcross, "'Do Thou Nothing without Counsel': Political Assemblies and the Ideal of Good Government in the Thought of Theodore Palaeologus and Theodore Metochites," *Al-Masaq* 20 (2008): 89–118.

82   The following is taken from Kaldellis, "Greek Sources."

83   Monfasani, *George Amiroutzes*, 7.

84   A. Moulakis, "Leonardo Bruni's Constitution of Florence," *Rinascimento* 26 (1986): 166, 168; also R. and F. Masai, "L'oeuvre de Georges Gémiste Pléthon,"

possible, then, that Laonikos knew this text at Mistra, in Plethon's possession. Bruni's treatise was likely meant to "explain" Florence to the visiting Byzantine dignitaries and intellectuals, but its subsequent popularity in the west indicates that western readers were also drawn to his curious attempt to transpose Italian republicanism, with its ancient roots, back into a Greek idiom. Laonikos devotes a full paragraph to the constitution of Florence at the point in his narrative where the Council moves there. Did he use Bruni's treatise?

There are tantalizing hints of a relationship, but nothing conclusive, and verbal resonances are countered by serious differences. For example, Laonikos says that the magistrates were chosen from among the common citizens and the leaders of the guilds (but he does not say that they were nine): τοὺς δὲ ἄρχοντας αἱροῦνται ἀπὸ τοῦ δήμου, δημότας τε ὄντας καὶ τεχνῶν τινων ἐπιστάτας. Bruni, who wishes the constitution to appear more moderate, fudges matters when he says that only two of the nine were chosen from this class: δύο μόνον εἰσί δημοτικοὶ ἀπὸ τῶν τεχνῶν (19). Roughly the same words, then, but different facts. Ioannes VIII, in the *chrysoboullon* that he issued at Florence granting legal privileges to the Florentine authorities, specifies that they were nine, i.e., "the Gonfaloniere di Giustizia and the other eight who are with him, the first among the guilds"[85] (the Gonfaloniere is called σημαιοφόρος in all these texts). Bruni distinguishes between the two Consigli—of the Popolo with three hundred members and the Grandi with two hundred (28–30)—but Laonikos fuses them into one of five hundred. Both authors have important matters

BAcBelg (1954): 548; F. Masai, *Pléthon et le platonisme de Mistra*, 68; Diller, "Autographs," 38–39.

85   Ioannes VIII, *Chrysoboulla regarding the Florentines*, 335. For the context, see J. Gill, *The Council of Florence* (Cambridge, 1961), 301.

referred first to the magistrates and then the *boule*, including matters of "war and peace": πόλεμον φέροντες ἢ εἰρήνην (Laonikos) / περὶ πολέμου τε καὶ εἰρήνης (Bruni). But these expressions were so conventional when it came to the business of any *boule* that there is no significant verbal parallel here.

The strongest parallel relates to the two foreign judges who were brought in to try cases impartially. Both authors explain the division of labor between the two in similar terms and in a similar grammatical construction, and then they offer the same rationale for them. There are, however, no exact verbal parallels. I quote the two passages (with translations of each in the notes):

Laonikos: καὶ ἄνδρες δύο πάρεστον αὐτοῖς ἐπήλυδες, οὓς μεταπέμπεται ἡ πολιτεία, τιμῶντες. τὸν μὲν δικαστὴν ἐφιστᾶσιν αὐτῇ τῶν ἐγκλημάτων τῆς πόλεως, τὸν δὲ ἐς τὸ τὰς ἄλλας δίκας δικάζειν τῆς πόλεως αὐτὸν ἀμφὶ τὴν τῆς πόλεως ἄλλην διοίκησιν ἔχουσιν. ἐπήλυδας δὲ οὗτοι ἐπάγονται τοὺς ἄνδρας αὐτούς, ὡς ἂν μὴ πολῖται, οἵ τε δικάζοντες δίκην τινά, ἐπὶ θάτερα ταλαντεύοιντο [6.12].[86]

Bruni: τῶν ἰδίων δὲ πραγμάτων δικαστήρια εἰσὶ καὶ νόμοι καὶ ἄρχοντες ἄλλοι, μήτε πολῖται οὗτοι ἀλλὰ ξένοι. αἱροῦνται γὰρ πρὸς ταῦτα ἄνδρες γνώριμοι καὶ εὐπάτριδες ἐξ ἄλλων τῶν πόλεων, μισθὸν ἔχοντες ἐκ τοῦ κοινοῦ, ἵνα ἐλθόντες δικάσωσιν ἐν τῇ ἡμετέρᾳ πόλει ... εἰσὶ δὲ οὗτοι ἄρχοντες δύο, ὧν ἕτερος μὲν ἐξουσίαν ἔχει περὶ τὰ δίκαια ἐν τοῖς πολιτικοῖς

---

86 "There are also two foreign men, whom the state invites in and honors. They appoint one as judge over the crimes that take place in the city, while they keep the other to preside over the other cases of the city, those that pertain to the rest of the city's administration. They bring these foreign men in so that their own citizens cannot show a bias in favor of one side or another, if they were to preside over a certain trials."

ἀγῶσι τε καὶ συναλλάγμασι καὶ τοιούτοις, ἕτερος δὲ μᾶλλον περὶ κολάσεις ἐστὶ καὶ τιμωρίας τῶν ἀσελγημάτων. [90–97].[87]

Bruni goes on, at greater length than Laonikos, to explain that this arrangement was designed to ensure impartiality and to prevent hatreds from arising among the citizens.

Another interesting feature that both texts have in common is their silence regarding Cosimo de' Medici, who had taken power in 1434, before the Council and Bruni's treatise. To be sure, Cosimo's power was notoriously unofficial and thus difficult to fit into a constitutional description without making Florence look like what Laonikos would probably have called a "tyranny." We can understand why Bruni would have wanted to suppress certain facts about political life in his city, but Laonikos had no reason to be inhibited, so this may indicate a reliance on Bruni as a source. As far as I know, no one has yet proposed a relationship between these two texts, and it should not be ruled out. It is difficult to explain the substantive differences, especially Laonikos's conflation of the two Councils. But he may have read Plethon's copy of the treatise at Mistra years before he wrote the *Histories*.

Compared to his accounts of Genoa and Florence, Laonikos's digression on Venice verges on being panegyrical. He discusses the city's origins, presenting it as the land of opportunity (4.21–22); its maritime expansion and wealth (4.23–24); heroic struggle against the Genoese in the War of Chioggia (4.25–27); expansion in mainland Italy (4.28); constitution (4.32–38); beautiful buildings and

---

87 "The laws and magistrates concerned with private law are different, the latter not being citizens, but foreigners. For this function, notable and well-born persons from other cities are chosen. They receive their salary from the community, to induce them to come to serve as judges in our city ... They are of two categories: one of them has authority over financial and commercial cases and the like. The other is responsible rather for the correction and punishment of evil-doers."

amazing sights, such as the Arsenal (4.38; only here in the entire *Histories* does Laonikos come close to an *ekphrasis*); and two failed attempts at revolution (4.40). All this basically follows the rules in the Byzantine rhetorical tradition for praising a city, even though Laonikos avoids overtly panegyrical expressions.[88] As it happens, Byzantine and post-Byzantine writers around the middle of the fifteenth century began to produce encomia of Venice, which had become a second home for some of them and the best hope for the survival of Greek culture abroad. In his famous letter of 1468 to the doge, Bessarion claimed that "as all peoples of almost the entire world gather in your city, so especially do the Greeks," and he called the city "another Byzantium."[89] Such attempts to make a home for the Greeks there after the fall of Constantinople may explain why Laonikos retroactively projects Greek migration to Venice to the days of its founding (4.22), thereby normalizing and legitimating their presence in the fifteenth century. Moreover, Venetian historiography liked to forget that the city had been subject to the Byzantines,[90] and Laonikos goes along with that too.

But Laonikos deviates from the general panegyrical context in subtle but significant ways. In a close reading and comparison of late Byzantine texts about Venice, Charis Messis has shown that, while panegyrics written by Greeks who had settled there stress Venice's intellectual merits and praise it as

88   The standard template against which scholars measure Byzantine panegyrics of cities is Menandros Rhetor, *Discourses* 32–75. For the later period, see H. Saradi, "The Monuments in the Late Byzantine Ekphraseis of Cities: Searching for Identities," *BSl* 69 (2011): 179–92.

89   For translation and context, see Geanakoplos, *Greek Scholars*, 35.

90   E. Cochrane, *Historians and Historiography in the Italian Renaissance* (Chicago, 1981), 65. For the emergence of the indigenous tradition, see T. S. Brown, "History as Myth: Medieval Perceptions of Venice's Roman and Byzantine Past," in *The Making of Byzantine History: Studies Dedicated to Donald M. Nicol*, ed. R. Beaton and C. Roueché (Aldershot, 1993), 145–57.

another Constantinople or Athens, Laonikos omits all reference to the theme of literary *paideia*, which was an essential aspect of Byzantine panegyrics of cities. Instead, he presents the education of the elite as geared entirely toward money-making and depicts the city as "a well-greased machine for the production of wealth." This is precisely why, having his choice of monuments to describe, he focuses on the Arsenal. These choices may not be devoid of implied criticisms.[91]

The Arsenal, after all, was whence the ships issued that sailed against Byzantium in the Fourth Crusade. In no fewer than three places, Laonikos emphasizes the Venetian role in the attack, which he presents matter-of-factly as an act of aggression: "At the instigation of the pontiff of the Romans, many westerners and especially the Venetians mustered a great expedition against the Greeks. They set out, came to Byzantion, and seized the city of Byzantion by force" (1.6); the Venetians "fought against the Greeks, defeated them in naval battles, and seized their capital; many westerners were with them then, but they were the leaders of the campaign against the Greeks" (4.24; and at 4.49). This is perhaps not a part of their history the Venetians liked to dwell on, though some were proud of it.[92]

By far the longest and most powerful speech in the *Histories* is that of Vettore Capello urging his fellow Venetians to respond with force to Ottoman attacks and provocations (10.37–42). It is

91   C. Messis, "De l'invisible au visible: les éloges de Venise dans la littérature byzantine," in *Villes de toute beauté: L'ekphrasis des cités dans les littératures byzantine et byzantinoslaves,* ed. P. Odorico and C. Messis (Paris, 2013), 175–79 . Not all texts of this period were panegyrical, of course. Messis discusses the mixed reactions of Syropoulos; also H. A. Klein, "Refashioning Byzantium in Venice, ca. 1200–1400," in *San Marco, Byzantium, and the Myths of Venice,* ed. H. Maguire and R. S. Nelson (Washington, DC, 2010), 193–210.

92   C. Freeman, *The Horses of St. Mark's: A Story of Triumph in Byzantium, Paris, and Venice* (New York, 2004), 92.

basically a Philippic, rousing an overly cautious republic against an unscrupulous and grasping tyrant.[93] Moreover, the last books of the *Histories* depict Mehmed as an increasingly cruel, unreliable, and sexually insatiable tyrant,[94] confirming Vettore's picture. It is tempting to conclude that Laonikos, writing in the opening phases of the first Venetian-Ottoman war (1463–79), saw in Venice the last hope for the liberation of the Greeks and the triumph of a western republic over "barbarian" tyranny.[95]

There may be some truth in this, but the full picture is more complicated. Vettore himself admits in his speech—or is made to admit, by Laonikos—that the Venetians basically sat back and did nothing as the Turks conquered Byzantium, the Peloponnese, and Bosnia: "We failed in all of these instances and it has brought us great shame and an evil reputation among other people throughout Europe, to the effect that for the sake of trade and shameful profit we are willing to abandon kindred races to be destroyed by this sultan" (10.41). This can serve as a standard by which to look back and interpret past Venetians actions and inactions, with unflattering results. It also makes one less sanguine about future prospects, Vettore's rousing speech notwithstanding—all the

---

93   Nikolaos Sekoundinos (Sagundino) and Bessarion seem to have noticed the relevance of Demosthenes's rhetoric to the contemporary situation in the east: Bisaha, *Creating East and West*, 80–81, 113; M. Meserve, *Empires of Islam in Renaissance Historical Thought* (Cambridge, MA, 2008), 112 and 298 n. 195; H. Lamers, "Reinventing the Ancient Greeks: The Self-Representation of Byzantine Scholars in Renaissance Italy" (Ph.D. diss., Leiden University, 2013), chap. 3.

94   See the last section of chap. 4.

95   For Laonikos writing as a Greek, see chap. 5; for the Turks as barbarians, see the fifth section of chap. 4. At 6.55, Laonikos reports the papal legate's cynical cancellation of the Hungarian king's oath to keep peace with Murad II, before the Varna Crusade (the legate was cardinal Giuliano Cesarini). Of course, Laonikos rarely expresses open disapproval, but he does later praise Cesarini, who died at Varna, in lofty terms (7.12).

more so if the reader recalls the fate of Athens after Demosthenes's *Philippics* were delivered. Laonikos notes that the first vote over war after Vettore's speech was tied (10.43), which does not bode well for Venetian resolve. This hostile view of Venice's motives and policies were actually part of the broader political scene, as we see in Pius's *Commentaries*, which offers the same hostile interpretation as does Laonikos's Vettore.[96] And when, in the *Histories*, Venice sends ambassadors to Hungary to seek an alliance for the coming war, Matthias Corvinus gives them an earful: "You seem to have forgotten that we have often invited you to join us in war against the Turks and yet you have not wanted to assist us, even when the great pontiff pleaded with you. Instead, you made treaties with the barbarian and totally disregarded us" (10.46). The envoys secure the alliance but we, the readers, come away with serious doubts about Venetian prospects.

We do not know when Laonikos finished writing up the opening phase of the war—i.e., the events of 1463 and early 1464—so we also do not know the degree of hindsight shaping his account. It cannot have been later than early 1468, and I suspect that he stopped writing in 1464, that is, just as he was learning about the events themselves. At any rate, Laonikos presents the Venetian invasion of the Peloponnese as a fiasco of unrealistic expectations, inadequate preparations, and insubordination and even betrayal.[97] This explains the tenor of the speech made by Asanes

96 Pius II, *Commentaries* 3.35; at 3.28, he drives home their former subjection to Byzantium.

97 For the opening phase of the war, see R. Lopez, "Il principio della guerra veneto-turca nel 1463," *AVen* ser. 5, 15 (1934): 45–131; T. Stavrides, *The Sultan of Vezirs: The Life and Times of the Ottoman Grand Vezir Mahmud Pasha Angelović* (Leiden, 2001), 150–53. Despite the furious battle recounted by Kritoboulos, *History* 5.1, Laonikos is supported by the other sources in claiming that the Venetians abandoned the Isthmos without a battle.

on the sultan's behalf to the people of Mistra, whose opening words are: "O people of Mistra, you see the depths to which Venetian affairs have fallen since they decided to go to war against the sultan here" (10.59). This is the last speech in the work, and the *Histories* ends after only one unpolished paragraph.

In sum, Laonikos may have admired some aspects of Venice's commercial republic, but it is hard to believe that he regarded it as a serious contender for the role of liberator. Vettore's powerful speech in favor of war serves as a contrast to what the Venetians had actually been doing all along and makes the anticipated failure of their invasion seem all the more abject. It certainly is the most forceful, and possibly personal, speech in the whole *Histories*, but so is Perikles's Funeral Oration in Thucydides and it is followed directly by the historian's account of the plague, which reveals how hollow the lofty rhetoric ultimately proved to be.[98]

---

98   W. R. Connor, *Thucydides* (Princeton, 1984), 63–72; C. Orwin, *The Humanity of Thucydides* (Princeton, 1994), 173–75, 182–84.

Religion, Islam, and the Turks

Laonikos was the first author from a Christian society to present Islam not as a theological error or religious abomination, but as a valid religious culture, presenting the facts dispassionately and finding it overall to be just. His approach was ethnographic, not religious. He also gave an account of Turkish history that the Turks themselves might well have accepted (had they been able to read it). As we will see, he was not entirely uncritical of them, but no one in the *Histories* escapes unscathed, and he saves his most bitter criticism for the leaders of his own people. He praises many Turkish leaders and achievements, but few Greeks.

In his representation of both Islam and the Turks, Laonikos was unique in the Byzantine and western traditions. He certainly owed this accomplishment to his imitation of Herodotos, which was not just "literary." What Laonikos found in Herodotos was a non-Christian way of viewing cultural difference. Yet this pluralistic approach was probably not achieved by Laonikos's unaided moral imagination. In a later chapter, I will consider the influence of his teacher Plethon, who shaped his view of Greek history, ancient and modern. Just as Plethon had given Laonikos his own personal copy of Herodotos, so too he passed on to him a philosophical ethnography and view of the world's religions that we find on display in the *Histories*. Unfortunately, we can merely glimpse Plethon's own thoughts, because his major work, the *Nomoi* (*Laws*), was burned by his enemy Scholarios after his death. Only fragments survive, but from them and from Plethon's surviving works we can still recognize the outlook that mostly governs Laonikos's practice as a historian. Plethon was also a Platonic neo-pagan who rejected Christianity and was probably neutral when it came to its struggle against Islam.[1] It is tempting, therefore, to see Laonikos as a pagan disciple of Plethon, given how discreet and aberrant he is when it comes to religious questions. We should not incautiously regard him as a "Christian author," but, as I labelled him above, only as an author from a Christian society. What he wrote is what he imagined Herodotos would have written about Islam. This alone makes the *Histories* a fascinating artifact.

Laonikos's Religious Outlook

Laonikos never discloses any attachment to a particular religious tradition. He sees the world as divided between Muslims and Christians: "for the entire known world is divided between two religions, that of Jesus and their religion [Islam], which sets itself against the other; for no other religion apart from these is established in the form of a kingdom or any other type of state" (2.50). There is the "faction of Muhammad" (2.50) and the "faction of Jesus" (2.55), just as there is "the religion of Muhammad" (2.33: θρησκείᾳ τῇ Μεχμέτεω) and "the religion of Jesus" (3.28: ἐς τὴν

---

1   The main studies of Plethon's thought are Masai, *Pléthon*; B. Tambrun, *Pléthon: Le Retour de Platon* (Paris, 2006); and N. Siniossoglou, *Radical Platonism: Illumination and Utopia in Gemistos Plethon* (Cambridge, 2011). Thinkers of Laonikos's generation who were associated with Plethon were also accused of being pagans (e.g., Iouvenalios, Raoul Kabakes, and Michael Apostoles).

τοῦ Ἰησοῦ θρησκείαν). These factions are supposed to be at war (though their members often fight among themselves). Laonikos twice refers to Jesus as a god (3.40, 3.42) and as a lord (3.41, 8.58), but these are formally correct titles from an ethnographic point of view; they imply no personal commitment. There is one passage that refers to "the religion of *our* Lord Jesus Christ" (9.35) and plays up the miracles that converted the Georgians away from their false religion, which tripped at least one scholar into thinking that Laonikos was a Christian. This passage had already been shown to be an interpolation.[2] Laonikos himself never refers to "Christ" or to "Christians" and avoids all the polemical Christian terminology used in that passage by the interpolator.

If Jesus is the "lord" and "God" of the Christian faction, Muhammad is the "hero" of the Muslim faction.[3] It is not clear what this term means or how much of its ancient religious valence Laonikos was adopting.[4] Perhaps it was meant to convey some of the sense of "Prophet." Laonikos says that Muslims regard Jesus also as a "hero" (3.17), and elsewhere he refers to the canonization of Bernardino of Siena as follows: "When he died, the Italians bestowed on him the honors of a hero and built shrines for him" (8.58). His Herodotean filter evidently converted "Prophet" and "saint" to "hero." The other term that Laonikos uses for Muhammad is the classical concept of the "lawgiver" (νομο-θέτης),[5] and many ancient heroes were lawgivers. I will discuss this term below in connection with Plethon, for Laonikos had

2 Christian: Reinsch, "Ἡ θεώρηση," 78. Interpolation: H. Ditten, "Βάρβαροι, Ἕλληνες und Ῥωμαῖοι bei den Letzten byzantinische Geschichtschreiber," in *Acts of the XIth International Congress of Byzantine Studies*, vol. 2 (Belgrade, 1964), 295–97 n. 161; idem, "Korruptel Χωρόβιον," 62–64; and Kaldellis, "Interpolations."

3 *Hist.* 2.50–56 (*passim*), 3.14, 3.18, 3.60, 7.21, 7.31, 8.17, 9.65, 9.66, 9.72.

4 R. Parker, *On Greek Religion* (Ithaca, 2011), chap. 4.

5 *Hist.* 1.10, 3.14, 3.17, 3.18.

its application to Muhammad from him. Here I note only that he regarded Jesus as an equivalent lawgiving-figure. When discussing the Russians, Laonikos says that "in their customs and way of life they follow the laws of Jesus, and incline more to the Greeks and do not follow the pontiff of the Romans" (3.26). Muslims and Christians have separate laws and customs (cf. 2.33 for Muslim "customs"). These concepts authorize an ethnographic and historical approach to religion, rather than a theological one. Laonikos places religion under the category of custom, not truth (or Truth).

Laonikos knew that there were other religions in the world. He refers to "to the religions that are recognized by us these days, I mean those of Jesus, Muhammad, and Moses" (3.29), but he never mentions Jews. The contradiction between these *three* religions and the division of the world into *two* religions above (at 2.50) is only apparent: he was there referring only to states that follow specific religions, and there was no Jewish state. The reference to Moses occurs in a passage that introduces pagans. In 3.29, he says that the Samogitians (a Lithuanian people)

> believe in the gods Apollo and Artemis. They follow the ancient Greek way of life and customs...Next to them are the Bohemians who have the same beliefs as the Samogitians...They have a capital city that is prosperous and populous; it is called Prague, and it has not been long since many of the inhabitants of this city stopped worshipping fire and the sun...There is also, so I have learned, an Indian race beyond the Caspian Sea and the Massagetai which practices that same worship of Apollo. That race believes in other gods too, Zeus and Hera, as will be made clear later in the narrative.

Let us take these in order.

Laonikos knows that the Lithuanians were Catholics (3.30), and he says nothing about their recent pagan past. The Samogitians, however, had begun to convert in 1416, so his information about them is out of date. It is his reference to Bohemia that is most puzzling, for Bohemia had converted in the ninth century. Ditten argued that Laonikos misunderstood the Hussite movement, or was given distorted information about it, presumably from a Catholic source,[6] though in that case he seems to have again formatted that information to his Herodotean template ("worshipping fire and the sun"). Catholic propaganda did present the movement as "entangled in the putrid errors of paganism,"[7] though mostly as heretical (and rarely as reformist). Laonikos refers to Bohemian paganism later in the *Histories*, in connection with the missions there of Giovanni da Capistrano (8.49, 8.58), but it is important to stress that he has consistently obliterated the polemical strains that must have run through his Catholic informant's account. As for Indian paganism, he discusses it in connection with Timur's invasion of India-China (he blurs the two). He uses Greek religion as a template but does not editorialize, even when he notes that they sacrifice children to Artemis (3.67). In sum, paganism is an oddity for Laonikos, especially in a European context, but he does not have a theological bias against it.

---

6   Ditten, *Russland-Exkurs*, 58. Yet Aeneas (Pius II) does not accuse the Hussites of paganism in his *Historia Bohemica*; see T. A. Fudge, "Seduced by the Theologians: Aeneas Sylvius and Hussite Heretics," in *Heresy in Transition: Transforming Ideas of Heresy in Medieval and Early Modern Europe*, ed. I. Hunter et al. (Aldershot, 2005), 89–101.

7   Martinus V, *"Inter Cunctos" Bull* (1420), translation by T. A. Fudge, *The Crusade against Heretics in Bohemia, 1418–1437* (Aldershot, 2002), 46.

His own religious views are difficult, if not impossible, to discern. Almost all references to God are made by speakers in the *Histories*, not Laonikos himself, and the exceptions are bland and predictably Herodotean. Referring to the great ambitions of Timur, he calls them "plans that fall rather under the jurisdiction of the fortune that is granted by God" (2.58). The hubris and downfall of Bayezid provided Laonikos with a perfect opportunity for Herodotean divine rhetoric: "But at that moment, when he had reached an extraordinary degree of power, it came about that Bayezid was chastened by God, as he had been presumptuous about his kingdom" (2.59).[8] And Timur, his conqueror, harps on this theme after the battle: "For God is accustomed to cut down to size those who think highly of themselves and are all puffed up" (3.60). This tells us less about religion and more about Herodotean imitation.

There is one passage, however, where Laonikos comes close to showing his hand. In a digression on the tides of the river Thames, which is itself in the British digression of Book 2, Laonikos claims that the moon has been stationed to preside over the motion of the waters by God (2.41). This, too, is rather banal, as is the subsequent explanation of the phenomenon in purely physical terms, leaving us to wonder how exactly "God" and the material world interact and where they intersect. This is a common problem in Byzantine thinkers who wrote physics and theology.[9] But that is not what is interesting about this passage. Laonikos begins by talking about how the motion of the moon affects the waters, and then he adds a secondary motion caused by the winds. In all this, of course, he was striving to emulate

---

8   Cf. T. Harrison, *Divinity and History: The Religion of Herodotos* (Oxford, 2000).

9   For Psellos, see A. Kaldellis, *Hellenism in Byzantium: The Transformations of Greek Identity and the Reception of the Classical Tradition* (Cambridge, 2007), 202–5.

the tenor of Herodotos's physical-geographic inquiry into the annual flooding of the Nile. But when he then mixes the two motions together, his prose becomes extremely convoluted and opaque (2.42):

> It happens that the winds contribute to this process too and move the waters still more, from wherever the latter originally receive their motion. This movement of the waters may, then, feature a dual motion that goes against the motion of the totality of the sky, becoming both spontaneous and violent, so that if this motion does not attain a harmonious unison, it becomes extremely varied. This is most pleasant to contemplate, view, and hear, and is in accordance with one of the rules of the Soul of this Universe, namely that this Soul takes pleasure in perceiving how different motions may be conveyed and borne along with each other into a certain uniform harmony.[10] Therein lies also the source of the soul's motion, which in turn moves our bodies on this dual course, namely to grow and to decline. Moreover, our individual soul receives the impulse for its motion as it is borne along with the Universe. For all living things, birth and growth necessarily follow the spontaneous motion, while decline and death are caused by the violent and compulsive one.

This passage (which continues in the same vein) merits a more detailed investigation by scholars who study medieval theories of the soul and of motion (both physical motion, i.e., in space, and generation vs. corruption). These were topics of heated debate during Laonikos's lifetime, for example, between Plethon and

---

10   This passage is probably corrupt, and seems also to have a lacuna.

Scholarios,[11] in the lectures of Amiroutzes,[12] and in the correspondence of Michael Apostoles on Crete.[13] What is tucked away in the folds of this tortured prose, however, is an unmistakable reference to the Neoplatonic concept of the World Soul (ἡ τοῦ παντὸς τοῦδε ψυχή), with which the soul of the individual is somehow attuned. This concept was explicitly associated with pagan Platonism by orthodox thinkers, who rejected it. "The soul of the All" and "the harmony" between it and the human soul were features of Plethon's pagan metaphysics.[14] Previous scholars have written that Laonikos appears to have been ignorant of or uninterested in Plethon's esoteric doctrines,[15] but I suspect that he has here shown his hand as a disciple of his philosophical paganism. He would, in this case, not be the first philosophically inclined thinker to place his heterodoxy in a cloud of confusing syntax,[16] nor the first in the classical tradition to place it in an account of faraway places—indeed, the very edges of the earth, for the farther we go from the center the easier it is to disclose certain things.[17]

Situating Laonikos in a relationship with Plethon helps us to understand his ethnographic practices, including his view of

11   Plethon, *Reply to Scholarios regarding Aristotle* 31 (τὸ περὶ τοῦ οὐ διττοῦ σοι τῆς κινήσεως). For lunar motions in Plethon, see M. V. Anastos, "Pletho's Calendar and Liturgy," *DOP* 4 (1948): 189.

12   Monfasani, *George Amiroutzes*, 39, 172–77.

13   See Appendix 1.

14   For the debate over the World Soul, see Siniossoglou, *Radical Platonism*, 82, 171, 183 n. 60, 185, 187, 257–61. Amiroutzes may have taken aim at it: Monfasani, *George Amiroutzes*, 97 n. 63.

15   E.g., E. Darkó, "Neue Beiträge zur Biographie des Laonikos Chalkandyles," *BZ* 27 (1927): 280; Woodhouse, *Plethon*, 40, 223.

16   Cf. A. Kaldellis, *The Argument of Psellos' Chronographia* (Leiden, 1999), 117–27.

17   Cf. A. Kaldellis, *Procopius of Caesarea: Tyranny, History, and Philosophy at the End of Antiquity* (Philadelphia, 2004), 75, citing previous studies; J. Romm, *The Edges of the Earth in Ancient Thought* (Princeton, 1992).

Islam. Philosophical Platonism recognized and accepted the existence of different national religious traditions, which were integrated into a single framework. This was how ancient Platonism absorbed Herodotos and the ethnographic tradition generally.[18] Following in the footsteps of the ancient Neoplatonists, Plethon had also practiced philosophical ethnography by synthesizing into a Platonic framework the (putative) religious beliefs of barbarian nations, which could be ascribed to their original lawgivers. Plethon favored Zoroaster for this role, but seems to have recognized a plurality of national lawgivers, who could be worked up into an overarching and exoteric system of loosely compatible approaches to God, though the true, esoteric system would be known only by the philosophers themselves.[19] In his funeral oration for Helene Palaiologina, he cites as witnesses to the immortality of the soul the Iberians, Celts, Tuscans, Thracians, Greeks, Romans, Egyptians, Medes, and Indians.[20] Most of these names recur in the *Histories*, though Laonikos is referring to their modern counterparts while Plethon probably meant the ancient versions. (But like Laonikos, Plethon appears to have been uninterested in Judaism.) It was probably this perspective that enabled Plethon to call Muhammad the "leader and

18   This was explicit in the thought of the emperor Julian, especially in his *Against the Galilaians*; see R. Smith, *Julian's Gods: Religion and Philosophy in the Thought and Action of Julian the Apostate* (London, 1995); for Plethon, see Tambrun, *Pléthon*, 69–80, 85–89.

19   Examples of this method include Porphyrios's *On Abstinence from Killing Animals* and Iamblichos's *On the Mysteries*; see J. M. Schott, "Porphyry on Christians and Others: 'Barbarian Wisdom,' Identity Politics, and Anti-Christian Polemics on the Eve of the Great Persecution," *JEChrSt* 13 (2005): 277–314. For Plethon, see Woodhouse, *Plethon*, 62–73; Tambrun, *Pléthon*, chap. 2 for Zoroaster and others; and below.

20   Plethon, *Monodia for Helene Palaiologina* 279. Discussion in Woodhouse, *Plethon*, 65–66.

lawgiver [νομοθέτης] of the Arabs," a title with philosophical implications.[21] The question of whether Plethon's thought owed anything to Islam has been raised but not debated extensively. At any rate, Plethon "understood that Islam was a way of life as well as a religion" and "there is nothing in [his] work to match the conventional vituperation of Orthodox theologians against Islam."[22] In sum, it may not have been only the belief in the World Soul that Laonikos owed to Plethon: the latter's entire philosophical approach may have enabled Laonikos's reactivation of Hellenic ethnography.

As noted, with the exception of the (admittedly vague) ascription of the downfall of Bayezid to the will of God, there are no cases of divine intervention in the *Histories*. Laonikos is also most un-Herodotean in his general avoidance of omens, miraculous events, dreams, and the like. Herodotos held it as axiomatic that signs presaged all great events (6.27; cf. 6.98), a notion accepted, for example, by Laonikos's contemporary historian of Mehmed, Kritoboulos. But in this respect Laonikos is fairly rigorous. Two

---

21   Plethon prepared a summary of the first two centuries of the Arab conquests drawn from Byzantine sources: *Muhammad the Leader and Lawgiver of the Arabs*; see Diller, "Autographs," 37; F. Klein-Franke, "Die Geschichte des frühen Islam in einer Schrift des Georgios Gemistos Plethon," *BZ* 65 (1972): 1–8. The terms ἀραβάρχης τε καὶ νομοθέτης are restored at the beginning of the text by D. Dedes, "Die Handschriften und das Werk des Georgios Gemistos (Plethon)," Ἑλληνικά 33 (1981): 67; cf. Woodhouse, *Plethon*, 19; for the concept of the *nomothetes* in Plethon, see Th. S. Nikolaou, Αἱ περὶ πολιτείας καὶ δικαίου ἰδέαι τοῦ Γ. Πλήθωνος Γεμιστοῦ (Thessalonike, 1989), 119–21.

22   Woodhouse, *Plethon*, 72; at 71–72, he summarizes the debate to that time on the question of Islamic influences in Plethon, citing previous scholarship. A. Asakoy does not reach more definite conclusions in "George Gemistos Pletho and Islam," in *Proceedings of the International Congress on Plethon and his Time, Mystras, 26–29 June 2002*, ed. L. Benakis and C. Baloglou (Mistras, 2003), 339–53; for his political proposals, see Necipoğlu, *Byzantium*, 275. See below for the concept of fate.

omens—perfectly natural events—are reported in connection with Bayezid's defeat at Ankara (3.51) and carefully attributed to others; one omen before the second battle of Kosovo (the Turks cheering, 7.42); and the story of the ox and the dismembered corpse (10.57), which was held to presage events that are not disclosed in the narrative of the *Histories*. That is all.

Laonikos mocks the Turkish diviners who plied their trade in the public markets, claiming "higher" access; he judged that the feats of tightrope walkers were more impressive (8.70). He makes an odd skeptical comment regarding the French belief in Joan of Arc during the Hundred Years' War: "facing such catastrophe, the French now turned to religion—indeed, people generally turn to religion at such a time—when a certain woman of considerable beauty claimed that she was in communication with God" (2.37). The word for religion here is *deisidaimonia*, which is commonly translated "superstition" but can also mean "religion."[23] It appears in only two other passages in Laonikos, in one of which it clearly means "religion" (2.16), while in the other it clearly means "superstition" (2.55), making it hard to decide which he meant in the third passage about the French.

Laonikos's stance toward prophecies was also ambiguous. He mocks, in a Thucydidean manner, the prophecy that the Turks would be turned back when they reached the forum of Tauros in Constantinople on 29 May 1453 (8.20).[24] But he seems to have accepted the papal prophecies that were attributed to Joachim of Fiore (6.29) and those attributed to the Byzantine emperor Leon

23   Cf. D. B. Martin, *Inventing Superstition from the Hippocratics to the Christians* (Cambridge, MA, 2004), 6–8, 18–20, and *passim*.

24   Cf. Thucydides, *History* 2.54; Prokopios, *Wars* 5.24.28–37 (and 5.7.6–8). For Laonikos and oracles, see C. J. G. Turner, "Pages from the Late Byzantine Philosophy of History," *BZ* 57 (1964): 359.

the Wise (886–912) (8.33), which were, in fact, textually related. The papal prophecies, contained in a series of manuscripts called the *Vaticinia de Summis Pontificibus*, were loosely based on the Byzantine Oracles of Leon the Wise that circulated from the twelfth century on, and were being attributed to Joachim by the early fifteenth. Laonikos does not seem to be aware of the textual relationship between his two prophets, and he devotes much more attention to the Greek ones attributed to Leon, which unfortunately survive only in late copies (none before the sixteenth century). As this genre was frequently reworked, we cannot easily reconstruct the versions circulating in his time. The passage in question follows his account of the fall of Constantinople:

I am amazed that some do not believe that the prophecies of the Sibyl came true, given that the list of the kings who ruled over the territory of Byzantion that was drawn up, as they say, by King Leon the Wise, ends right before this king and the patriarch who died in Florence, in Tuscany [Patriarch Gregorios III]. That list does not include King Konstantinos, since he perished at the hands of the barbarians and did not die while ruling the kingdom, or Gregorios, the one who went to Italy.[25] Entries were assigned in this book for each king, one after the next, down to the death of this king, and for the patriarchs who held the high priesthood of the city, whether they were more or fewer than the kings. Many other amazing deeds are attributed to this king [Leon VI], as he was an expert in the ways of the stars and souls and familiar with their powers. [8.33]

25 The unionist patriarch Gregorios III Mamas left Constantinople in 1451 for Rome and did not return; he died in 1459.

Such oracles and esoteric knowledge regarding "the power of stars and souls" fit perfectly with Plethon's thought.[26] In his discussion *On Fate*, a chapter of his *Laws*, Plethon claimed that the gods do reveal part of their foreknowlege to select mortals;[27] elsewhere in that mostly lost book he devoted considerable attention to the philosophy (or religion) of the stars and souls. Plethon also paid much attention to the *Chaldaean Oracles*.[28] The siege and fall of Constantinople led to an explosive production of oracles predicting that event, as well as the City's eventual reconquest by the Christians; some of these were based on the tradition of Leon the Wise.[29] Unfortunately, it is difficult to match up Laonikos's description of this table of oracles with the versions that have come down to us, given that his version featured both emperors and patriarchs, and scholarship on the oracles has overlooked his testimony.[30]

26   Ioannes Zonaras, *Chronicle* 16.13 (v. 3, 445) notes Leon's love of esoteric knowledge, his ability to prophesy, and his study of the motion of the stars.

27   Plethon, *On Fate* in PG 160:962–63 = *Laws* 2.6 (p. 70).

28   Tambrun, *Pléthon*, 91–104, 142–44; P. Athanassiadi, "Byzantine Commentators on the Chaldaean Oracles: Psellos and Plethos," in *Byzantine Philosophy and Its Ancient Sources*, ed. K. Ierodiakonou (Oxford, 2002), 237–52.

29   M. Philippides and W. Hanak, *The Siege and the Fall of Constantinople in 1453: Historiography, Topography, and Military Studies* (Farnham, 2011), 219–31.

30   Versions of the Leon Oracles in PG 107:1121–58; and J. Vereecken and L. Hadermann-Misguich, *Les Oracles de Léon le Sage illustrés par Georges Klontzas: La version Barozzi dans le Codex Bute* (Venice, 2000), who crucially overlook Laonikos at 24–25; cf. C. Mango, "The Legend of Leo the Wise," *Zbornik Radova Vizantinološkog Instituta* 6 (1960): 77 (who identifies the emperors and patriarchs in Laonikos differently from me); and P. Alexander, *The Byzantine Apocalyptic Tradition* (Berkeley, 1985), 125, 130–36. H. Grundman proved that the *Vaticinia* derive from a Byzantine source: see M. Reeves, *The Influence of Prophecy in the Later Middle Ages: A Study of Joachism* (Oxford, 1969), 193; eadem, "Some Popular Prophecies from the Fourteenth to the Seventeenth Centuries," in *Popular Belief and Practice*, ed. G. J. Cuming and D. Baker (Cambridge, 1972), 109–13. For the date of the pseudo-Joachim prophecies and their Byzantine original, see eadem, *Joachim*

To conclude, Laonikos has a detached view of both Christianity and Islam. His ethnography reflects a philosophical view of the world that recognized many founders and lawgivers, each for a different people, and in one passage he nods towards non-Christian Platonic metaphysics. In all this, as in his interest in occult oracles, Laonikos reveals himself a disciple of Plethon.

The Representation of Islam

Book 3 is the Asian and Muslim book of the *Histories*, and is chiefly devoted to the wars of Timur. In one sense, it is a long digression, occasioned by Timur's conflict with Bayezid, so only the account of the Ankara campaign toward the end of the book is part of the main narrative of the *Histories*. This digression, in turn, occasions secondary digressions, including one on Arabia and Islamic culture in general (3.13–20) and another on the Mamluk sultanate (3.39–42). In these passages, Laonikos matter-of-factly reports on Muslim beliefs, practices, and institutions. Much of his information is banal, e.g.: "They have priests who ascend to a conspicuous position in a tower that is built in front of the shrine and there pray to God in a loud voice and always recite the customary prayers, calling them out in order to be heard" (3.15). But "banality" is relative. The Christian world had "known" such basic facts about Islam for eight hundred years and yet no one had seen fit to record them in a dispassionate, ethnographic account, not in Byzantium and not in the medieval west. By presenting the basic facts in this

---

of Fiore and the Prophetic Future: A Medieval Study in Historical Thinking, 2nd ed. (Sutton, 1999), 75–78, 98–100; M. H. Fleming, *The Late Medieval Pope Prophecies: The* Genus nequam *Group* (Tempe, 1999). Laonikos's account (in 6.29) of Joachim's illumination (in the Cistercian monastery at Sambucina, Calabria) echoed western traditions and was itself used by later western writers: Reeves, *Influence of Prophecy*, 102–3.

way, Laonikos normalized Islam, making it a part of the world that one could discuss in non-polemical tones. I am not saying he got all his facts right—the number of prayers per day is five, not four (3.15). His presentation of the five Pillars of the Faith is unsystematic. But in a world of centuries-old prejudice, his very banality was revolutionary.

"Islam" for the Christian world had never been just another culture to be set next to its neighbors, but a polemical literary construct to which the "facts," whether known or not, were irrelevant. In both Byzantine and western literature, and in narrative tales or theological disputation, Muslims existed in order to be overcome by Christians or as the instruments of God's anger at the Christians. In neither case did they enjoy much agency of their own, or exist for themselves in a world of their own that was not governed by Christian concerns. I have studied the Byzantine material in a separate book on Byzantine writing about foreign peoples.[31] Despite their proximity to centers of Arab and Muslim power, the constant exchange, communication, and conflict between them, and the near-permanent presence of Muslims in Constantinople itself, Byzantine writers had astonishingly little to say about Arab and Islamic culture. They seem not to have regarded it as a "culture" to begin with, rather as a set of theological errors to be refuted in logical order.[32] Two of the emperors who appear in the

---

31   Kaldellis, *Discours ethnographique.*

32   J. Meyendorff, "Byzantine Views of Islam," *DOP* 18 (1964): 113–32; A. T. Khoury, *Polémique byzantine contre l'Islam: VIIIᵉ–XIIIᵉ s.* (Leiden, 1972); R. G. Hoyland, *Seeing Islam as Others Saw It: A Survey and Evaluation of Christian, Jewish and Zoroastrian Writing on Early Islam* (Princeton, 1997); A. Ducellier, *Chrétiens d'Orient et Islam au Moyen Age, VIIᵉ–XVᵉ siècle* (Paris, 1996); and, for a neglected source (Eustratios of Nikaia), M. Trizio, "A Neoplatonic Refutation of Islam from the Time of the Komneni," in *Knotenpunkt Byzanz: Wissensformen und kulturelle Wechselbeziehungen*, ed. A. Speer and D. Wirmer (Berlin, 2012), 145–66. The main sources for the middle period are in R. Glei and A. T. Khoury, *Johannes Damaskenos*

Histories wrote anti-Muslim tracts (Ioannes VI Kantakouzenos and Manuel II Palaiologos). The latter, considered a humanist among Byzantine authors, wrote in a letter "that the false and evil teachings of Islam must be clearly revealed for what they are," so that Muslims could not claim on the Day of Judgment that they didn't know.[33] In historical narratives, Byzantines tended to depict Muslims as the "enemies of Christ"—often paradoxically sent by God to punish Christians—or as just secular opponents, stripped of religious affiliation in a political contest defined by power relations. I have suggested a number of reasons why Byzantine thinkers failed to come to terms with Islam as a living cultural system. These include the ideology of victory on which the genres of ecclesiastical and imperial historiography were premised: this could not accommodate what had happened in the seventh and eighth centuries. Moreover, the cardinal distinction between True and False religions prevented most Byzantines from adopting a Herodotean approach ("to each his own").

There has recently been an explosion of interest in medieval (i.e., western) views of Islam.[34] These studies generally conclude

---

und Theodor Abu Qurra: Schriften zum Islam (Würzburg, 1995); K. Förstel, *Niketas von Byzanz: Schriften zum Islam* (Würzburg, 2000); and idem, *Schriften zum Islam von Euthymios Zigabenos und Fragmente der griechischen Koranübersetzung* (Wiesbaden, 2009). For Byzantine views of the Arabs, see E. M. Jeffreys, "The Image of the Arabs in Byzantine Literature," in *The 17th International Byzantine Congress: Major Papers* (New Rochelle, 1986), 305–23; N. A. Koutrakou, "The Image of the Arabs in Middle-Byzantine Politics: A Study in the Enemy Principle (8th–10th Centuries)," *Graeco-Arabica* 5 (1993): 213–24; S. Vryonis, "Byzantine Attitudes towards Islam during the Late Middle Ages," *GRBS* 12 (1971): 263–86.

33   J. W. Barker, *Manuel II Palaeologus (1391–1425): A Study in Late Byzantine Statesmanship* (New Brunswick, 1969), 136. Manuel's treatise, which drew attention when it was referenced in 2006 by Pope Benedict XVI, is his *Dialogue with a Persian*.

34   Older studies include N. Daniel, *Islam and the West: The Making of an Image* (Edinburgh, 1960; 2nd ed. Oxford, 2009); R. W. Southern, *Western Views of Islam in*

that medieval authors did not aim to record what they knew about Islam as a cultural system or as a practiced religion. They either "refuted" it on theological (and usually rhetorical) terms or constructed fantastic narrative images to serve in the ongoing articulation of Christian identies and attributes. There were few texts in which one could find valid information about "*realexistierenden* Islam,"[35] even in areas where both Christians and Muslims lived, such as Spain. The study of Islam "did not actually include an interest in it for the sake of understanding the religion or culture, but rather in spreading distorted propaganda for political purposes."[36] Laonikos knew some of these western texts and their motifs, for example, the tales of conquest in Spain by Charlemagne and his Paladins (2.32–33). In his digression on Arabia, moreover, he rejects the notion that Muhammad's tomb was suspended in mid-air (3.20), but this was not something that he would have learned from a Muslim. It was, in fact, a hostile fiction that appeared in the *Roman de Mahomet* and other western texts.[37] Interestingly, it is also the only instance in the *Histories* where Laonikos rejects the testimony of his sources,[38] and his likely purpose is to counter an anti-Muslim calumny (though we cannot rule out the possibility that he took this story to be of

the Middle Ages (Cambridge, MA, 1962); more recent studies include D. R. Blancs and M. Frassetto, eds., *Western Views of Islam in Medieval and Early Modern Europe: Perception of Other* (New York, 1999); J. V. Tolan, *Saracens: Islam in the Medieval Imagination* (New York, 2002); Akbari, *Idols in the East*; J. C. Frakes, *Vernacular and Latin Literary Discourses of the Muslim Other in Medieval Germany* (New York, 2011).

35   Frakes, *Muslim Other*, 71–72.

36   Ibid., 153; cf. 160, 165.

37   Tolan, *Saracens*, 122, 143–44, 147; Akbari, *Idols in the East*, 226–27, 231–32; in detail, A. Eckhardt, "Le cercueil flottant de Mahomet," in *Mélanges de philologie romane et de littérature medieval offerts à Ernest Hoepffner* (Paris, 1947), 77–78.

38   See p. 42 above.

Muslim origin, and so by countering it he was rejecting what he thought was an credulous Muslim claim).

There is nothing monstrous, evil, Satanic, or fantastic about Muslims in Laonikos.[39] His Muslims do not have different kinds of bodies, as they do in much western literature, making them effectively a different species.[40] He does not seek to denigrate them (or any other people) in order to affirm his own way of viewing the world. In the *Histories*, they emerge as ordinary people with their own religion, and they are not defined in relation to Christians but on their own terms. So much so, in fact, that Laonikos has gone to the trouble of inventing a putative kingdom to serve as their geographical and ethnic point of reference, a place that did not exist in his time or any other before the twentieth century, the "kingdom of Arabia," with which Timur allegedly went to war (3.13). Laonikos focalizes his digression on Islam on this putative kingdom, concretizing it as the culture and religion of the Arabs—a religion that is shared, however, by many other peoples, including the Turks. This focalization serves the organizational requirements of Herodotean ethnography: there has to be a named people and place behind every social system such as a religion, especially one that has its own "lawgiver." But it is not only for Islam that he practices such invention. We will see in the next chapter that his view of Catholic Europe is structured around a non-existent people, the "Romans," who serve as a taxonomic and relational standard for the west, but are themselves fictitious.

Laonikos, then, invents "Arabia" in order to ethnographically embed his account of Islam. His geography of that land (in 3.13) focuses on Arabia Felix (modern Yemen), and thus Laonikos

---

39 Cf. Frakes, *Muslim Other*, 64, for medieval literature.
40 Cf. Akbari, *Idols in the East*, 159–60.

presents his Arabs as quite prosperous.[41] The war of Timur against the Arabs that he recounts is fictional (3.14), but it allows his Arabs to take center stage and claim priority among all people who follow Muhammad, who was one of their own. This makes them "the fathers of all who worshipped according to the hero's religion" (3.14). He then discusses Muslim prayer (3.15) along with sexual, marriage, and family customs (3.16). He says that Muslim prayer took place on "the day of Aphrodite," i.e., *venerdì* in the Romance languages (English Friday). It is possible that Laonikos is using the Romance name of the day to channel an old Byzantine accusation against Muslims that the veneration of the Ka'aba was really about Aphrodite.[42] It was a slander known in the west too that Muslims "worschippe Venue, and therfore it is that Saracens holdeth the Fridy holy."[43] If this is what lies behind the allusion, it would be the only instance of anti-Muslim polemic in the *Histories*, and even so it is extremely covert. But the likely audience of the *Histories* was not composed of Muslims: Laonikos had no reason to be circumspect. We will see that he says harsh things about Mehmed II, the sultan at the time he was writing, so he evidently had no fear of offending Turkish authorities. It may just be, then, that in his antiquarian manner he had no other way to say "Friday." Greek *Paraskeuê*, for instance, was too unacceptably Christian a way to refer to the sixth day of the week.[44]

41   For its image in ancient literature, see J.-F. Breton, *Arabia Felix from the Time of the Queen of Sheba (Eighth Century B.C. to First Century A.D.)*, trans. A. LaFarge (Notre Dame, 1999).

42   For other sources, see Meyendorff, "Byzantine Views of Islam," 118–19; Khoury, *Polémique byzantine*, 162–63, 240–41, 275–78.

43   Ranulf Higden, *Polychronicon* (fourteenth century), quoted by Akbari, *Idols in the East*, 243; and cf. 275 and 277 for Roger Bacon; also Tolan, *Saracens*, 73.

44   See the fourth section of chap. 5 for Laonikos's use of western day-names.

Laonikos peppers his presentation of Islam with ambiguous sentences, so it is not clear whether he is offering praise or mild criticism. Are Muslims doing good things but in a bad way, bad things but in a good way, or just their own things? I suspect that this is Laonikos's way of making us think of Islam on its own terms. For example, what are we to make of the following? "Their lawcode promotes indolent mildness yet also enthusiasm for God, and especially constant study" (3.15: ἀνίει τε τὴν νομοθεσίαν ἔστε τὴν ῥᾳστώνην καὶ τὴν τοῦ θείου βακχείαν μέντοι, συνεχῆ δὲ ὡς μάλιστα μελέτην). It is hard to translate this sentence. Each of its terms is loaded, but it is not clear how they are supposed to be combined here, or to what overall effect. If we knew in advance that he was praising the religion or criticizing it we would translate them in more pointed ways for or against, but he gives us no signals as to his overall intent.

Laonikos introduces a notorious topic, Muslim polygamy, in a similarly ambiguous way (3.16):

In other matters in their way of life and overall conduct nothing is regarded as so reprehensible that it would prevent them from living pleasurably; thus, they do not curb nature in any way. For they marry more than one wife and have concubines from among their captives, however many as each man is able to support and feed.

The start of this passage would seem, from a Christian perspective, to contain criticism—for there are things that give pleasure but are reprehensible, such as having many concubines—but the practice under discussion turns out to accord with "nature." Do Christians, then, "violate nature" with their restrictions? Perhaps this ambiguity reflects back on Laonikos himself, revealing his standards of judgment to be non-Christian. Are we perhaps seeing what Herodotos would make of Muslim sexual and marital practices? He certainly would not have abhorred them. From the surviving table of contents of Pḷethon's *Laws*, we know that chapters were included on the topics of the cohabitation of one man with several women and on the sharing of women, but unfortunately we do not know what was said about them. Plethon's launching point was certainly Platonic rather than Islamic, but his position either way would not have been Christian.[45]

I have not found the source for the "three spleens" that Laonikos says are necessary for Muslim divorce (3.16; cf. 2.54). This refers to the rule of triple *talaq* (the divorce is final if the husband says "I divorce you" three times to his wife). Laonikos knew the rule that a Muslim man could not take back a woman whom he had divorced unless she had first remarried and been divorced by another man. This is in the Quran, but I do not think he had it from there, even though there were Greek translations.[46] He characterizes this second, interlude marriage as "adultery," which sounds like the type of hostile interpretation that a Christian polemicist might offer,[47] but it may be how some Muslims viewed it. He first discusses the rules of Muslim divorce when he reports the insults that Bayezid sent to Timur: among them was that Timur should renounce his wife three times, which, as an insult, meant that she would have to sleep with another man before he could take her back (2.54).

Laonikos then discusses the prohibition of wine, Ramadan, circumcision, burial customs, dietary prohibitions, and beliefs regarding God, the angels, Jesus, and Muhammad (3.17). His

45   Plethon, *Laws* 3.16–17; see Anastos, "Plethon's Calendar," 301–2.

46   *Quran* 2.230; for the translations, see C. Simelides, "The Byzantine Understanding of the Qur'anic Term *al-Samad* and the Greek Translation of the Qur'an," *Speculum* 86 (2011): 887–913.

47   For Arethas and Euthymios Zigabenos on this divorce rule, see Förstel, *Schriften zum Islam*, 30–35, 68–69; cf. 94.

reporting on these points is mostly sound, but there are errors too. The notion that Muslims believe that "at the end of this world, when all people who have ever lived are judged, they say that Jesus will judge the world," is based on prior Byzantine discussions of Islam that misunderstood the beliefs in question (albeit possibly based on actual variants within Islam).[48] But Laonikos does not use it polemically. He probably assumed that the beliefs themselves were being reported correctly and discarded the context of theological disagreement. I have been unable to find his source for the "fiery minds" (i.e., angels) who serve God. We must remember, however, that Laonikos lived in the fifteenth century, not in the days of classical Islam. Centuries of religious contact and exchange certainly led to idiosyncratic combinations of beliefs among both Christians and Muslims, and Laonikos's oral informants are beyond our reach. He may have been told things that we regard as errors but were beliefs actually held by some Muslims. And my focus on these passages should not be taken to imply that Laonikos's discussion of Islam consists of such problematic reporting, for most of it is generally valid.

Laonikos does, however, frame his account of Islam with vague and often inaccurate notices about the life of Muhammad and the early expansion of the Arab armies. For example, the following generalization is typical of Laonikos's prose: Muhammad "was declared lawgiver and they obeyed him wherever he led them. They entrusted their affairs to him and allowed him to govern them in whatever way he deemed best" (3.18). As for inaccuracies, Muhammad did not lead armies against Egypt. Laonikos could have consulted any number of histories from which he would have learned the basic facts about Muslim expansion, but evidently he

48   Simelides, "Byzantine Understanding," 894. *Quran* 4.158 says only that Jesus will testify against his persecutors on the Day of Resurrection.

did not. As it happens, Plethon had made a brief summary of those very events drawn from prior Byzantine historians, but Laonikos reveals no knowledge of it. I have not been able to find the source for the strange idea that Muslims do not enslave Armenians because an Armenian once prophesied to Muhammad his future glory (3.18). The closest comparandum I have found is the tale told in Armenian sources that Muhammad studied with an Egyptian (or Syrian) Christian heretic who made such a prediction (and Muhammad later murdered him).[49] But the tale circulated widely and was not Armenian in origin.[50] Perhaps its "Arian" heretic protagonist was changed to an "Armenian" at some point before Laonikos. As for the *hajj*, to which he devotes an entire section (3.20), it was not in honor of Muhammad and not held at his tomb (which is in Medina, though placing it in Mecca was an error made by many Christians). In sum, Laonikos does report a great deal about Islam that does not come from Muslim sources, but he seems to have removed their polemical edge. Perhaps he was trying to adjust for the obvious bias of his sources, but at the same time he did not try to explicitly correct those sources by citing Muslim authorities. At the end of his discussion, he finds that Muhammad's "lawcode bears the mark of a just man, not someone who became a tyrant" (3.18). Likewise, Arabia "is inhabited by men who are the most just and extremely wise in matters of their religion" (3.13).

As far as I know, for all his mistakes there is nothing quite like Laonikos's impartial account of Islam in any prior literature produced by Christian writers, and I suspect that Laonikos was able to write it because he saw the world, or was trying to see it, not as

49   R. W. Thomson, "Armenian Variations on the Bahira Legend," *Harvard Ukrainian Studies* 2–4 (1979–80): 884–95.

50   Tolan, *Saracens*, 52, 139, 150, 204–5.

a Christian but through the pluralist lenses of Herodotean eth-nography and Plethonian ethno-philosophy. This was an extraor-dinary feat of moral imagination and authorial repositioning. Laonikos's Islam is not a foil for or distortion of Christianity,[51] and it was not evil: his Muhammad was "just" and his Muslims are exactly what modern scholars have been looking for in vain in medieval texts, that is "Muslims per se . . . living their lives without necessary relation to the projected needs or desires of Christian Europeans."[52] Laonikos, I propose, was not writing as a "Christian European" but as a "New Greek" living under Muslim rule.

By way of concluding this discussion, there is one passage in the *Histories* that has been read by historians as linking together Islam, Laonikos's Herodotean project, and Plethon's philosophy; it involves the concept of fate. Before the second battle of Kosovo (1448), Laonikos recounts the single combat between a Hungarian champion and the Turkish youth İlyas who bested him. When İlyas was later questioned by the sultan Murad about where he had learned to fight, he said it was from a rabbit (7.43). "A rabbit?" Yes, he said, for when he had gone hunting he once saw a sleeping rab-bit, yet he missed it with all his arrows. The rabbit then ran away:

> At that point I realized that all my arrows had been in vain, as it had been fated [εἱμαρμένον] for that rabbit to live on. From that moment on, O sultan, I made a resolution to fear neither sword, spear, or arrow, for if it is fated [πεπρωμένον] for me to live on, no spear can claim my life. That is why I came out in confidence, O sultan, against the Hungarian, as I knew that, if I were fated [πεπρωμένον] to live, the Hungarian could do me no harm.

51 Cf. Frakes, *Muslim Other*, 81, for medieval literature.
52 Ibid., 101.

Laonikos then adds in his own voice that "this race is unnaturally devoted to the belief in fate [εἱμαρμένη], like others who adhere to the religion of Muhammad" (7.44). Laonikos uses these terms only here, and nothing in the *Histories* indicates that he too saw events as "fated" to happen, with the exception of one passage regarding the fall of the Peloponnese (8.43), though this copies a Herodotean formula used by many later Greek historians ("it had to happen") and cannot justify pinning a philosophy of history on him. His preface, at least, suggests that he thought in terms of "virtue" and "chance,"[53] and he does not elsewhere use the alleged belief in fate to explain even the actions of his Muslim characters. The mother of Uzun Hasan, in the powerful speech that she addresses to Mehmed II (9.72), alludes to the good and bad "fates" or "lots" (*moirai*) that God dispenses to people, but as she develops her admonitions her theology is rhetorical and impossible to formalize.[54] Laonikos's contemporary Doukas noted the Turkish belief in kismet: he has Mehmed I declare that "everything that has been written on the forehead of each person by the finger of God must absolutely come to pass" (19.12).

Now, Plethon's *Laws* included a chapter *On Fate* (2.16: εἱμαρμένη), which affirms a strongly deterministic view of the world. It had circulated as a separate treatise.[55] This too has been used to infer an Islamic influence on Plethon, though strong arguments favor a Hellenic, specifically Stoic, pedigree for this concept.[56] Unfortunately, Laonikos does not correlate the Islamic notion of

53 See the first section of chap. 5.

54 Cf. Turner, "Pages," 360.

55 Plethon, *On Fate* in PG 160:961–64 = *Laws* 2.6 (pp. 64–78); summary in Woodhouse, *Plethon*, 332–34. Plethon touched on this issue also in his *Reply* to Scholarios: Woodhouse, *Plethon*, 305–6.

56 Anastos, "Plethon's Calendar," 299–301; Siniossoglou, *Radical Platonism*, 313–23.

fate with any such concept that he may have learned from Plethon nor does he explain exactly how that notion may have affected the course of Ottoman expansion, given that he mentions it in only that one passage. Be that as it may, his stance as a historian of a foreign culture broke with the Orthodox view that consistently condemned the notion of fate, and here his Herodotean and Plethonian education played a decisive role again. He was at least prepared to make Hellenic sense of Islamic beliefs.

Laonikos as an Early Ottoman Historian

The *Histories* may range from Britain to Mongolia, but Laonikos was first and foremost a historian of the Ottoman Turks. His narrative follows the sequence of the sultans, and the majority of his information is about the Turks and told from a Turkish vantage-point, including the capture of Constantinople. Yet academic specialization and linguistic barriers have relegated Laonikos to the Byzantine side of things, and so he remains underutilized by historians of the early Ottoman state, even when he provides evidence that would be central to modern debates, if only it were better known. For example, there is much controversy about the role in Ottoman expansion of the light cavalry raiders: were they holy warriors or opportunistic plunderers and slavers, or both? Laonikos's strong support for the more cynical interpretation has not been brought into the debate. He is also one of the first authors to tell us, among other things, about the recruitment and training of janissaries and the organization of the sultan's camp and army.

More importantly, however, he offers us a view of early Ottoman history that comes from Turkish oral sources, and this at a time before that history had really begun to be written down by the Ottomans themselves. In other words, whether his testimony on specific facts and events is, after scrutiny, found to be inaccurate or partial, he remains an important, albeit overlooked, witness to early Ottoman traditions. Thus he can and should be regarded as an "Ottoman" historian, for all that he was writing in Greek and transposing what his sources told him into a classical idiom. Even through this filter, we can sometimes discern traces of Turkish tradition. Laonikos's importance as an Ottoman historian is, in fact, greater than most scholars might assume, given that he has now been dated to no later than the 1460s, with much of his research probably already complete in the late 1450s. This makes him one of the earliest Ottoman historians in any language.

It has long been understood that Laonikos had Turkish informants for Ottoman history, as he offers us information and traditions that are not recorded in Byzantine and western sources.[57] We do not know whether he understood Turkish. It has been doubted on the basis of alleged errors, but they are few and concern technical terms or nuances (Yıldırım is "Thunderbolt" not "Hurricane")—and he may have had reasons to render them the way he did. The question of the language in which he received Turkish traditions must, then, remain open. He himself claims to have had access to the sultan's budget officers (8.78) and to the contractors who ferried his armies across the Danube in 1462 (9.90). Marios Philippides has also suggested to me the possibility that Laonikos interviewed renegades, converts to Islam who became functionaries at the Porte, such as Thomas Katabolinos/Yunuz Beg, whom Laonikos mentions once (9.84–85). He devotes a separate paragraph to this group and the Turkish names that they took

57 Unfortunately, we have only dated, preliminary, and limited discussions: A. Nimet, *Die türkische Prosopographie bei Laonikos Chalkandyles* (Hamburg, 1993); and Baştav, "Türkischen Quellen," 38–42, who offers mostly general parallels, which could have come from reporting on the same events.

on (8.72; cf. 10.13). These men, native Greek-speakers, continued to maintain close relations with the Orthodox community.

But Laonikos did not use Turkish (or eastern) sources exclusively for the history of the Ottomans: he synthesized them with western and contemporary Byzantine views. The following reading of Book 1 (primarily) aims to identify the range of his sources and to show, wherever possible, how he transformed "barbarian" oral traditions into classicizing historiography. There is scope for further research in this direction, and it should be undertaken jointly by Ottoman and Byzantine historians, now that we have a translation of the *Histories*. It may be that the following discussion merely touches the surface, as I will be using only certain early Ottoman sources for my comparisons (effectively ending with Aşıkpaşazade, who wrote after Mehmed's death in 1481). I will be introducing each of these as well as western sources when they become relevant to the discussion. But later Ottoman sources, which I cannot read, reflect earlier traditions too.[58]

Before launching into an analysis of the Turkish material in the first books of the *Histories*, it is worth noting that Laonikos made no use of prior Byzantine historiography on the Turks, whether the Turks of Central Asia in the early period (such as we find in Menandros), the Seljuks (in Ioannes Skylitzes), or the Ottomans (in Nikephoros Gregoras and Ioannes Kantakouzenos).[59] As far as we know, he had never read them (he does not mention any

---

58   The standard surveys of early Ottoman historiography are H. İnalcık, "The Rise of Ottoman Historiography," in *Historians of the Middle East*, ed. B. Lewis and P. Holt (London, 1962), 152–67; and V. L. Ménage, "The Beginnings of Ottoman Historiography," in *Historians of the Middle East*, ed. Lewis and Holt, 168–79.

59   For Laonikos's ignorance of Gregoras, see Kaldellis, "Greek Sources"; for his ignorance of Byzantine ethnography, Nicoloudis, *Laonikos*, 166 n. 66 (who, however, believes that Laonikos had Gregoras). For prior Byzantine accounts of the Turks, especially Skylitzes, see Kaldellis, *Le discours ethnographique*, chaps. 2 and 8.

ancient historian either, but it is certain that he had read some).
Nor does he show any interest in his teacher Plethon's theory that
the Turks were really the Paropamisadai whom Alexander the
Great had shut in within a mountain range.[60]

The first theory that Laonikos gives of the origin of the Turks,
attributing it to others, is that they were a branch of the Skythians
(probably here meaning the Mongols) (1.9). As it happens, this is
the theory given at the very beginning of the *Epitome on the Family
of the Ottomans* written in Latin in 1456 by Nikolaos Sekoundinos
(Sagundino) for Aeneas Sylvius, the future Pius II (this treatise
actually began to be printed together with Laonikos's *Histories* in
1553).[61] In fact, there are so many parallels in the first section that
there must be a dependence here:

> *Hist.* 1.9: Some believe that the Turks are descendants of
> the Skythians, which is quite a reasonable conjecture about
> them, given that their customs are not all that different and
> that their languages are even now closely related. They say
> that the Skythians burst out of the Don region ... and sub-
> jugated Greater Asia ... and then the land of the Persians,
> Medes, and Assyrians. After this they attacked Asia Minor,
> specifically Phrygia, Lydia, and Kappadokia, and made
> these lands subject to themselves ... They tend to follow
> the ways and customs of the nomadic Skythians and have

---

60   Plethon, *Advice to Theodoros II regarding the Peloponnese* 114–15; more information about this theory was given in 1472 by Theodoros Gaza in a letter to Filelfo,
On the Ancient Origin of the Turks, in PG 161:997–1006. Gaza knew the evidence of
Skylitzes ("Skylax") regarding the Seljuk Turks: M. J. Heath, "Renaissance Scholars
and the Origins of the Turks," *Bibliothèque d'humanisme et Renaissance* 41 (1979):
459–60; J. Hankins, "Renaissance Crusaders: Humanist Crusade Literature in the
Age of Mehmed II," *DOP* 49 (1995): 138; Meserve, *Empires of Islam*, 15, 123–42.

61   P. D. Mastrodimitris, Νικόλαος Σεκουνδινός (1402–1464): Βίος καὶ ἔργον (Athens,
1970), 171.

clearly not settled down in any particular part of Asia. And
they also add that the barbarian nations of the Turks who
live in Asia Minor, I mean in Lydia, Karia, Phrygia, and
Kappadokia, speak the same language and have the same
dress as the Skythians who roam the lands from the Don
into Russia.

Sekoundinos 1–2: Six hundred years ago and more the
nation of the Turks originated from the Scythians, who
had been accustomed to live across the Don, everywhere
in Asia, in no specific capital, no cities, and no firm or long-
term homes but wandered over the open fields... They
first moved through the Pontus and Cappadocia and gradually infiltrated the other neighboring parts. In addition,
the same point is argued by the similarity of [style of] life,
customs, clothing, care of the body... and the greatest
proof of all: the related languages and manner of speaking... They occupied and subjected not only the Pontus and
Cappadocia but also Galatia, Bithynia, Pamphylia, Persia,
farther Phrygia, the Cilicians, the Carians, and that [part
of] Asia that is known as Minor.[62]

Sekoundinos had a fascinating life.[63] A Greek from Euboia who
knew Latin, he was in Thessalonike when it was taken by the Turks

---

62   Text and translation in M. Philippides, *Mehmed II the Conqueror and the Fall
of the Franco-Byzantine Levant to the Ottoman Turks: Some Western Views and Testimonies* (Tempe, 2007), 56–87, here 56–57; cf. Meserve, *Empires of Islam*, 75, 106–12, who
shows that Sekoundinos was echoing views of the Turks expressed previously by
his patron Aeneas, specifically regarding their Skythian origin. Meserve and Bisaha,
Creating East and West, supersede (and cite) previous scholarship on western views
of the Turks at this time. The Skythian angle had first been explored by Heath,
"Renaissance Scholars."

63   Mastrodimitris, Νικόλαος Σεκουνδινός; Philippides, *Mehmed II*, 6–16.

in 1430. He was the official translator at the Council of Ferrara-Florence, and knew Kyriacus of Ancona. He worked alternately for the papacy, Venice, and Alfonso V, and wrote a vivid and influential portrait of Mehmed II, whom he met on a mission in 1453. He lost most of his family in a shipwreck in 1460; accompanied Mehmed's army when it seized Trebizond in 1461; and died in Venice in 1463. There were many opportunities during his travels for him and Laonikos to meet and they probably had common acquaintances. A link can be established. In 1452, upon the death of Plethon, Bessarion wrote a letter to Sekoundinos praising Plethon and asking him to convey a consolatory poem to his sons, presumably at Mistra. It is likely that Laonikos (also named Nikolaos) was there at the time, just over twenty years old. Bessarion says that Sekoundinos had personal experience of Plethon's wisdom, implying a stronger prior acquaintance than just the Council, which was now so many years in the past.[64] Sekoundinos seems to have spent the 1440s working for the Venetians in nearby Euboia,[65] and he was briefly involved in the philosophical dispute over Plato and Aristotle that raged in Italy in the 1450s.

The problem is that, with two possible exceptions, there are no further parallels between Sekoundinos's treatise and Laonikos's *Histories*. The two texts recount Ottoman history after that very differently.[66] Strange as it is, Laonikos must have used only the

---

64   Bessarion's letter is in C. Alexandre, *Pléthon, Traité des lois* (Paris, 1858), Appendix XVII, 407–8 (the verses themselves are Appendix XVI, 406); cf. Mastrodimitris, *Νικόλαος Σεκουνδινός*, 44–45.

65   Mastrodimitris, *Νικόλαος Σεκουνδινός*, 51.

66   The two exceptions: both Sekoundinos (7) and Laonikos (2.13, 2.20) anachronistically depict Sigismund as Roman emperor at the time of the Nikopolis campaign; and both use a similar phrase for the accession of Mehmed II, and only for him: cf. Sekoundinos 9 ("he arranged the entire realm in accordance with his inclinations") with *Hist.* 7.65 ("he made arrangements concerning his rule which he believed would be advantageous for the time being").

first page of the *Epitome*, but at least we are able here to identify the man behind one of Laonikos's vague citations ("some believe"). If the connection holds, however, we can postulate Sekoundinos as a potential source of information for Laonikos about the west, for example, about Alfonso V, to whom Sekoundinos reported in 1454 and 1455–56. Moreover, Sekoundinos also wrote a (still unpublished) essay on the history of the Hexamilion wall,[67] a topic to which Laonikos devotes a paragraph in the *Histories* (4.19). There might have been some influence here, but in which direction? Laonikos's digression is based on Herodotos and the Justinianic inscription that was found at the site, which he possibly saw for himself in 1446.[68] Moreover, Sekoundinos's essay was meant to preface his translation of an oracle regarding the wall, but Laonikos says nothing about the oracle.

Let us return to the question of Turkish origins. Meserve has shown that a Skythian background for the Turks was being deployed by the humanists before Sekoundinos wrote his *Epitome*, and that it was part of an effort to cast the Turks as barbaric. After he lists some alternative theories about the origins of the Turks (see below), Laonikos dons his Herodotean cap and weighs the alternatives (1.10):

> I am not able to say with certainty how much truth each of these views contains or to what degree one should trust in each. But this much, at least, can be said, that it would be better to side with those who ascribe a Skythian origin to these people, because the Skythians who even now remain in the

---

67 Mastrodimitris, Νικόλαος Σεκουνδινός, 166, 220–21; Meserve, *Empires of Islam*, 112 and 298 n. 196.

68 The discovery of the inscription is reported by Sphrantzes, *Chronicle* 4.2. The inscription was almost certainly placed on display.

eastern parts of Europe in the so-called Horde[69] have no difficulty in understanding the Turks of Asia. Both nations have one and the same way of life and use the same dress even now ... The name Skythian itself obviously designates anyone who follows a nomadic way of life and spends most of his time doing this.

Laonikos sides with the humanist version, ostensibly on the grounds of language and anthropological taxonomy. But he seems to be conflating two different types of argument. One is to say that the Turks are related to the Skythians as a specific ethnic group (i.e., the Mongols) on the grounds of language and material culture, and another is to use "Skythian" as a generic term for all "nomadic" peoples, as he does at the end of the passage quoted above. Are Skythians an *ethnos* or a type? In Herodotos, they are a people who happen to be nomadic, but in the Byzantine tradition their name came to stand for all nomadic peoples and thus for the very antithesis of "civilized" life. The Skythians were the most frequently invoked anthropological category because they were the archetypical Other—whether they were Goths, Huns, Avars, Magyars, Pechenegs, Mongols, or whoever: their precise identity (e.g., "language") did not matter.[70] (Prokopios had claimed that whoever lived north of the Black Sea was a Skythian and that a secondary name was added to distinguish them.)[71] In Laonikos, these two approaches dovetail.

Did any of this entail a negative view of the Turks? The Turks are "the barbarians" in the world of the *Histories*, but what did "barbarian" mean exactly for Laonikos? Margaret Meserve emphasizes

---

69   I.e., the Golden Horde.

70   Kaldellis, *Discours ethnographique*, chaps. 9–10.

71   Prokopios, *Wars* 8.5.5–6.

that the western humanists seem not to have read Herodotos by this stage (the mid-fifteenth century), so their view of the barbarians "ultimately perpetuated a medieval Christian image of barbarity: the Turks were a monstrous, inhuman scourge, sent by a vengeful, interventionist God against a sinful civilization."[72] This was certainly not Laonikos's view of the Turks. The difference may lie in the fact that Laonikos did read Herodotos and was deeply influenced by him. Herodotos did not intend to exalt the Greeks over all other peoples. He viewed almost all nations as having good and bad qualities and none of his ethnographic types fit the later "Christian" image of barbarity. Laonikos's Skythians (Mongols) are likewise but one people among many in the world, not Gog and Magog. He may have linked the Turks to the Skythians, but this does not mean that he saw them as essentially *barbaric*. So, too, he may agree with the humanists on the facts of a Skythian origin, but he breaks with them when it comes to their interpretation.

A crucial factor that sets Laonikos apart from the humanists is his subsequent use of actual Turkish sources, to which no humanist seems to have had access. For instance, among the alternative theories that Laonikos records regarding Turkish origins is that they "came to this land from Koile Syria and Arabia, rather than from the Skythians, and that they did so in the company of 'Umar, who succeeded as lawgiver [i.e., of the Muslims after Muhammad]" (1.10). This was an idea with which some Turkish historians were already flirting. Among them was Enveri, who finished his epic poem, the *Düsturname*, in 1464, exactly when Laonikos was finishing the *Histories*, and was likely in the same place too, post-conquest Constantinople. Enveri's patron was Mahmud Pasha, whose power Laonikos highlights (at 8.71), and who had participated in the campaigns against Wallachia,

---

72   *Empires of Islam*, 152–53.

Lesbos, and Bosnia (in 1462–63).[73] Through the careful structure of his poem, Enveri makes the Ottomans to be the successors of the Prophet and "names the proto-ancestor of the Ottomans as a companion of the Prophet called 'Iyad."[74] 'Umar, of course, was an archetypical figure in Muslim literature and a touchstone for comparison. In the early fifteenth century, the poet Ahmedi wrote a world history posing as an Alexander epic (the *İskendername*), which he intended to dedicate to Süleyman (1402/3–1411), the son of Bayezid. The last part of it contains an Ottoman history, where he compares the justice of Osman to that of 'Umar.[75] We already see the Turkish viewpoint entering Laonikos's synthesis, even if he opts for the Skythian thesis here.

Having settled the question of ultimate origins, Laonikos turns to more proximate times and the origin of the Ottomans specifically (1.11): "The Turks, being large and having spread far and wide, are divided into separate tribal groups, including, among others, that of the Oğuz, a noble people not to be despised." He traces a sequence of Oğuz leaders from father to son: Gündüz-Alp, Oğuz-Alp, Ertoğrul, and finally Osman. We note, first, that Laonikos's account verges on the panegyrical—indeed, his narrative of the earliest Ottomans highlights their nobility and achievements—and, second, that these names could have come only from Turkish sources. In fact, it was precisely in the early fifteenth century that an Oğuz connection (though the Kayı branch) began to be promoted, so Laonikos again emerges as in tune with current Turkish

73 C. Kafadar, *Between Two Worlds: The Construction of the Ottoman State* (Berkeley, 1995), 69–70; Stavrides, *Sultan of Vezirs*, 294–96.

74 Lowry, *Nature*, 79, with references; also C. Imber, "Canon and Apocrypha in Early Ottoman History," in *Studies in Ottoman History in Homour of Professor V. L. Ménage*, ed. C. Imber and C. Heywood (Istanbul, 1994), 128.

75 K. Sılay, "Ahmedi's History of the Ottoman Dynasty," *Journal of Turkish Studies* 16 (1992): 137; discussion by Lowry, *Nature*, chap. 2.

historical thinking.[76] He also knew that the earliest of these figures were active under the umbrella of Seljuk power, specifically one of the last Seljuk sultans of Rum, 'Ala' al-Din Kay-Qubad III (on and off the throne between 1284–1303), whom he names (1.12–13). Laonikos knows that it was the death of 'Ala' al-Din—i.e., the collapse of Seljuk power in Asia Minor—that enabled the rise of the Ottomans. Ottoman historians did not place these figures in a direct genealogical sequence, but it is the same men whom they associate in service to the sultan 'Ala' al-Din, probably as a way of generating legitimacy for the Ottomans by association with the last Seljuks.[77] This theme, then, could have come only from Turkish sources. Another major difference is that some Ottoman historians, notably Ahmedi, highlight the *gazi* (i.e., holy warfare) aspect of this early expansion, whereas Laonikos occludes it entirely. This is a much-debated topic in modern scholarship, and we will return to it below.

Among the early Ottoman historians, the most detailed account of those years is found in the work of Aşıkpaşazade. He claims that when he was sick in 1413 he stayed at the house of Yahshi Fakih, the son of Orhan's imam, where he read a history of the Ottomans down to Bayezid written by his host. He then incoporated this history into his own work, which goes down

76   A. Gallotta, "Il 'mito oguzo' e le origini dello stato Ottomano: una riconsiderazione," in *The Ottoman Emirate (1300–1389)*, ed. E. Zachariadou (Rethymnon, 1993), 41–59; Imber, "Canon and Apocrypha," 135 ("the tradition had emerged by the first quarter of the fifteenth century"); idem, "Ottoman Dynastic Myth," *Turcica* 19 (1987): 16–20; Kafadar, *Between Two Worlds*, 94–96, 122.

77   In Ahmedi, 'Ala' al-Din is served by Gündüz Alp and Ertoğrul, the father of Osman: Sılay, "Ahmedi's History," 136; Lowry, *Nature*, 18. In Aşıkpaşazade (on whom see below), Gündüz is Osman's brother: E. A. Zachariadou, Τὸ χρονικὸ τῶν τούρκων Σουλτάνων καὶ τὸ Ἰταλικό του πρότυπο (Thassalonica, 1960), 66–67, 135, 138. Legitimacy: Imber, "Ottoman Dynastic Myth," 13–15.

to 1485, though he made additions to it himself.[78] Aşıkpaşazade is generally considered the first proper prose historian of the Ottoman Empire, and I mention him here precisely to highlight how *different* his account of the early years is from that of Laonikos. The former provides a wealth of names for Osman's companions, for the places involved, which are clearly in northwest Asia Minor, and of anecdotes and stories that had clearly once circulated orally. Laonikos, by contrast, strips events down to their bare essential outline, recounting them in his abstract prose. He lacks a prosopography or a real sense of place, as his narrative hovers vaguely over all of Asia Minor. This is not to say, however, that either historian is more accurate. Some traditions recorded by Aşıkpaşazade probably promoted the interests of powerful families, and he gives the Ottomans too much agency by omitting their supporting role in the Byzantine civil wars and the earthquake of 1354, which allowed them to claim the fort of Kallipolis without a fight.[79] Plenty of politics is behind Aşıkpaşazade's account.

Laonikos, by contrast, modeled the career of Gündüz-Alp on Deiokes the Mede in Herodotos.[80] We are in a different discursive world here that expects other sensitivities from its readers. But then, turning to Ertoğrul (1.12), Laonikos seems to have transferred to him the epic tales that were being told about Umur Beg, emir of the coastal beylik of Aydın (1334–48). Umur's Aegean

---

78 V. L. Ménage, "The *Menaqib* of Yakhshi Faqih," *BSOAS* 26 (1963): 50–54; E. Zachariadou, Ἱστορία καὶ θρύλοι τῶν παλαιῶν σουλτάνων, 1300–1400 (Athens, 1991), 42; see H. İnalcık, "How to Read Ashik Pasha Zade's History," in Imber and Heywood, eds., *Studies in Ottoman History*, 139–56. Coming from a field where scholars can doubt whether Ovid really went into exile, I am surprised at how readily Ottomanists believe Aşıkpaşazade's account of his embedded source.

79 Zachariadou, Ἱστορία καὶ θρύλοι, 54, 56.

80 See p. 42 above.

raids were mentioned by Kantakouzenos, but Laonikos was clearly using Turkish tradition here. Our main source for Umur is Enveri's *Düsturname*, which was finished in 1464 (see above),[81] though the tales about Umur must have been circulating for some time already.[82] There is no mistaking the parallels. Laonikos mentions the Hebros river (by Ainos), the Peloponnese, Euboia, and Attica as the targets of Ertoğrul's raids. According to Enveri, Umur raided the Aegean and Euboia;[83] the Peloponnese, probably in 1335;[84] arrived at Athens at the request of the Catalans, but then raided Attica;[85] and went to Thrace many times in the early 1340s to aid Kantakouzenos.[86] The feat that both Laonikos and Enveri highlight is the sailing of ships up the Hebros river.[87] I have no good answer for why Laonikos made this switch (Ertoğrul for Umur), nor am I prepared to say that he was working specifically with Enveri's material.

Laonikos's Osman is a less colorful figure in comparison. The historian knows about the dynasty's connection to Söğüt, but Osman "was not terribly successful as a leader; still, he had a most liberal disposition and, making indulgent use of the local resources, he made every possible effort to win over the townspeople" (1.13). Laonikos says little about his reign and nothing about his famous dream (we have seen his absolute aversion to

---

81 The basic study, using both Enveri and the Byzantine sources, is P. Lemerle, *L'émirat d'Aydin, Byzance et l'Occident: Recherches sur "La Geste d'Umer Pacha"* (Paris, 1957).

82 Zachariadou, Ἱστορία καὶ θρύλοι, 41.

83 Lemerle, *L'émirat*, chap. 4, here 75–88.

84 Ibid., 102–6.

85 Ibid., 122, 250 (possibly in 1339–40).

86 Ibid., 177 (by Ainos with Kantakouzenos in 1344).

87 Ibid., 169–73; s.v. Maritza river in the index of the Mélikoff-Sayar edition, esp. 101.

dreams, anyway).[88] But one part of Laonikos's assessment (just quoted) does resonate with Ottoman tradition, namely that Osman, "upon taking his father's place [in Söğüt], began to get along well with those unbelievers who were his close neighbors."[89]

One of Laonikos's greatest errors is that he intrudes Orhan's son, the *gazi* raider Süleyman, into the sequence of Ottoman rulers—that is, between Orhan and Murad I—when, in fact, he died before Orhan (in ca. 1357; Orhan died in ca. 1360). Laonikos is quite vague about the length of Süleyman's putative reign, which is compounded by his decision to use no dating system. His chronology becomes so confused that he has Süleyman lead the Turks at the battle of the Černomen (Marica), which occurred in 1371 (1.34). This confusion is especially unfortunate, for Laonikos is our main source for this crucial battle, which shattered Serbian power in Thrace. But it is precisely this foregrounding of Süleyman, to the extent of making him an independent ruler, that most reveals Laonikos dependence on Turkish tradition. Ahmedi highlights Süleyman's raids in the Balkans in order to play up the *gazi* aspect of Ottoman warfare, and likewise gives him more space than he does Osman or Orhan. Ahmedi even calls him a great sultan.[90] One might well have concluded from such accounts that he was a separate ruler in the sequence (Sekoundinos, by contrast, reports

88   For the dream, see Aşıkpaşazade in Kreutel, *Vom Hirtenzelt*, 24–27; and Zachariadou, Ἱστορία καὶ θρύλοι, 131–32; Kafadar, *Between Two Worlds*, 8–10, 29–30, and *passim*. For a critical study of the Ottoman sources about Osman, see C. Imber, "The Legend of Osman Gazi," in Zachariadou, ed., *Ottoman Emirate*, 67–75.

89   Aşıkpaşazade in Kreutel, *Vom Hirtenzelt*, 23; trans. from Lowry, *Nature*, 68–69.

90   Lowry, *Nature*, 20; see Sılay, "Ahmedi's History," 138. On the other hand, the tradition recorded in Aşıkpaşazade does not place so much emphasis on Süleyman in Thrace and makes sure to note that he was under the orders of his father Orhan: Zachariadou, Ἱστορία καὶ θρύλοι, 188. For Süleyman in Ottoman historiography generally, see İnalcık, "Conquest of Edirne"; Kafadar, *Between Two Worlds*, 115.

nothing about Süleyman). On the other hand, Laonikos's account of the fall of Adrianople (1.35), which he also anachronistically places under Süleyman, does not sound like anything in Turkish tradition, probably because it is patterned on a classical source, most likely Herodotos.[91]

There are moments in the *Histories* where Laonikos indirectly alludes to Turkish sources, offering us glimpses into the material he was working from. The most direct reference is in 1.51, which cites stories about the vizier Hayreddin (Çandarlı Kara Halil Hayreddin Pasha, 1364–87) and collections of his sayings, some of which he goes on to record; unfortunately, their vigor and even sense is obscured in Laonikos's classical Greek rendition.[92] This happens in many places in the *Histories*, where Laonikos reports an anecdote or saying that just does not make much sense the way he describes it, for example, the comment made by Bayezid to Timur about the hawks and hounds (3.60), and possibly the reference to the hare and the hounds after the Revolt of the Princes (1.48: depending on how it is translated).[93] We are dealing with colorful anecdotal material of Turkish provenance that did not survive the transition to Laonikos's prose, mixed in with a Byzantine-style rhetorical exercise (an *ethopoieia*) on the theme of Bayezid's captivity.[94] The Turkish original only haunts the text here; it is no longer alive.

91   See p. 43 above; for the contemporary sources, see İnalcık, "Conquest of Edirne."

92   F. Taeschner and P. Wittek, "Die Vezirfamilie der Gandarlyzade (14./15. Jhdt.) und ihre Denkmäler," *Der Islam* 18 (1929): 74 n. 1.

93   The Revolt is possibly fictional, a conflation of separate events: P. Katsoni, *Μία επταετία κρίσιμων γεγονότων: Το Βυζάντιο στα έτη 1366–1373* (Thessalonike, 2002).

94   Cf. Barker, *Manuel II*, 513–18 for versions by Manuel and others. "What Bayezid said in his captivity" was a theme that attracted writers in many languages at the time.

At 1.35, Laonikos notes that "there is said to have been a man with this sultan [Süleyman] who was a most remarkable military strategist and an extraordinary leader in battle and during assaults." This is a patent reference to a *gazi* warrior of the oral tradition, whether Evrenos, Lala Shahin, or Hajji-Il Beg, whose name also did not make the cut when Laonikos condensed his material. He is alluding to traditions like that when he refers to "Evrenos's remarkable deeds in Europe that are well known" (4.62). The phrase ἔργα ἀποδεδειγμένα ἄξια λόγου alludes to the title of the *Histories* itself and so possibly to another composition. Evrenos was the greatest of the *gazi* raiders and his exploits were celebrated throughout the Balkans, in the same way, perhaps, that those of Charlemagne were celebrated throughout Spain, Italy, and France (2.32). Laonikos may look like Thucydides on the surface, but behind that surface we can glimpse the unclassical materials that modern historians often wished had survived instead.

Laonikos devotes a whole page to Evrenos (4.62–63), noting among other things his close connection to the town of Giannitsa. He there calls him by the strange name Evrenos Hajji Therizes, which can also be translated Hajji Evrenos the son of Therizes or even Evrenos the son of Hajji Therizes. Now, the name of Evrenos's father is normally given as İsa Beg "Prangi" (whose exact meaning is disputed), and "Therizes" is how Laonikos renders the name Firuz,[95] so there is an odd mistake here somewhere. As it happens, Evrenos's tomb at Giannitsa was discovered in 1974, and the tombstone records his name as *Haci Awranuz bin İsa*: "Hajji Evrenos the son of İsa" (he had apparently gone to Mecca during his long, long life).[96] "Therizes" is a plausible phonetic mistake for "bin

95   Nimet, *Türkische Prosopographie*, 46.

96   V. Demetriades, "The Tomb of Ghazi Evrenos Bey at Yenitsa and its Inscription," *BSOAS* 39 (1976): 328–32; Lowry, *Nature*, 58–61.

İsa," so Laonikos is possibly giving the form of the name given on the tombstone (Aşıkpaşazade calls him Gazi Evrenos, not Hajji). With the Justinianic inscription at the Hexamilion, then, this would be another instance of epigraphic research on his part (after all, he had taken Kyriacus, "the first epigraphist," on a tour of Sparta). But this visit to Evrenos's tomb is hypothetical, though Laonikos knew about his connection to the place and could easily have visited it.

We also need to give Laonikos the benefit of the doubt when he claims to report Turkish traditions, even (or especially) when they do not match what is reported in the limited range of extant Turkish sources. His most explicit claim concerns the death of Murad I at the battle of Kosovo (1389). The Turkish version of events, he says, is that Murad won the battle and was killed by an anonymous Serb in the pursuit, while the Greek version is that he was first killed by Miloš, whereupon Bayezid killed his own brother, assumed command, and defeated the Serbs (1.56–57). At the beginning of the next book, Laonikos casts doubt on what he has dubbed the "Greek" view by wondering how Bayezid could have killed his own brother while he was in battle formation and how Miloš could have been allowed to approach Murad with a spear (2.2). He seems to side with the Turkish version, though we wonder why he calls the second version the "Greek" one, given that no Greeks were involved. In fact, no two versions of the event in any of our sources are identical. The earliest Turkish source, Ahmedi, which is also the earliest source generally (first decade of the fourteenth century), claims that Murad won the battle but stayed behind with some slaves while his army was giving chase. An (unnamed) infidel soldier who had hidden among the bodies jumped up and stabbed him with a dagger.[97] The version in

97   Sılay, "Ahmedi's History," 142.

Aşıkpaşazade is closer to what Laonikos calls the Greek view.[98] So is the version in Doukas.[99] The *Anonymous Bulgarian Chronicle* written in the first half of the fifteenth century seems to fuse the two versions: Murad was winning when Miloš ran him through with a spear; thus, in its narrative it is like the "Turkish" version, except the anonymous Serb is Miloš.[100]

A great deal has been written about this battle, which continues to haunt Balkan politics. I cite these different versions not—God forbid—because I want to find the truth about what happened, but only to situate Laonikos's report within a field of competing versions to which it is difficult to assign ethnic labels. Yet Laonikos's clearly did. What he calls the "Greek" version of events has become canonical and seems to have been accepted by Aşıkpaşazade, writing almost a century after the battle. But we need to believe Laonikos that a Turk told him the "Turkish" version, even though it is not reported outside the *Histories*. Ahmedi's version comes close, the difference being whether Murad had joined the pursuit after the battle or stayed behind. Laonikos is here reporting an alternate Turkish version.

We can also discern the moral concerns of Islamic historiography at work in some passages of the *Histories*, specifically in the

---

98   Aşıkpaşazade in Kreutel, *Vom Hirtenzelt*, 94–95. It is like the "Turkish" version in that it places this event after a great battle in which Murad was victorious, but it does not have Murad engage in heroics during that battle; he is found by Miloš in his tent.

99   Doukas, *History* 3.1–3 (except Miloš uses a dagger, not a spear).

100   In his recent edition and translation, and in a series of prior articles, Nastase argues that this was basically a translation of a chronicle written by the Byzantine scholar Ioannes Chortasmenos. I remain skeptical: Kaldellis, "Greek Sources." The Serb versions have Miloš kill Murad on the day before the battle, with Bayezid in command on the next day, when the battle was fought: J. Fine, *The Late Medieval Balkans: A Critical Survey From the Late Twelfth Century to the Ottoman Conquest* (Ann Arbor, 1994), 409–10.

idea that Muslims should not make war against other Muslims. The debate between Timur and Bayezid hinges on that issue, and an interesting, pious intervention is made by Timur's wife, who tries to shield Bayezid from Timur's wrath, seeing as he was fighting against the infidels (2.50–56). The same theme recurs when Mehmed II attacks Uzun Hasan: he is deterred by the latter's mother, who makes similar arguments in a long and powerful speech (9.72). The speeches are invented by Laonikos, of course, but are designed to echo Muslim themes. For example, Ahmedi's chief moral purpose was precisely to steer future sultans away from warfare with fellow Muslims.[101] The theme of the mother/wife who reproaches her son/husband for attacking a rival who is promoting Islam also seems to be staple of Islamic historiography.[102] Another form of Islamic moralizing emerges from the attention that Laonikos devotes to the drinking parties of (the real) sultan Süleyman (4.7), which were so notorious as to have inspired Turkish literature (by Ahmedi).[103]

Without giving an exhaustive commentary on Laonikos's history of the early Ottomans, I have tried to tease out the sources that he might have used from his hints, the indirect traces that they left in his text, and the testimony of Turkish historians. We can also gain a sense for how he might have reworked these materials into his classicizing template. At times, this drained the original stories of their vigor and cultural specificity, but Laonikos also peppered his narrative with set-pieces (siege accounts, speeches,

101   Lowry, *Nature*, 17, 25.

102   For example, the wife of the Seljuk sultan 'Ala' al-Din uses similar arguments to protect Osman in Khwandamir (trans. Thackston, p. 273: he is recounting the origin of the Ottomans). For the theme in Christian literature about Muslims, see Tolan, *Saracens*, 115.

103   Ocak, "Social, Cultural and Intellectual Life, 1071–1453," in Fleet, ed., *Cambridge History of Turkey*, 1:419.

and battles) drawn from the world of classical historiography. To give another example of the latter, Murad's use of the wind to defeat the emirs in Asia Minor in battle (1.43) is not found in Turkish sources, as far as I know, however it may remind some readers of Hannibal at the battle of Cannae.[104] In some matters he is more reliable than the Turkish historians and in others less, but he deserves to be considered not only as a valid historian of the early Ottomans but as a historian who transmits parallel *Turkish* versions of events, which sometimes tally with and at other times diverge from those in linguistically Turkish sources. He deserves a place in surveys of Ottoman historiography.

In an important article, Colin Imber argued that Ottoman scholars should not limit themselves to the "canonical" Turkish sources, but take in the evidence of the so-called "apocrypha," that is, four histories of the Turks written in Italian, Czech/Polish, and Arabic, which often reflect authentic Turkish material.[105] He does not mention Laonikos, who is not yet on this field's radar. Yet he wrote earlier than or as early as the others and was drawing on authentic material. I would argue, moreover, that he belongs in the "canonical" category.

I would like to offer, in conclusion, a biographical image of how we might view Laonikos as an Ottoman historian. It may be fictional, but it is something that could easily have happened and it allows us to reposition Laonikos out of the humanist niche into which scholars have been so keen to place him and into a different

104   So noted by the French translator of the sixteenth century: B. de Vigenère, *L'Histoire de la décadence de l'empire grec, et establissement de celuy des Turcs, par Chalcondile Athenien* (Paris, 1577), 22.

105   Imber, "Canon and Apocrypha." Fleet does not include Laonikos in her survey of literary sources for early Ottoman history, though she does include other Byzantine historians: "The Turkish Economy, 1071–1453," in Fleet, ed., *Cambridge History of Turkey*, 1:228.

place where he might rub shoulders, literally, with Turkish historians. A contemporary event that Laonikos describes with unusual
vividness and detail is the ceremony organized by Mehmed II for
the circumcision of his sons, in 1457 at Adrianople (8.69–71). This
was when Laonikos was gathering the materials for the *Histories*,
and the nature of his account has led some scholars to suspect
that he was present and has left us an eye-witness account.[106] It
was not unusual for the scions of prominent provincial families
to be invited to such events (Athens had been annexed from the
Acciaiuoli enemies of the Chalkokondylai only one year before, in
1456, and this might have generated an invitation). But Laonikos
was not the only Ottoman historian present. He might have literally rubbed shoulders with Aşıkpaşazade, who wrote an eyewitness
account of the same ceremony in his own history.[107] Aşıkpaşazade
tells us that among the dignitaries present were the Persian scholar
al-Bistami (whom, as we have seen, Laonikos praised and may
have known)[108] and Şükrullah, court physician, diplomat, and
chronicler.[109] Let us, then, keep that image in mind, of these men
standing side-by-side, or face-to-face, looking out at the spectacle
of Ottoman power, and use it as a counter-weight to the humanist context into which Laonikos is often pressed. His context
and native environment were not those of his cousin Demetrios.
Might Aşıkpaşazade, Şükrullah, and Laonikos have spoken to
each other? I picture here the first international conference of

---

106   E.g., Baştav, "Türkischen Quellen," 37.

107   Aşıkpaşazade in Kreutel, *Vom Hirtenzelt*, 208–10; cf. Babinger, *Mehmed*, 149,
who uses Laonikos's testimony but oddly seems to deny its existence ("we have no
independent account," etc.).

108   See pp. 12–13 above.

109   For Şükrullah, who finished his history in 1459, see S. N. Yildiz, "Historiography XIV: The Ottoman Empire," in *Encyclopaedia Iranica* (www.iranicaonline.org/
articles/historiography-xiv, accessed 26 November 2013).

Ottoman historians. Each would go on to write Ottoman history in a different language (Turkish, Persian, and Greek, respectively) and according to different cultural conventions. Maybe they never met, but it is not too late for us to start a conversation among them.

Ottoman Institutions and the "Raiders": *Gazi* or *Akıncı*?

Laonikos is a primary source not only for the events of early Ottoman history but for Ottoman institutions as well, though he has been underutilized in this respect too. In a sense, Laonikos provides an extended institutional ethnography of the Ottoman Turks, not just a history, though it is dispensed in small installments throughout the *Histories*. For example, he discusses the organization of the sultan's "Gates" (i.e., his roving military court, which we might also translate as his "Porte" in anticipation of later usage), including the origin, recruitment, and training of the janissaries (5.11); the order of rank of people at the Porte and how they pitch tents on campaign (5.12–13); the military hierarchy (5.14); cannons (5.15–16); the way the Porte deploys for battle (7.4); the fires that Turks light two days before an attack, their religious hymns, and people who accompany the army of the sultan to perform various necessary tasks (7.21); the provisioning of the sultan's camp and the camels and pack animals that they bring with them (7.22, 8.4); the religious instructions by which the *zahids* exhort soldiers before battle "reminding them of their beliefs regarding death, namely that the hero [Muhammad] had promised happiness for those who died fighting, and of their other beliefs" (8.17); the royal customs of circumcision, weddings, and the games and acrobatic displays of such occasions (8.69–71); the organization, revenues, and expenses of the Ottoman empire (8.73–78); and the horse relay of the Ottoman post (9.89). His evidence on these topics is only erratically cited in the scholarship, in many cases not where it is crucial for the discussion at hand.[110] I will focus here on the institution of the light cavalry raiders, who are central to modern discussions of early Ottoman expansion.

A debate has raged in recent times between historians who view the light cavalry raiders as holy warriors, *gazi*, men who were religiously motivated by the desire to increase the power of Islam—a thesis that goes back to Paul Wittek—and those who see them as raiders, *akıncı*, men who were materially motivated by the desire for plunder and who were often not even initially Muslims.[111] Cemal Kafadar has also plausibly argued that these same people may have been viewed in different ways, depending on the context and the audience, as nothing precludes economically motivated religious warfare.[112] I will put my cards on the table and state that I am skeptical of theories that ascribe a primary religious motivation to groups that are engaged in military and other self-aggrandizing behaviors (so I find myself also at odds with much recent revisionist scholarship on the Crusades). I am not persuaded that we must regard religious devotion in the Middle Ages as always sincere and heartfelt, despite much recent insistence on that point, and I am willing to see a great deal of cynicism in its manipulation to achieve worldly ends. Besides, in this instance we have no evidence that comes from the raiders

110 The discussion of the training of the janissaries in P. Fodor's otherwise useful chapter, "Ottoman Warfare, 1300–1453," in Fleet, ed., *Cambridge History of Turkey*, 1:207, overlooks Laonikos's early evidence. There are other places where Laonikos could have been used: 211 (the *azaps*) and 220 (pack animals).

111 The key studies in this debate are conveniently cited by Meserve, *Empires of Islam*, 259 n. 3, though she omits the most important recent argument against the *gazi* hypothesis: Lowry, *Nature*, esp. 46–47. Wittek and his context are incisively discussed by C. Heywood, *Writing Ottoman History* (London, 2002), chaps. V–VII.

112 Kafadar, *Between Two Worlds*.

themselves. What we are dealing with exclusively is their representation in texts, which leads us to the politics of the authors in question. The texts from which we must approach this problem are not anthropological interviews or case-studies. They were written to promote specific ideological agendas, among them the anticipatory or retroactive justification of war.

To be sure, a *gazi* ideology hovered over the expansion of the Ottoman state, but I am not convinced that it can be used to explain anyone's motivation in a straightforward way. There are texts whose authors (e.g., Ahmedi) we can literally catch in the act of painting what were being called *akıncı* in the colors of the *gazi*.[113] The Greek sources never mention the *gazi* or their ideology. Lowry, a proponent of the *akıncı* interpretation, quotes Doukas on these raiders, who even uses the correct term (23.8: the raids are called ἀκκήν, i.e., *akın*). But, in reality, the most important source *in all languages* on this issue is Laonikos. At one point, Lowry even relies on Spandugnino whose "work predates all but the very earliest Ottoman chronicles" and so "warrants its serious consideration."[114] But Laonikos is also early and he offers far more information about the activities of these raiders. He is also a reporter who has established a prima facie case for objectivity and detachment. He understood that Muslim rulers felt pressure to wage war against Christians rather than other Muslims. I do not see anything that would have prevented him from saying that the Turks regarded these raiders as holy warriors carrying on the war against the infidels. But at no point does he suggest that there was anything remotely religious about the motivation of the *akıncı*, a group that he discusses extensively and presents as purely predatory.

113   Imber, "Canon and Apocrypha," 136.
114   Lowry, *Nature*, 65.

Laonikos names this group after the Herodotean term for light cavarly, ἱπποδρόμοι (or "cavalry raiders"), which is perhaps why his evidence has not yet received attention; he does not use a technical Turkish term for them. When he first introduces them, he says that

> The cavalry raiders of this people, as they are called, receive neither wages nor office from the sultan, but they are always striving for plunder and loot and thus follow wherever someone leads them against an enemy. Each rides one horse and brings along another to carry the loot. When they enter enemy territory, they receive a signal from the general to mount the horses that they have been leading, and they ride with all their might; nothing holds them back. Dispersing into groups of three, they seize captives and anything that might be useful. I know that this is how those with Murad, the son of Orhan, and those at this time who crossed over into Europe with Bayezid used to behave when they charged and so made their living, and some of them quickly became very wealthy by doing this. They settled throughout Europe, from the city of Skopje to the land of the Serbs and that of Bulgarians, and throughout Macedonia, and after that many settled in Thessaly. [2.47]

The raiders were basically paramilitary slave-drivers. They were drawn by the prospect of easy plunder against weak opponents: "others flooded into this area for the same reason when they learned that they could conveniently plunder the land for slaves and property taken from the enemy, especially where the enemy put up no resistance" (2.49). We must remember that when Laonikos says, as he often does, that a city or region was "enslaved" he does not mean only that it was "conquered," though it can mean just that. The expanding Ottoman Empire was in some respects a vast slave emporium, with huge profits generated by the sale, in both domestic and foreign markets, of human beings captured in raids and wars (these sales were facilitated by the massive slave trade networks established by the Venetians and Genoese, as far as the Black Sea and Caucasus). Laonikos is explicit about this aspect of Ottoman expansion on many occasions. The greatest leader of the raiders was Evrenos:

> When he was appointed general, many members of that race, including the cavalry raiders of Europe, would immediately join up to follow him wherever he might lead them, and they carried off huge profits. He attacked Venetian territory and enslaved their land, leading away so many slaves that he enriched his Turkish followers and made them very wealthy in a short time. [4.62]

Or again:

> The Turks advanced into the land and plundered it often, leading away as many slaves as they could and filling Asia and Europe with Hungarian slaves. [5.50]

His neutral language should not be taken to signify indifference to what was going on. In Books 9–10, which are more openly critical of Mehmed II, he indicts these operations in the Peloponnese and then Bosnia as a criminal racket:

> Zağanos settled down to survey the affairs of the Peloponnese and generated huge profits, for both himself and the lords of the Peloponnese, from the slaves that they were secretly exporting and conveying to Thessaly; he also exacted gifts from the Peloponnesians. [9.61]

The Turks who live next to this land have led away a great many slaves from it. They were plundering slaves and transporting them on to Europe and Asia from all the cities there of which we know. And from the time that he settled the city of Skopje, İsa, the son of Ishak, who supervised that city on the sultan's behalf, plundered the land of the Illyrians for a long time and more thoroughly than anyone else of whom we know, and carried away more slaves than one would have ever expected that land to provide. [10.20]

There is no room for religion in this interpretation.

At the same time, Laonikos allows us to see that Evrenos especially was covered in glory by his distinguished career (4.62–63). In this respect, he allows the Turks to glorify their own. He has no trouble acknowledging martial glory, even when it was at the expense of the Greeks. This was not because he was a passive transmitter of the material that he found in his Turkish sources, for he had total control over what went into his work. But he wanted his readers to see what the Ottoman conquests looked like to the Ottomans, just as he makes us witness the siege of Constantinople from a Turkish point of view. His use of the rhetoric of glory is actually quite neutral. He is just as likely to praise native rulers who gloriously resist the Turks and defeat their armies, e.g., Arianiti (5.42) and Skanderbeg (passim). But alongside the glorious battles and campaigns, there was a dark side to Ottoman expansion. Laonikos understood that the whole operation was based on slavery. And, in his classical scheme of things, was not a regime that enslaved its subjects the essence of barbarian despotism? "Slavery" was not just a way to describe the relationship between the Ottomans and the peoples they had conquered but also, in one striking passage, the relations at the Porte itself. Mehmed, Laonikos reports, would strike blows upon his

Vizier Mahmud, but "this is not regarded as a particularly shameful thing in the sultan's Porte, for these men associated with him in his rule are the sons of slaves and not of Turks" (9.88). Yet we never hear anything in the *Histories* about those authentic Turks, who were presumably exempt from such treatment.

East and West, Asia and Europe: The Turks as Barbarians

The "barbarians" in the *Histories* are primarily the Ottoman Turks. The term is also used of other Muslim peoples in Asia, such as the Black Sheep Turks and Timurids (2.8, 9.27), the Muslims of North Africa and Spain (2.18, 2.32–33, 5.73), and of Muslims in Asia, generally (3.19, 3.28). In one passage, Laonikos seems to define barbarians as "the enemies of Jesus" (8.49), though this was in relation to the crusading activities of Capistrano. This usage has, nevertheless, created the impression that Laonikos saw the world as divided between Christians and barbarians and that his text thus reflects a Christian ideology.[115] There is one passage in which he calls the Germans barbarians, but it has been changed by his modern editors, precisely so as not to spoil the tidiness and ostensible Christian bias of his usage.[116]

At first sight, religion does seem to be the dividing factor between barbarians and non-barbarians in the *Histories*, and Laonikos believed that Christendom and Islam were engaged in conflict on many fronts, including Spain, the Baltics, the Balkans, and the Levant (3.28). But are we authorized to understand his barbarians as "infidels," given that there is no religious polemic in his work and he does not use the terms "infidel" or "Christian"?

---

115 Ditten, "Βάρβαροι," 291–95.
116 *Hist.* 4.24; see p. 184 below.

I propose that Muslim-Christian is, in fact, a secondary distinction compared to the guiding narrative axis of the *Histories*, which, as Laonikos's preface explains, is the conflict between barbarians and Greeks. The *Histories* replays Herodotos in the present, albeit with a different outcome. The preface outlines the parallel histories of the ancient Greeks and the Asiatics (i.e., the barbarians), and then of the Romans, who later joined in the struggle against the Persians.[117] The main body of the work then extends into the present that same history of conflict between the Greeks and the Asiatic "barbarians," who are (this time) the Turks. They are divided by religion too, but that is incidental. The Herodotean polarities are more important than the Christian ones.

In other words, Laonikos's modern barbarians are secular Muslims, just as Laonikos's narrative is generally secular. There are non-Muslim "barbarians" in the *Histories*, namely, the Persians of Xerxes who attack Greece (4.19; a reference to Herodotos). It was western writers, such as humanist scholars[118] (and perhaps also modern historians), who could not see past the religion of the Turks. For Laonikos that was not so important an issue. He was not writing crusading historiography, and if he were in favor of a war against the Turks it would be for secular reasons. In moments of hyperbole, Byzantine humanists could also claim that beyond the borders of the Roman state there lived only beasts with human form.[119] But this is not the outlook of Laonikos or his genre. We have to revisit his Herodotean experiments to access his meaning. Writing secular history meant using classical paradigms, hence

---

117   See the first section of chap. 5.

118   Meserve, *Empires of Islam*, 9.

119   Theodoros Metochites, *Second Imperial Oration* 14 (pp. 376–87); see I. Ševčenko, "The Decline of Byzantium Seen through the Eyes of Its Intellectuals," *DOP* 15 (1961): 178.

the barbarians, on the one hand, and the Greeks (and Romans), on the other. These Greeks and Romans are now Byzantines and Catholic Latins. The barbarians were once the Persians and are now the Turks. These classical terms are the axis of the *Histories* and not a classical disguise for a Christian worldview.

The most common polarity in the *Histories* is not between Christians and Muslims, but Europe and Asia. Europe in Laonikos occasionally refers to the entire continent but usually to the Balkans and more specifically to the Ottoman territories in the Balkans, i.e., the *beylerbeyilik* of Rumeli. Likewise, as a technical term Asia refers to *beylerbeyilik* of Anatolia, i.e., Asia Minor, but occasionally to a broader unit. "The rulers of Asia"—all Muslims, presumably—are in one passage reified as a cultural unit bound together by common customs (2.51: the royal gift of robes, but this too may have been lifted from Herodotos).[120] One of the most common verbs and significant actions in the text is "to cross over" from Asia into Europe or the reverse. Just as Herodotos begins his *Histories* with stories about the mutual hostilities between the Greeks of Europe and the barbarians of Asia, so too Laonikos begins by recounting how the Greeks penetrated deep into Asia on multiple occasions (1.3) and also how the Persians "crossed over into Europe" (1.4). The Fourth Crusade caused the Greeks to cross over into Asia briefly (i.e., to the empire of Nikaia), but then they returned to Europe (1.6). The Herodotean background of these oscillations explains how Ottoman Turks and Achaemenid Persians are linked as "barbarians." Laonikos compares Murad I to Cyrus in his mildness (1.42), which is an early sign that barbarians are not all bad, or not in all respects. Laonikos's Turks are "barbarians" because they replay the role of Herodotos's Persians, but Herodotos hardly demonizes his Persians.

---

120   Cf. Hdt. 9.109–10.

These parallels indicate that Laonikos's Turks are not dehumanized, but rather are made comprehensible, just as Herodotos creates Persian characters that Greek readers could understand. Herodotos also presents Xerxes's expedition against Greece from the Persian point of view: we follow his army from Asia into Europe and witness their perplexity at the strangeness of some Greek customs. As far as I know, it has not been noticed that Laonikos also presents major actions, including the siege of Constantinople in 1453, from the Turkish point of view. We are made to stand outside and look at the walls, rather than at the cannons from the inside. The *Histories* is not a fully Hellenocentric narrative. Like Herodotos, Laonikos breaks up Greek history and presents it in bits and pieces, in interludes from his main Turkish theme. When he refers to the king (*basileus*) without qualification, he usually means the sultan. This is not a question of a theory of legitimacy, which Laonikos altogether lacks, but of narrative focus.[121] His main difference from Herodotos is, of course, that Asia prevails this time over Europe.

A great irony in the work is that the most aggressive sultan, Bayezid, fails to recognize that Asia can prevail. Even as he is conquering all of Europe, he learns that he is about to be attacked from Asia by Timur. "Bayezid planned to defend himself against this invader, reasoning, based on ancient history, that the kings of Asia had never prevailed over those of Europe in the past, while it was the latter who had set out against Asia and stripped its leaders of their kingdom" (2.58). In a reversal of roles, Bayezid is identified with Europe and the Greeks. When he marched against Timur, "he cited Alexander, the son of Philip, who took the Macedonians with him and crossed over into Asia, blaming Darius [III] for

---

121 *Pace* Moustakas, "Byzantine 'Visions' of the Ottoman Empire," 224; see the fourth section of chap. 3.

Xerxes's war against the Greeks. Alexander defeated him in an attack with a smaller army and subjected Asia to himself" (3.49). In this iteration of the ancient narrative, Timur is the Asiatic and, of course, he prevails, for that is what this new *Histories* is about. Timur has already been cast as a temporary stand-in for Herodotos's Persians: Laonikos tells us that his campaign against the Skythians was motivated by a desire to outdo Darius I (3.22), as if Timur too thought in Herodotean terms. So he is cast here as a new Darius (I), just as Bayezid imagines that he will defeat another Darius (III). Timur's campaign against the Skythians is told in Herodotean terms,[122] except that he wins, which again reinforces the reversal narrated in these *Histories* (Darius I had famously failed against the Skythians). Laonikos even says that "he hired a large number of Persians because they were very experienced when it came to the Skythians" (3.22). Laonikos is presumably referring to the wars in Herodotos: he really does mean "Persians" and "Skythians," and not (say) Muzaffarids and the Golden Horde! Readers of Herodotos have seen all this before.

At the Ottoman council of war before the battle of Ankara, İbrahim gives sensible arguments against offering battle in one of the most lucid and well-constructed speeches so far (3.52). Bayezid counters with a series of delusional claims based on classical history: Xerxes was defeated by a smaller number of Greeks, and a small army under Alexander defeated Darius III; so too will he now defeat the Chaghadai (3.53)—as if smaller armies always win. Bayezid has now identified completely with the Greeks, whom he has conquered; he calls his own side "we in Europe." But the *Histories* is devoted to the thesis that Asia can conquer Europe; relying on classical precedents is dangerous. Bayezid does not know that the Greeks never had virtue in proportion to their

---

122   See the third section of chap. 2.

fortune (1.3).[123] His fate is their fate: defeat and enslavement, and the women are taken by the victor.

After the defeat of Bayezid, the Byzantines become the Greeks again and the Turks the Persians. But there are few specific allusions after that. Replaying ancient roles becomes explicit again when Laonikos rehearses the history of the Hexamilion wall (4.19: it was originally built to keep out Xerxes), but that's it. As for the theory that viewed the Turks as Trojans and the fall of Constantinople as payback for the fall of Troy—a theory promoted by many in both east and west, which would fit nicely with the theme of Asia-and-Europe in the *Histories*[124]—Laonikos mentions it after his account of the Fall (8.30), only to ascribe it to westerners and tacitly dismiss it. It is unclear why he drops the system of East-West or Asia-Europe comparisons that he had developed so artfully in the first three books.

So just how "barbaric" are his Turks anyway? At least two scholars have come away from the *Histories* thinking that its intent is to praise the Turks, even to exalt the deeds of Mehmed.[125] This goes too far, possibly confusing Laonikos with Kritoboulos and, at any rate, overlooking the biting criticisms of Mehmed made in the later books. I will argue, instead, that Laonikos, like Herodotos,

123   See chap. 5.

124   Philippides and Hanak, *The Siege and the Fall*, 37–38, 197–214; previous scholarship is cited conveniently by Kafadar, *Between Two Worlds*, 159 n. 11. The most graphic development of the thesis was by Filippo da Rimini, who reported that the sultan raped a woman on the altar of Hagia Sophia to pay the Greeks back for their rape of Cassandra in a sanctuary. Kritoboulos is especially fond of both Persian and Trojan comparisons for Mehmed's Turks (*History* 1.4.2, 1.42.7, 1.68.4, 2.14.1, 4.11.5–6, 5.16.4). Heath, "Renaissance Scholars," and Meserve, *Empires of Islam*, chap. 1, have questioned the popularity of the Trojan thesis in the west, compared to the Skythian thesis.

125   Geanakoplos, *Interaction*, 217; Moustakas, "Byzantine 'Visions' of the Ottoman Empire," 224.

was not unmoved by the heroism and dynamism that the Turks displayed during the course of their expansion, but also that he was critical of the destruction that they visited upon the people they conquered. "Criticism" is, however, a term that should be qualified. As the next chapter will show, no one in the *Histories* is more criticized than the Greeks, the group to which Laonikos belonged, and especially the Greek leadership. But they are criticized for their colossal incompetence. The Turks, by contrast, are occasionally criticized for their exploitation of subject populations and abuse of power. They are not dehumanized as savage, ferocious, and beastly, as in humanist rhetoric.[126] On the sole occasion when Laonikos uses such language it is a metaphor to describe the rapacious action of human agents and not a way to dehumanize them (9.53; see below). His "barbarians" are not a different species: they have the same virtues and vices as others. Most of the criticism in the *Histories* is directed personally, if in measured tones, at Mehmed himself.

I will examine Laonikos's increasingly negative portrait of Mehmed in the next section. Here I will discuss his presentation of the other sultans and aspects of the Ottoman system that troubled Laonikos. To repeat, there is nothing here to show that his barbarians are "barbaric" in an essentializing or polemical way.

The semi-legendary founders of the Ottoman Empire receive largely favorable press. Günduz-Alp was just, his son Oğuz-Alp more tyrannical (1.11), but these figures are basically Herodotean calques. Ertoğrul was dynamic as a conqueror, but raiding and enslaving make their first appearance here, and these are behaviors that will receive more criticism later. Laonikos puts his finger on the mechanism that propelled Ottoman expansion in the following passage: "because he soon made his followers rich by

<hr>

126   Meserve, *Empires of Islam*, chap. 2.

plundering, nomads flocked to him in great numbers to fight alongside him and keep up the war against his neighbors" (1.12). It is an analysis on which modern historians have not been able to improve much, except if you believe that this raiding was religiously motivated. Laonikos, at any rate, believed that the engine of Ottoman expansion was raiding for slaves and plunder, and that success attracted even more light cavalry raiders. Ertoğrul's son Osman was liberal, a good politician (1.13), and "marched out and performed great and glorious deeds" (1.15). Laonikos does not shrink from praising the glorious deeds of the barbarians: "We have discovered that he was extremely courageous in all circumstances, and because of this he was generally believed to have supernatural powers." Here also Laonikos has condensed away the colorful and extravagant information in his sources. He also presents Osman as a founder in the classical tradition: "he arranged matters as excellently as possible for his people and set up its government in the most suitable way. He instituted a superb administration around himself which they call the 'king's Porte'" (1.15). This intimidated his subjects and servants alike. We see already that the Ottoman system is based on fear. It is the negative aspects of this analysis that will come together in a magnified way under Mehmed, but here they are present only potentially.

Laonikos offers a mixed picture of Murad I. He too basically raided and plundered in order to enrich his followers (1.37). He "performed great deeds and displayed the same sort of decency as Cyrus, the son of Cambyses. He thus treated the rulers of the Serbs, Bulgarians, and Greeks whom he had subjected to his authority in the most equitable and liberal way" (1.42). But he was cruel in punishing the followers of his rebel son Sawji, forcing fathers to kill their own sons and laughing during the executions (1.48). Laonikos's obituary of Murad is mixed, stressing his tireless energy and greatness, but not without criticism: "He always seemed rabid for battle and insatiable when it came to spilling blood everywhere" (1.58). It seems that Murad was lenient with those who submitted to him, but violent against those who resisted or rebelled against him: "He surpassed previous kings in terms of the slaughter he caused. But he spoke very politely when dealing with those under his power and with great moderation to the sons of rulers" (1.59). This mixed image was not necessarily at odds with Turkish tradition. Ahmedi also praised Murad as a warrior, but said of him that he cut off many heads and threw them to the sky (but he may have meant this too as praise).[127] No one can take issue with Laonikos's verdict on Bayezid, "a man who, wherever he went, had shown great daring and remarkable boldness. He displayed great daring in his accomplishments in Asia and Europe . . . But he was impetuous, so that he listened to no one else, and advanced confidently against the enemy" (3.65). Ironically, this makes him look just like the French knights he defeated at Nikopolis (cf. 2.20).

Laonikos's obituary of Murad II is by far the most positive: "He had been a just man and favored by fortune. He had fought in defense and did not initiate acts of aggression, but he would immediately march against the one who did. If no-one challenged him to war, he was not eager to campaign; yet he did not shrink from that when it came to it" (7.63). In many ways, this is the picture of an ideal monarch, not a "barbarian" in the negative sense, and it was probably meant as a contrast to the current one, Mehmed II. Murad II wins epic battles in the *Histories*, and his campaigns "brought glory to his rule" (5.35). Still, there is an undercurrent of cruelty that bursts out sometimes. When he took the Hexamilion wall, he butchered three hundred captives and then "bought about six hundred slaves and sacrificed them to his father [Mehmed I], performing an act of

127   Sılay, "Ahmedi's History," 139.

piety through the murder of these men" (7.26)—a rare piece of sarcasm.[128] This points forward to the behavior of his son Mehmed, an increasingly cruel butcher and rapist.

The Classical Tyranny of Mehmed II

Book 8, which includes the fall of Constantinople and the successful defense of Belgrade against Ottoman attack (in 1456), is relatively neutral when it comes to the reign and personality of Mehmed II. But Books 9–10 relentlessly highlight attributes that cast Mehmed as an oriental despot: cruelty, a love of executions and torture, treachery and the violation of agreements, rule by fear, and sexual aggression on a vast scale. It is perhaps not coincidental that these books recount the final campaigns in the Peloponnese, where Laonikos grew up, and many of these cruel acts take place there. It is in Book 9 that Laonikos sets his objective stance aside and begins to make critical comments.

The defenders of Kastritsi, for example, surrendered on terms, but Mehmed "led them all to one place where he butchered them, a total of three hundred, and on the following day he had their lord's body cut into pieces" (9.44). Mehmed then took Gardiki, and when his soldiers entered they "killed without mercy, as the sultan had instructed them, the men, women, pack animals, and livestock, sparing none" (9.45). The sultan then exterminated all the captives from Leontarion by issuing an order that basically institutionalized terrorism in the Ottoman camp:

> The sultan then proclaimed throughout the camp that whoever had taken a captive slave had to return him immediately

---

128   Cf. S. Vryonis, "Evidence on Human Sacrifice among the Early Ottoman Turks," *Journal of Asian History* 5 (1971): 140–46; Kafadar, *Between Two Worlds*, 54.

or else the slave would be ordered to kill his master, and then the slave too would be killed. After that there was nothing more scarce in the camp than slaves from that city. For more than one thousand and two hundred had been taken away. He led them all to one place there and killed them, so that not a single inhabitant of the city of Leontarion was left alive, whether man or woman. Later I learned that the bodies of the slain inhabitants were about six thousand, and many times that number for the pack animals. [9.46]

He later considered whether to kill the population of other towns, but sent them on to Constantinople instead (9.47).

At Kalavryta in Achaïa, meanwhile, Zağanos killed everyone "on the sultan's instructions" (9.49). He also made an agreement for the surrender of Santamerion, but

when he received it, it became apparent that he had deceived them, for on the following day he allowed his army to enslave all who remained in their place in the city, and he killed many there. When this was reported to the other cities, namely that there was nothing firm in their dealings with the sultan, they all rushed to defend themselves in their own cities, and none of the towns was any longer willing to submit. Shortly after that, Zağanos, who committed these acts at Santamerion, fell into disfavor and lost his command. [9.50]

The sultan required Zağanos to release of all the slaves from Santamerion (9.52), because he feared that the Greeks would now be less willing to surrender, as Laonikos does report. But Laonikos then contradicts himself and says that the Greeks "wanted to rush and surrender themselves before the sultan could arrive and capture them, enslaving some and slaughtering the rest" (9.53). It is at

this point that he delivers his harshest criticism of Ottoman policies, comparing them to wild beasts, one of his rare literary images:

> Like wolves attacking defenseless flocks of sheep, they never
> have their fill of murder. The people there suffer piteously at
> the hands of these beastly wolves, and so the Peloponnese
> was horribly destroyed, ruined by the sultan's men, with
> people dying everywhere in horrendous ways. [9.53]

Then the dynamic changes again and the Greeks become unwilling to surrender, because they do not trust the sultan's word (9.54,
9.61). This shift might reflect lack of attention and inconsistency
on Laonikos's part, or it may be his way of conveying the chaotic
and uncertain situation that the Peloponnesians faced. What
was one to do? Surrender and hope the agreement would hold?
Or fight on, but to what end? (Kritoboulos, Mehmed's panegyr-
ist, tried to put the best face on this chaos, by claiming that the
sultan's "terrorism" aimed at these peoples' "salvation.")[129] The
problem was that Mehmed himself continued to execute those
who came to him to make a treaty (9.51). Laonikos comments
in his own voice that "those who trusted in his word perished
through his deceit" (9.57).

In Book 10, Mehmed continues to saw people in half, a form of
execution that he preferred, because he had ascertained through
study that it prolonged the agony: "This was the most violent form
of death that he had devised for his enemies, to cut the body into
two. They make the cut at the diaphragm, whence it happens that
the victim lasts for a long time during his execution" (10.11; also
10.56 for the execution in this way of 500 people). He also continues to violate oaths of safety that he himself or Mahmud Pasha

129   Kritoboulos, *History* 3.22.4–5.

had given to lords who surrendered on terms, culminating in the infamous execution of the king of Bosnia (10.32–35).

This relentless litany of slaughter, cruel executions, and broken agreements gradually establishes a powerful negative portrait of the sultan. But there is one moment, mastefully recounted by Laonikos, that offers psychological insight into his character and suggests that Mehmed was not a typical Turk. Other Turks did not necessarily share his glee in torture and death; at worst, they wanted to profit by making and selling slaves. Mehmed's rival in cruelty was, of course, Vlad III Ţepeş ("the Impaler"), known today as Dracula. Laonikos says that Vlad killed his enemies "by impalement, along with their sons, wives, and servants, so that this one man caused more murder than any other about whom we have been able to learn" (9.83). He was originally Mehmed's protégé, but turned against him. In 1462, Mehmed invaded Wallachia and reached Vlad's capital at Târgovişte. The Ottoman army advanced to the field where Vlad had impaled his enemies. Laonikos paints the gruesome tableau, but note the different reactions of the Turkish soldiers and Mehmed (9.104):

> The sultan's army entered into the area of the impalements, which was seventeen stades long and seven stades wide. There were large stakes there on which, as it was said, about twenty thousand men, women, and children had been spitted, quite a sight for the Turks and the sultan himself. The sultan was seized with amazement and said that it was not possible to deprive of his country a man who had done such great deeds, who had such a diabolical understanding of how to govern his realm and its people. And he said that a man who had done such things was worth much. The rest of the Turks were dumbfounded when they saw the multitude of men on the stakes. There were infants too affixed to

their mothers on the stakes, and birds had made their nests in their entrails.

The Turks manage to see the human beings in all that carnage, their humanity and suffering emphasized by the sight of women and infants spitted together, an image of new life turned into its opposite. The reaction of the Turks is of disgust; they see what is wrong. But that is not at all Mehmed's reaction. He stands in admiration of Vlad's ruthlessness. He sees only a Machiavellian lesson here. "Teach me," he seems to be saying, or, "if only you still worked for me." Mehmed is basically a psychopath: a disturbed personality, he has no ability to empathize with the sufferings of others. Fear and terror are just methods of rule for him.

This is linked to another "barbaric" aspect of the Ottoman regime that is revealed in the final books, an aspect that Mehmed only exemplifies. I mean the system of incentives by which the sultans lead their armies. There is, of course, the promise of material gain, especially slaves, which I have discussed. But along with the carrot comes the stick. As in the armies of Xerxes in Herodotos, the belief pervades the Ottoman high command that the common soldier fights primarily out of the fear of punishment. Kasim states this directly to Murad II: "If we do not fight, our morale, grounded in the fear that we have of our sultan, will crumble" (6.36). A fleeing Turkish commander is brought back to the fight by a reminder of the horrible death that he will suffer at Mehmed's hands: he "will be far more ill-disposed toward you than the enemy would be, and will deliver you immediately over to a horrible death" (9.106). Before the final assault on Constantinople in 1453, Mehmed himself gives what might have been a rousing speech to his soldiers, but it seems to rely on two alternatives. On the one hand, "whomever I notice turning back to the tents and not fighting at the walls, not even if he flies away like the birds will he be able to escape and not suffer a horrible death." On the other hand—these are the final words in his speech—"you will obtain valuable slaves, both women and children, and there is much wealth in the city" (8.15). Like Xerxes, Mehmed has a mechanical-instrumental view of the motivation of his soldiers. There is no higher purpose. After that, "he sent a messenger around in the camp announcing that the assault would be at dawn and promising gifts for valor in battle, but the penalty for anyone who did not fight would be death" (8.17).

This contrasts to what Laonikos says of the Greeks, on this tragic occasion, if not any other: "Many Greek men who were brave fought and died on behalf of their country rather than witness their own wives and children being taken captive" (8.21). At 8.22, he recounts the noble, patriotic deaths of individual Greek heroes. These contrasts give substance to the dichotomy between Greeks and barbarians.

Vlad the Impaler also emerges as Mehmed's idol as a motivator. During the campaign, a captive Wallachian said that

> he knew exactly [where Vlad was] but would tell them nothing whatsoever about it, because he feared Vlad. They said that they would kill him if he did not tell them what they wanted to know, but he said that he was more than ready to die, and would not dare to reveal anything about that man. Mahmud was amazed by this and, while he killed the man, he commented that with such fear surrounding him and an army worth the name, that man would surely go far. [9.102]

Vlad teaches the Turks another lesson in fear and terrorism; Mehmed's servant and chief "slave" is suitably impressed.

Finally, tyrants were, according to classical notions, sexually aggressive, transgressive, and insatiable. Not only does their power give them the ability to indulge desires that are unthinkable for most people, their abnormal sex lives distort the public sphere by making it accountable to personal whims and sexual politics that should be confined to the private sphere. In Herodotos, for example, *eros* is mentioned only in connection with forbidden love or desire for power.[130] Likewise in Laonikos, sexual desire appears usually in destabilized situations and is associated with political upheaval and assassination, especially in his many Italian "sex-stories."[131] Laonikos, of course, did not disapprove of sex any more than Herodotos did. Rather, along with the ancient Greeks, he believed that its appearance on the stage of politics and world history was never a good thing.

In the final books of the *Histories*, Mehmed personally rapes his way through a good portion of the populations that he conquers. It is not only queens and princesses that end up in his bed, but thousands of children are carted away to swell the corps of palace slaves who provided for his various needs, to "attend upon his needs," as Kritoboulos put it, too discreetly.[132] Hostage royalty would serve him in bed and then be appointed to rule over

---

130   S. Benardete, *Herodotean Inquiries* (The Hague, 1969), 136.

131   *Hist.* 2.12: the widow of De Luis has an affair with a priest (which facilitates the invasion by Bayezid); 4.54–55: Esau has an affair with the wife of Preljubović (leading to the latter's murder); 4.58: Antonio I of Athens steals a bride at a wedding (this is the only story that does not have an unhappy ending, except for the groom, of course); 5.8: Ioannes VIII spends time with the daughter of a priest with whom he was infatuated (and so does not prevent Murad from crossing over into Europe); 5.65–66: Ladislao is poisoned by the maiden of Florence; 6.8–9: the wife of the lord of Ferrara has an affair with his illegitimate son (the lord executes them all); 9.15–16: the widow of Nerio II is infatuated with Bartolomeo Contarini (who kills his Venetian wife to marry her); 10.30: the king of Bosnia is smitten by a Florentine prostitute (causing political instability in the region and in his kingdom). Ditten, *Russland-Exkurs*, 4, notes that these stories may allude to Boccaccio; Herodotos suffices.

132   Kritoboulos, *History* 1.74.3; see the far less favorable account of this practice written by the interpolator in Laonikos (probably Georgios Amiroutzes), at *Hist.* 9.79–80.

their native lands, creating a strange mix of sexual and imperial politics. Laonikos is explicit about this (and its homosexual implications) in his account of the relationship between Mehmed and the Wallachian prince Dan, the brother and rival of Vlad III (9.82; cf. 8.71–72). At first, Dan did not understand that he was supposed to put out, and fled, but in the end he came around and submitted. Laonikos goes on to add (9.82):

> The sultan was used to having relations no less with men who shared his own inclinations. For he was always spending his time in the close company of such people, both day and night, but he did not usually have relations with men who were not of his own race, except for brief periods of time.

In true Herodotean form, the tyrant's desires are politically disruptive and even deadly. Zağanos's daughter had been pledged to a Mahmud (probably the later Vizier), but when Mehmed saw her he took her for himself, and Zağanos had to give Mahmud another daughter (8.31). In this case, the potential repercussions of sexual tyranny were countered by another aspect of oriental despotism: servility, specifically that of Mahmud, who, as we saw, would endure even physical blows at the hands of his master (9.88). But other victims did not have even that option. Laonikos recounts the tragic story of Notaras, who would not give his son up to the tyrant's lust (8.28–29), and claims that Mehmed murdered most of the Greek aristocracy that survived the fall of Constantinople "at the instigation of a Greek who had come there from abroad and with whose daughter the sultan was sleeping, being madly infatuated with her. He cultivated her relatives, driven by his lust. And so, they say, Mehmed obeyed this man in killing the Greeks" (8.29). The murders were real, though the alleged motive was more Herodotean than historical.

Laonikos's account of Mehmed is a checklist of the attributes of a classical tyrant. The Ottomans in the *Histories* play the structural role that the Persians do in Herodotos and so they are "barbarians" and have barbaric traits. But this label is not their destiny or their essence. They have good and even glorious qualities as well as savage and tyrannical ones. In the final books of the *Histories*, Mehmed increasingly exemplifies the latter traits. But he does not stand in for all Turks. In many cases, they are just as much the victims of his tyranny as anyone else, and in a crucial moment, namely in Vlad's forest of victims, Laonikos emphasizes the humanity of the common Turk in order to highlight Mehmed's disturbing view of absolute power and his utter ruthlessness. Finally, it is worth noting that not once does Laonikos associate the negative traits that Turks occasionally display with their religion, not even in the case of Mehmed. For Laonikos, Islam is just another religion, no worse or better than any other. He never links it to the slave-trade or the character of Mehmed. In this, he stood apart from everyone else who was writing about these people and events at that time, and also from those who would write about them for a long time to come.

Between Greeks and Romans

Greeks and Romans:
A Reading of the Preface

The *Histories* is not a continuation of a previous Byzantine work: it does not pick up at the point where a predecessor left off. Laonikos separates himself from the sequence of Byzantine history and the tradition of Byzantine historiography altogether. He begins, rather, at the beginning. If he were a Christian author, he would have begun with Adam, as did Doukas, his contemporary historian of the fall of Byzantium. But Laonikos's theme is the fall of the Greeks and the rise of the Turks (1.1), so he begins with the prehistory of the Greeks, which for him means Dionysos and Herakles; he races through ancient Greek history and recounts the interactions between Greeks and Romans down to the Council of Ferrara-Florence (1.3–7). He then goes back to trace the origins of the Turks (1.9–11).

In his Greek prehistory, and in accordance with his metanarrative of recurring conflict between Europe and Asia, Laonikos draws attention to Greek expansion in both the east and the west, led by Dionysos and Herakles (1.3). He probably learned of the historical role of this mythical pair from Diodoros of Sicily.[1] He then refers to the Peloponnesian War and Alexander the Great. At the end of this section he makes a remarkable statement: despite their success, "the virtue of the Greeks was everywhere lacking in comparison to the fortune they enjoyed, and nowhere commensurate to it." We will soon learn that the virtue of the ancient Romans was "in proportion to their fortune" (1.5), and virtue and fortune are conjoined again in the case of Murad I (1.47, 1.58). As we will see, the Greeks (Byzantines) in Laonikos's narrative have a virtue-deficit, so much so that Ottoman generals have to give them remedial lectures in how to govern their affairs (Turahan at 8.39, 8.41). Laonikos did not write his *Histories* to make the Greeks look good.

J. Harris has argued that Laonikos owed the distinction between virtue and fortune to the emerging concepts of Renaissance humanism, assuming that he was in touch with western intellectual developments.[2] I do not believe this was necessarily the case. The concepts *arete* and *tyche* pervade classical literature. In fact, Plutarch had written essays debating whether the successes of the Romans and of Alexander the Great were due more to fortune or to virtue. In both cases, he boringly finds that both played a role.[3] Plutarch is likely the source of Laonikos's categories and

1   H. Inglebert, *Interpretatio Christiana: Les mutations des savoirs (cosmographie, géographie, ethnographie, histoire) dans l'Antiquité chrétienne, 30–630 après J.-C.* (Paris, 2001), 469–70. See below for further use of Diodoros by Plethon and Laonikos.

2   J. Harris, "Laonikos Chalkokondyles and the Rise of the Ottoman Empire," *BMGS* 27 (2003): 163–70; idem, "The Influence of Plethon's Idea of Fate on the Historian Laonikos Chalkokondyles," in Benakis and Baloglou, eds., *Plethon and his Time,* 215. *Pace* Harris, I would not characterize Laonikos's position as "that fortune tends to be found where there is virtue" (cf. Kaldellis, "Laonikos," 165), given that his ancient Greeks had fortune without virtue. Moreover, Harris seems to be unaware of Plutarch's essays (see below).

3   Plutarch, *On the Fortune of the Romans* (= *Moralia* 316c-326c); *On the Fortune or Virtue of Alexander* (326d–345b). Justin, *Epitome of Pompeius Trogus* 30.4.16, says

statements, given that he uses them in connection with the same people. Plutarch was used extensively by Plethon.[4] Also, in his brief eulogy of Helene Palaiologina, Plethon noted that "it would be difficult to find in all of recorded history any state in which virtue and good fortune came together and lasted for as long as they did as the ancient Roman polity."[5] Helene died in 1450, so this work was probably composed and delivered while Laonikos was still with Plethon at Mistra. It makes the same statement regarding the Romans that Laonikos would later make.

A similar observation with regard to the Greeks and Romans had been made in the early fourteenth century by the statesman-philosopher Theodoros Metochites. He said that he admired the *tyche* of the Greeks, given that so many of their writings survived when their deeds were in fact not that outstanding. We know their deeds in detail, but they are not that amazing.[6] He then goes on to compare them to the Romans, whose glory, he says, was truly incomparable. The deeds of the Romans surpassed their *tyche*. What Metochites admires about the Greeks, however, is their wisdom and language, just as Laonikos praises their language in his preface too, right before doubting their virtue. This agreement between Laonikos and Metochites is especially significant if the latter did, indeed, stand at the head of a philosophical tradition in late Byzantium that led to Plethon; its channels and history have yet to be fully explored.[7] Yet Metochites regarded his superior Romans as the ancestors of his own people, whom we

---

that the Romans owed their success to fortune, not virtue; for the Macedonians, he says the opposite (7.14).

4   Anastos, "Pletho's Calendar," 206–9, 289; Woodhouse, *Plethon*, 18, 26, 58–59, 68, 221.

5   Plethon, *Monodia for Helene Palaiologina* 272.

6   Theodoros Metochites, *On Character or on High Culture* 22, 24.

7   A preliminary outline is given in Siniossoglou, *Radical Platonism*.

call the Byzantines; he meant to shame the latter, his readers, by this comparison. Laonikos also put down the Greeks in order to shame his readers, but he saw them as Greeks, not as descendants of the Romans.

After discussing the undeserving successes of the Greeks, Laonikos turns to Asian affairs, to present the other side of his geographical divide (1.4). Here he eschews the history of the Old Testament and utilizes Hellenic sources. He races through the Assyrians, Medes, and Persians (the latter being important because they "crossed over into Europe"). A few generations later, Alexander brought the war to Asia. This back-and-forth sequence alludes to the opening of Herodotos, except with nations at war between Europe and Asia, rather than women being abducted. The spelling Arbakes (rather than Arsakes) and the link connecting him to Sardanapalos show that Laonikos's source here was Diodoros (following Ktesias), rather than Herodotos. Diodoros was also used by Plethon; a complete copy of the *Bibliotheke*, moreover, is said to have been in the palace library of Constantinople before the fall of the city.[8]

Enter the Romans, whose "virtue was in proportion to their fortune" (1.5). Laonikos jumps to the foundation of Constantinople, whose purpose, he claims, was to enable the Romans to fight against the Persians. This tendentious claim reinforces his theme of conflict between East and West. But we note that he names neither Constantine nor his city, which for Laonikos is always "the Greek city of Byzantion." He uses the name Constantinople only twice in the *Histories* (6.4, 10.41), the first likely a slip on his part and the second in a speech, reflecting the outlook of the

8   Arbakes and Sardanapalos: Diodoros, *Bibliotheke* 2.24–25; cf. Woodhouse, *Plethon*, 18–19, 221–22. Complete copy: Konstantinos Laskaris, *De scriptoribus Graecis Patria Siculis* in PG 161:917–18.

speaker rather than the author.[9] Laonikos would have wanted to eschew Constantine's Roman and Christian associations, which were central to Byzantine views of history. To counter them in his preface, Laonikos relies on the view of history in the *Donation of Constantine*: when the Romans crossed over to Thrace, "they entrusted Rome to their great pontiff," i.e., the pope. The *Donation* circulated in multiple Greek translations, though Laonikos could have consulted a Latin version—or none at all, for its basic theory was widely known. The text had already been exposed as a forgery by Makarios of Ankara in the east (ca. 1400) and by Lorenzo Valla in the west (1440).[10] By citing it, Laonikos makes the pope the arbiter of the succession among the Roman "emperors" (*basileis*) of the west and the standard for *Romanitas* more generally (though the *Donation* did not have to be read that way, even when taken at face value).[11] This does not mean, however, that Laonikos espoused a Catholic perspective. His move is strategic: it helps him to peel the Roman label from the Greeks: *Romanitas* was something the Romans left behind in Rome. Meanwhile, those Romans who made their capital at Byzantion mixed with the Greeks there and

> because many more Greeks ruled there than Romans, their language and customs ultimately prevailed but they changed their name and no longer called themselves by their hereditary one. They saw fit to call the kings of Byzantion by a title that dignified them, "emperors of the Romans," but never again "kings of the Greeks." [1.5]

9   See p. 19 above.

10   D. G. Angelov, "The Donation of Constantine and the Church in Late Byzantium," in *Church and Society in Late Byzantium* (Kalamazoo, 2009), 91–157.

11   For Laonikos's "Romans," see the next section.

We will see in the following chapter that this is tendentious and distorted as an interpretation of Byzantium. It deploys western prejudices to fashion a new Hellenic identity at the expense of the Roman identity of the Byzantines. Like the Neohellenism to which it gave rise, it emphasizes language to establish Greek continuity, while sweeping the Roman identity of the Byzantines under the carpet, as if it were a misunderstanding or misnomer. Neohellenists, starting with Laonikos and continuing today with nationalist historians, claim to know who the Byzantines had been all along better than they themselves had known: sure, they had *called* themselves Romans, but they *were really* Greeks on the inside. Laonikos perpetrated this distortion in order to construct a new Greek identity out of the ruins of the old Roman one, and many modern historians still do the same, either to maintain that identity or to prop up the western polemical claim on which it is based, that the Byzantines were not "really" Romans. That move was and is necessary in order to transfer the "imperial" Roman title and all its "rights" to the west. Byzantium was only a Greek kingdom all along.

By this move, Laonikos has invented a de-Romanized national kingdom of the Greeks whose capital was Byzantion. They differed from the Romans of the west in language and culture. We learn in the next section (1.6) that these Greeks and Romans also came to differ in religion and other matters. Laonikos does not name the religion in question, of course, nor can we press his language to conclude definitively that it was the Romans (Catholics) who deviated from the original common norm rather than the Greeks, though that is what he seems to be saying. Having deviated from the Greeks, the Romans then wanted to bring them into harmony with their religion, which the Greeks were unwilling to do. Eventually, the pope instigated what we call the Fourth Crusade and forced the Greeks to go over into Asia for a while. Laonikos speaks bluntly about these events and does not beat around the bush, as a Catholic, perhaps, might: the pope launched an attack against the Greeks because they would not accept his religion. Laonikos says the same later in the work (4.49). But he also makes the Greeks look bad when he jumps in the next section from the Fourth Crusade to the Council of Ferrara-Florence (1.7). Ioannes VIII wanted military aid against the Turks, so he took his bishops and learned men to Italy, where they hammered out an agreement with the Romans. However,

> when the Greeks got home they did not abide by what had been worked out in Italy and at the councils, holding that it would not be right at all for them to be fully united with the Romans, who did not make a proper affirmation of the faith. Thus the Greeks remained at odds with the Romans to the end. [1.7]

Laonikos repeats the same claim, when he concludes his account of the Council later in the work (6.16). Therefore, in his view when it comes to differences of religion—a religion to whose tenets Laonikos is indifferent—neither the Romans nor the Greeks act justly. His detached, candid perspective does not match what would have been said by partisans of either side. We can entertain the possibility that the student of Plethon was neutral here. His Hellenism was not defined by Orthodoxy. It was a national idea, and it had revolutionary implications.

Who are Laonikos's Romans?

Laonikos's contemporary Romans are an endlessly deferred signifier. His ancient Romans pose no difficulties, but his contemporary use of the label seems to point nowhere.[12]

---

12 See the third section of chap. 3.

According to the prehistory that introduces the *Histories*, ever since the Romans who settled in Constantinople effectively became Greeks, "the Romans and their great pontiff" in the west appoint kings for themselves among the French and Germans (1.6). Throughout the *Histories*, it is clear who the "great pontiff of the Romans" is—the pope. But of which Romans is he the archpriest? Here we can apply what I call the Daphnopates test. When, in the ninth century, Symeon of Bulgaria began to call himself emperor of the Romans, the Byzantine writer and diplomat fired back (to paraphrase): "Of which Romans exactly do you claim to be the emperor? Just because you rounded up some prisoners from among our people does not make you their emperor. If you capture some Arabs, that won't make you Caliph either."[13]

What do I mean that in Laonikos the "Romans" are a deferred signifier? At first sight, it seems as though his Romans are the Catholic world at large, the Church of Rome. The pope is their religious leader, and Union for the Greeks is with the "Romans" (1.7, 6.16, 8.17). In the fourteenth century, Kydones, a convert to Catholicism, had claimed that anyone who was worth anything in the west owed it to the Church of Rome.[14] Such an assertion points to a concept of a Roman Catholic west. In this same sense, Laonikos says that the Russians worship Jesus but "incline more to the Greeks and do not follow the pontiff of the Romans" (3.27); also that Monothelites "worship the religion of the God Jesus in other ways, that is, not according to the ways of the Romans or the Greeks" (3.40); "the Romans" believe that the capture of Constantinople was Asiatic payback for Troy (8.30); and Smyrna, when Timur attacked it, was held by "the Romans" (3.63; in fact, by a coalition of western powers, including the Knights of Rhodes, those Catholic warriors *par excellence*).

13   Theodoros Daphnopates, *ep.* 5 (pp. 58–59).
14   Demetrios Kydones, *Apologia for His Faith* 372.

Despite being themselves Romans, the Byzantines had long since referred to what we call Catholics as "Romans" in a religious sense or, more correctly, in a strictly ecclesiastical sense: this usage of "Roman" referred to the members of the Church of Rome.[15] The Byzantines also called Catholics "the Latins." Laonikos uses the term *Latins* twice, to characterize Orthodox reactions against the western Church (2.45, 6.16); it is not a term that he uses in his own voice. But what about his usage of the term "Roman"? How are we to understand the following ethnographic comparisons?

The Germans

As a political community they are organized in the same way as the Romans, whose customs and way of life they have adopted. They are also like the Romans in most other respects, and of all the people in the west they are the most pious followers of the religion of the Romans. [2.16]

The Hungarians

They are like the Germans in terms of weaponry and in way of life and customs, and favor a luxurious life as, they say, the French and the Germans do. They hold to the same religious practices as the Romans. [2.17]

The Wallachians

This people is like the Italians in its way of life and in other aspects. With respect to weapons and dress, they still, even now, use the same as the Romans do. [2.23]

---

15   Kaldellis, *Hellenism*, 339. See also the following chapter.

The Poles

> The Poles are next to the Russians and speak their language, but their customs and way of life are like those of the Romans. [3.30]

Only where the comparison is explicitly about religion does it make sense—and even then it is strange to say that Catholics are Romans in religion, if "Romans" *simply means* Catholics. In all other cases, it presupposes a Roman nation distinct from these others in the Catholic world that has its own political organization, customs, weapons, and material culture. But such a nation never appears in the *Histories*—or in history. To make matters worse, Laonikos does occasionally refer to a localized group of Romans, namely, those of the city of Rome, who have their own territory (5.64, 6.8), side with the Guelphs (6.18), and have their own noble families (6.27). But there is nothing distinctive about their culture in the way required by the above comparisons, and so they cannot hold up the other end. They are certainly not a people on a par with the Germans and the Poles; they are only one city in Italy (6.18).

It would resolve the logical problem—but create insuperable historical problems—to posit that Laonikos meant the *ancient* Romans here. But that does not seem likely. His "Romans" in these comparisons are quite an elusive standard, nicely reflecting, in fact, the elusiveness of the Romans in the western emperor's title *Imperator Romanorum*. Western theorists could never decide *of whom exactly* their emperor was the emperor, or who the Romans in his title were.[16] Daphnopates's question remained unanswered for them. The Byzantines never faced that problem: they were all

---

16   Folz, *Concept of Empire*; Arnold, *Medieval Germany*, 75–125.

Romans in a national sense, so their *basileus* was obviously "of the Romans." In the west, by contrast, that title was an ideal and principle of legitimacy masquerading as an ethnographic category, as in Laonikos. There were no real "Romans" to back it up, as the elusiveness of Laonikos's concept highlights.

There is a Byzantine text, however, that might help us to understand Laonikos's deployment of "Romans" in these ethnographic comparisons, though it does not resolve all the problems that this usage causes. The late sixth-century historian Agathias offered an ethnographic digression on the Franks, who, he says, were formally called Germans. He there presents the Franks as having a society almost identical to that of the Romans, by which he meant the Romans of the eastern empire ruled from Constantinople—i.e., his own people. What he says is remarkably similar to Laonikos's near-equation of Germans and Romans:

> The Franks are not nomads, as some barbarians are, but their system of government, administration and laws are modeled on the Roman pattern, apart from which they uphold similar standards with regard to contracts, marriage and religious observance. They are in fact all Christians and adhere to the strictest orthodoxy. They also have magistrates in their cities and priests and celebrate the feasts in the same way as we do; and, for a barbarian people, strike me as extremely well-bred and civilized and as practically the same as ourselves except for their uncouth style of dress and peculiar language [Agathias, *Histories* 1.2.3–4; trans. J. D. Frendo]

We should not read this passage through a positivist lens to correct its errors and try to ascertain where Agathias might have acquired such bizarre ideas. This passage is, instead, utilizing a trope of ethnographic discourse in which a foreign people is used as an ideal model for critiquing the author's own society. Agathias goes on, at great length, to explain how the Franks never fight civil wars and resolve their differences without bloodshed. For historians this is pure fiction, but the point of his comparison is not to give us the facts about Frankish society: it is, rather, to provide a vision of what Roman society could become, if it heeded Agathias's moral lessons. Agathias equates the Romans and the Franks precisely so that his Roman readers will notice the crucial differences.[17]

This is not exactly what Laonikos is doing, though he does say that the Germans are well governed (2.15), which he does not believe about the Greeks. It is possible that he found the equation of Germans and Romans in Agathias, but he has foiled the point of Agathias's comparison by relabeling the (Byzantine) Romans as Greeks, so he cannot anchor it on the eastern side.

In my chapter on Laonikos's digressions, I emphasized the relative quality of his ethnographies, how he will define one nation by comparing it to another. This chain of comparisons, at least for the west, often leads back to the Romans, but they appear to be a disembodied construct that is itself never defined. It is interesting to note in this connection that he also situates his abstract account of Islam and Muslim culture in an equally notional historical setting, a kingdom of Arabia that did not exist in the fifteenth century (3.13). His benchmarks for both the Catholic west and Islamic east are basically imaginary peoples and places. The leaders of these imaginary Romans are the emperor and the pope. Let us consider Laonikos's perception of them in turn.

Laonikos's "Roman emperors" appear especially in the context of warfare against the "barbarians," meaning mostly Muslims. In one place, he clarifies that this was their primary function: "the

17   Kaldellis, *Discours ethnographique*, chap. 3.

pontiff of the Romans had originally given this title to the kings of the French on account of the wars that they fought, frequently and with great courage, against the barbarians who crossed over from North Africa to Iberia" (2.18). But not in a single instance has Laonikos got this right from a historical point of view. Specifically, it is an exaggeration to say that the ancient Romans founded Constantinople to fight the Persians (1.5). Charlemagne had not been crowned at the time of his Spanish interventions (2.32), and no western Roman emperor subsequently campaigned against the Moors in Spain. Sigismund was not Roman emperor at the time of the Nikopolis campaign in 1396 (2.13; he would not obtain that title until 1433, almost forty years later). Friedrich III, whom Laonikos mistakenly calls Albert, never "set out to campaign against the Turks and Mehmed" (8.61). He made vague gestures in that direction, but was well known for his reluctance to act. However, many intellectuals at the time had called on him to do so, including Michael Apostoles, possibly another student of Plethon; Laonikos may be turning their exhortations into history.[18] None of the emperors after Charlemagne prevail over the Muslims in the *Histories*.

It is possible, moreover, that in one passage Laonikos did refer to the Germans as barbarians. In his Venetian digression, he refers vaguely to a war in which the Venetians helped to restore the pope when *basileus Barbarossa* had driven him into exile, referring probably to the Peace of Venice in 1177 that ended the conflict between Friedrich I Barbarossa and Alexander III (Laonikos would then be wrong that it was a naval engagement

18   Hankins, "Renaissance Crusaders," 120 (Poggio); Bisaha, *Creating East and West*, 37, 116 (Georgios of Trebizond), 60 (Bernardo Giustiniani); Meserve, *Empires of Islam*, 96–98; Apostoles: Geanakoplos, *Greek Scholars*, 96–97, either in the late 1450s or 1468: if the latter, it was probably too late for Laonikos to know about.

that settled the issue, for the battle of Legnano, 29 May 1176, was on land). However, the manuscripts do not have Βαρβαρόσσης βασιλέως, they have βαρβάρων βασιλέως (4.24). The emendation was made by T. L. F. Tafel (and then accepted by Darkó) on the assumption that Laonikos does not refer to western people as barbarians. I am inclined to think, however, that he probably did have "barbarians" (at any rate, not "Barbarossa") and the emendation is ideological and circular. Another of Plethon's students included all westerners among the "barbarians,"[19] while contemporary Italian historians could also look back and lump Barbarossa with the "barbarians," so I do not see why Laonikos could not have done so (or picked it up from them).[20]

The pope is the primary bearer of Roman identity in Laonikos. He confers imperial authority and is associated with the Roman name itself more than any other agent or institution in the *Histories*. But what was Laonikos's stance toward him? Almost all "Greeks" of his time were either pro- or anti-Union. Those who went to Italy or sought western patronage obviously were (or had to pretend to be) pro-Union, and Laonikos has usually been viewed against that background, in part because his career has been confused with that of his cousin Demetrios. But the *Histories* suggests a third alternative: Laonikos sided with neither party, probably because he was indifferent to Christianity. In this respect, he may have been a truer disciple of Plethon than anyone else.

We saw in the previous section that Laonikos presents the Fourth Crusade frankly as an act of papal aggression, but at the same time he makes the Greeks look bad for reneging on their

19   Hieronymos Charitonymos in PG 160:807c–d.

20   Cochrane, *Historians*, 118 (Bernardino Corio). An exact contemporary of Laonikos, Pius II had also pointedly contrasted the barbarian Germans to the Latin Italians: *Commentaries* 11 (43:735–36). In his polemics, Pius refers to his enemy Sigismondo Malatesta and the Venetians as barbarians.

consent to Union at Florence. He alludes to the religious differences between the two sides but never says what they are. In this respect he is unique among all authors of this period, who took formal positions. His seemingly long account of the Council in Book 6 is actually taken up with digressions on the various cities and powers in Italy and contains many sexual anecdotes.[21] What he says about the Council itself amounts to a brief and vacuous summary (6.13):

> Upon arrival there, the Greeks and the pontiff scrutinized their differences of religion for some time, trying to decide what would be best for them to declare, and finally they reached an agreement: both sides in harmony renounced their differences as both parties now held one and the same opinion and wanted no more innovations. They put this agreement in writing and called on the saints to witness that they were introducing no innovations regarding the faith.

How, then, does Laonikos represent the papacy itself? If he were writing against a western background (e.g., Venetian Crete, Venice) and with a western audience potentially in mind, we would expect him to be favorable, extremely so perhaps. But what we find instead is his usual neutrality, into which he mixes an unusual amount of sexual mockery directed against the papacy (see below). The Greeks may have reneged on the Council, but Laonikos also makes it clear that the pope was too involved in his Italian conflicts to send the aid on which Greek consent to Union was premised. Specifically,

> the Greeks immediately changed their minds and regretted having broken their agreement with the pontiff. But

he was not sending aid for the following reason. He was involved in a war that had broken out in Italy between him and the Tuscans over a territorial dispute, and he had to maintain an army, expenses, and a general. [6.25; cf. 1.8, 6.17]

Laonikos devotes an entire section to papal attempts at Crusade (8.62–64), which makes it clear that "they accomplished nothing worthwhile." And in the lead-up to the attack of the Venetians on the Ottomans in 1463, Laonikos recounts the response that Pope Pius II gave to their invitation to join them (10.43):

> But the pontiff responded by saying that it was first necessary to get rid of the "small barbarian" and only then go against the large one, meaning the ruler of Rimini [Sigismondo Malatesta], with whom he was then at war. He had fallen out with him in a way that it would be best to omit here. For such-and-such a reason he had brought charges against him and was at war. Thus the pontiff turned the Venetians down, having a civil war of his own to fight.

Yet this was the same pope who, we know, had previously complained "in a passionate and bitter letter after the Council of Mantua [1459] that the princes of Europe could not be brought to place the good of Christendom above that of their several principalities."[22] Did Laonikos intend the irony? That would require him to have known about Pius's letters and proclamations. At any rate, neither the emperors nor the priests of the Romans accomplish much against the Turks in the *Histories*. It was a way of saying

---

22   Hankins, "Renaissance Crusaders," 113. In his *Commentaries*, Pius rails against both the Venetians and Malatesta.

that Greeks who hoped for liberation after 1453 should look elsewhere for help (cf. 1.2).

Let us turn now to Laonikos's "digression" on the papacy itself, which is embedded in his general account of Italy. He begins with a pragmatic account of how a new pope is elected, and then cuts directly to this hilarious passage (6.27):

> They seat him upon a chair with a hole so that his testicles dangle down and can be touched by a man appointed to that duty, and in this way it becomes clear that he is a man. They believe that long ago a woman attained the high priesthood at Rome.[23] The uncertainty was due to the fact that almost all men in Italy and the western lands regularly shave their beards. She then became pregnant and when she went to perform the eucharist she gave birth to a child during the ceremony in full view of the congregation. It is for this reason, so that they may know for certain and have no doubts, that they do this touching, and the person doing the touching calls out, "Our lord is a man!"

No Catholic (or Unionist) would have devoted a substantial portion of his discussion of the papacy to this material: dangling testicles, beardless men, and pregnant women giving birth at the altar of St Peter's (the infamous *sedes stercoraria* has a claim on reality; Pope Joan less so, but this, at any rate, is her first appearance in Greek).[24] Here, in the most striking passage of its kind in the *Histories*, we have a comic and sexual freak-show. On one level, it reduces the workings and history of the popes to the oddest of Herodotos's observations, for example, that Egyptian women

23   A reference to the legendary Pope Joan.
24   A. Boureau, *The Myth of Pope Joan*, trans. L. G. Cochrane (Chicago, 2001), 21.

pee standing up while men squat. Moreover, it engages with the asymmetrical dynamic of the long-standing polemic between the Byzantines and Latins. Charis Messis has astutely observed that the Latins ascribed feminine vices to the Greeks (basically the same qualities that we consider "civilized" today), whereas the Byzantines attributed to the Latins hyper-masculine vices (blood-thirsty aggression, the will to dominate, etc.). From the rhetorical point of view, this contest favored the Latins: the "man" always wins. There was one respect, however, in which the Byzantines prevailed in the arena of masculinity, namely, they wore beards, whereas Latins tended to shave. This discrepancy actually troubled some westerners, who grew out their beards in response: according to the dominant logic, it was the Byzantines, a culture of eunuchs, that should lack this badge of masculinity.[25]

Laonikos's depiction of the papacy, that quintessential "Latin" institution, reveals a sharp understanding of this dynamic. With amazing precision, it targets the weak points of the pope's sexual persona, evoking precisely those castrating and feminizing polemics that the Latin world had for so long directed against Byzantium. Laonikos knew all the sore spots and struck with precision. This was payback. Laonikos was no Catholic.[26]

Hellenocentrism vs. Hellenocriticism

In his copy of Herodotos, given to him by Plethon, Laonikos commented at the end of the text on the amazing virtue that the Greeks

25   C. Messis, "Lectures sexuées de l'altérité: Les Latins et identité romaine menacée pendant les derniers siècles de Byzance," *JÖB* 61 (2011): 151–70.

26   I am not sure what to make of this, but Laonikos uses the same language to characterize the relationship between the pope and his cardinals as he uses for the sultan and the men of his Porte and janissaries: cf. 6.13 with 5.11–13. Are we to infer a parallel or is this just his usual minimalism?

had displayed in the wars recounted. But when he wrote the preface of his own *Histories*, he looked back at the long course of Greek history and noted that the Greeks had benefited more from fortune than their virtue. He was not referring specifically to events in Herodotos, but still it was a strikingly different reaction.[27] Of course, between the 1440s when he first read Herodotos and the 1460s, when he stopped working on his own *Histories*, everything had changed. The Greeks no longer had any state: Laonikos had seen the fall of Constantinople, the Peloponnese, and Trebizond.

Upon closer inspection, however, the two reactions are not so different and can be seen to reflect the same outlook. What the Greeks manage to do in Herodotos against the Persians is precisely what they fail to do in Laonikos against the Turks. Disgusted by the performance of his people, Laonikos could not but feel amazement at that single, glorious past success against the barbarian. There was nothing like it in Thucydides or any other historian. In fact, Laonikos's amazement at the virtue of Herodotos's Greeks does reflect a critical view of his own contemporary Greeks: he was amazed *precisely* because this was not what anyone who knew recent history would have expected of Greeks. This, I believe, reinforces the argument made above that Laonikos wrote this subscription while working on his own *Histories*, in a critical spirit formed by the disasters of the 1450s.

The critical tone of the preface of the *Histories* is reflected in the narrative. Laonikos is extremely critical of Greek leadership, more so than of anyone else. He is generally dispassionate when it comes to the failures and follies of other people, but Greek failures get him worked up. Still, he is no enemy of the Greek people; he is not writing a polemical history to, say, justify their conquest by the Turks. He is writing as a Greek frustrated by his own people's lack

---

27   For Laonikos's subscription to Laur. 70.6, see the fourth section of chap. 1.

of leadership. In the final books, he is also critical of the atrocities of the Turks and Mehmed, in particular. The difference is between disappointment (at the Greeks) and outrage (at the Turks). It is precisely in his Hellenocriticism that Laonikos, who might otherwise come across as anational, reveals his Hellenocentrism.

It is also reflected in the following comment in the preface (1.2):

> Let no one disparage us for recounting these matters in the Greek language, for the language of the Greeks has spread to many places throughout the world and has mixed with many other languages. It is already exceedingly prestigious and will be even more so in the future, when a king who is Greek himself, along with the kings that follow after him, will rule over a substantial kingdom. There the sons of the Greeks may finally be gathered together and govern themselves according to their own customs, in a manner that is most favorable for themselves and from a position of strength with regard to other peoples.

Laonikos is not looking forward to a revived "Byzantine" (i.e., Roman) empire or a western colonial protectorate to be established after a Crusade (the wish of many in the west), but to a national Greek state. Only one person had called for such a thing before, his teacher Plethon. But Plethon was hoping to make reforms within the Byzantine despotate of the Peloponnese, to change it in the direction of a national Greek state modeled on Platonic, utopian principles.[28] But after the 1450s, there was nothing to reform, so the project was deferred. Laonikos had to convert Plethon's exhortations into a national teleology and rebirth. He was not alone in this endeavor among Plethon's students and

---

28   See the next chapter.

associates. Bessarion wrote to Michael Apostoles asking him to find and gather manuscripts "for the sake of the Greeks who are left now as well as those who may have a better fortune in the future (for many things may happen in the course of the years)."[29]

In the meantime, as a historian Laonikos could only look back, and what he saw when he beheld the Greeks of his time was dispiriting. He criticizes them, and especially their leadership, at many points. Civil wars harmed their common interest (1.17). The early Palaiologoi failed to make good use of Turkish defectors (1.18, 1.21). The tone is set early in Book 1:

> They squandered the revenues of their realm by using them solely to gratify their own nobility, and neither enlisted an army nor hired foreign mercenaries. They showed no will to avenge themselves on the enemies who were attacking them. [1.21]

Laonikos badly misdates Serbian expansion under Dušan to the reign of Andronikos II, but does not hold back in his (fair) criticism of that emperor and his subjects:

> At this time the affairs of the Greeks seemed to have reached a state of ultimate peril, as they were undermining themselves by the indolence of their royalty. I am referring to the licentious and dissolute way of life to which the elder king Andronikos [II] had turned.[30] So the Greek people made a decision not to go out and attempt battle, but instead

---

29   Quoted by Geanakoplos, *Greek Scholars*, 81–82.

30   Laonikos means Andronikos II Palaiologos (1282–1328), although Stefan Dušan did not come to the throne until 1331, and his attacks on Byzantium followed in the 1340s.

decided that the surest way to keep safe, whatever this might mean, was behind their walls. [1.30]

Laonikos is also wrong about the marital histories of Ioannes V and his son Manuel II—he thinks that the former stole the latter's first bride[31]—but his verdict on Ioannes, one of the most ineffective Byzantine emperors, strikes the same chords (2.26):

> It is said that he lusted after women and perpetrated many indecent acts. He was attracted to singers and spent time with them, setting aside the work of the kingdom and paying little attention to it while enjoying such things.

Manuel II does not come in for criticism, although at the end of his reign his son Ioannes VIII had taken over and pushed for the disastrous policy of supporting the Ottoman claimant Mustafa (5.1):

> In this matter, out of sheer folly, the Greeks moved closer to utterly destroying their affairs and themselves, and they came very close to seeing their city enslaved by Murad.

Turning to the final years covered in the *Histories*, students of the Palaiologan Empire can find no more worthless characters than Thomas and Demetrios Palaiologoi, the despots of the Peloponnese. Laonikos exposes how their incompetence, sneakiness, and rivalry brought about the ruin and loss of the last Byzantine territories, including Mistra, where Laonikos himself was raised (8.37, 8.42–43, 9.1). So bad was their administration that Ottoman armies began to intervene not to conquer them but to prop them up, until it proved easier to simply annex their lands.

---

31   Barker, *Manuel II*, 475.

Laonikos even includes two speeches (set in 1454) by Turahan Beg with advice to them on how to govern (8.39, 8.41).

All this is without parallel in the *Histories*. No other people conquered by the Ottomans (and there are many) come in for such patronizing criticism. But only someone who identified with the Greeks would be critical of them in this way. Along with the teleological Hellenism of the preface, this enables us to situate Laonikos more solidly within the fluid and hybrid identity-formations that were being tossed up in the rapidly changing circumstances of the fifteenth century. Laonikos himself had a complex cultural background. Nevertheless, the Greeks seem to have been his primary point of reference, for all that he structured his narrative around the Turks and devoted most of his digressions to the west. Of course, following Plethon, he had his own distinctive view of who the Greeks were.

Laonikos does not imbue the fall of Constantinople (or of Trebizond) with great pathos. Some noble deaths are briefly mentioned (8.18, 8.21–22), as is the family tragedy of Notaras (8.28–29). Otherwise the treatment is Thucydidean. The fall of the Peloponnese, by contrast, elicits passionate complains about Turkish cruelty and rapaciousness (9.53).[32] Here Laonikos reveals his attachment to the Peloponnese (while his other home, Athens, had made a smoother transition to Ottoman rule). In two instances, he has sultans campaigning in the Peloponnese execute three hundred captives (7.26: Murad II, followed by another six hundred sacrificed; 9.44: Mehmed II). The number, of course, has symbolic importance in the context of a Neo-Persian invasion of Greece, and may have been introduced or invented by Laonikos to highlight the difference between Leonidas's men and the Greeks of waning Byzantium. Interestingly, Laonikos also has Giustiniani

---

32   See the fourth and sixth sections of chap. 4.

bring three hundred men with him to defend Constantinople in 1453 (8.17). The sources give conflicting figures for the size of his force; this one may have again suited Laonikos because of its symbolic associations.[33]

Laonikos's pervasive criticism of the Greeks does not set him outside the Greek national community that he, Plethon, and others were trying to bring into existence out of the ruins of the Roman Orthodox community of Byzantium. He was hardly the first historian in the Byzantine tradition whose narrative offered a damning condemnation of the failures of imperial policies. In their own ways, Psellos (1060s), Attaleiates (1070s), Choniates (1200s), and Pachymeres (1300s) had done just that. The Byzantines had a tradition of writing intelligently about their own imperial failures, and Laonikos fits right in, though I can find no sign that he knew their works.

An interesting bridge between those historians, who had recounted the imperial collapses of the eleventh and twelfth centuries, and the failures of the Palaiologan era, is provided by Bessarion, also a student of Plethon, albeit from two generations before Laonikos. In ca. 1436 he wrote an encomium of his native city of Trebizond that praises its ancient and recent history. When he reaches the eleventh century, in explaining how his city eventually became independent under its Komnenoi rulers, he accuses the rulers in Byzantium of being "deeply asleep" and "living indolent lives while the enemy fought vigorously against

33   Kritoboulos, *History* 1.25.1, 1.25.4 says 400. Marios Philippides informs me (pers. comm.) that the figures in the sources are incomplete and unreliable, and that historians have to estimate the size of the foreign forces. He, too, independently, suspects Laonikos's figure as being Herodotean. The sixth-century historian Agathias, *Histories* 5.19.1–2, also used it in a similarly pointed way: W. Treadgold, *The Early Byzantine Historians* (New York, 2007), 288–89.

them."[34] They squandered public funds on personal indulgences and neglected the armies, living in "luxury and indolence."[35] Bessarion was discussing the eleventh century and may have drawn on Psellos or Attaleiates, but his words might be read as an indirect indictment of how the Palaiologoi were again rapidly losing territory to another vigorous enemy from the east (a development that Bessarion hints at toward the end).[36] In another work addressed in ca. 1444 to Konstantinos Palaiologos (when he was despot of the Peloponnese), Bessarion notes that the Turks are prevailing over the Greeks and have grown to great power "because of our negligence and indolence."[37] He had used the same language in his encomium of Trebizond to explain the eleventh century.

Though the explanatory schema was fairly conventional and moralistic, this was also how Laonikos viewed Palaiologan failures, as we saw. Bessarion's texts were certainly available at Mistra and similar indictments must have been circulating in Plethon's circle. What is most distinctive about Laonikos's scheme is that he scrupulously avoids any intimation that decline was the result of God's anger at sin, the mode of explanation preferred in Orthodox circles.[38] Plethon also avoided supernatural explanations and famously wrote policy memos to the emperors and

34 Bessarion, *Encomium for Trebizond* 57. For *ekphraseis* of late Byzantine cities, see Saradi, "The Monuments."

35 Bessarion, *Encomium for Trebizond* 57–58.

36 Ibid. 69.

37 Idem, *Address to the Despot Konstantinos* 33; see S. P. Lambros, "Ὑπόμνημα τοῦ καρδιναλίου Βησσαρίωνος εἰς Κωνσταντῖνον τὸν Παλαιολόγον," *Νέος Ἑλλ.* 3 (1906): 12–50; and Necipoğlu, *Byzantium*, 273–74. For late Byzantine views of decline, see Ševčenko, "Decline of Byzantium"; S. Vryonis, *The Decline of Medieval Hellenism in Asia Minor* (Berkeley, 1971), 408–21.

38 For Orthodox views of decline, see the sources in S. Vryonis, "Crises and Anxieties in Fifteenth-Century Byzantium: And the Reassertion of Old, and the

despots on how the situation might be salvaged (these influenced Bessarion' address to Konstantinos). More than any philosopher in Byzantium, Plethon made concrete proposals for the reform of the state in order to achieve what he insistently and repeatedly called *epanorthosis*, or "restoration" (which included reining in monastic properties).[39] By Laonikos's time these proposals were obsolete, for there was no state left to restore. But the project of Hellenic revitalization lived on. Laonikos's task was to chronicle the collapse that most thinking people had long been expecting.

The 1460s called out for a critical approach to recent history. Kritoboulos asks the readers of his *History* of Mehmed not to reproach him for exposing the failures of his own people. It was not his *intention* to do so, he explains, thereby intimating that it was, in fact, a prominent part of his project. He reminds us of the element of chance in history, which cannot be controlled by human beings, but concludes that, if it turns out that the rulers did not use their power properly, such failures should be ascribed to them alone and not the entire Roman *genos*. Kritoboulos was in a position to read and use Laonikos. Many of his criticisms, especially of the despots of the Peloponnese, are similar to those in Laonikos, but this need not indicate his dependence on him; the facts in this case were pretty clear.[40] Where Kritoboulos and Laonikos differed was primarily in their conception of what their own *genos* was exactly, and we will turn to this question in the next chapter to better appreciate the revolutionary intention behind the *Histories*. It is, in its way, the first history of the "modern Hellenes."

Emergence of New, Cultural Forms," in *Islamic and Middle Eastern Societies: A Festschrift in Honor of Professor Wadie Jwaideh*, ed. R. Olson (Brattleboro, 1987), 100–125.

39 Siniossoglou, *Radical Platonism*, chap. 7; Necipoğlu, *Byzantium*, 274–76.

40 Kritoboulos, *History* 1.3.1–7. For Kritoboulos and Laonikos, see Kaldellis, "Date."

The Intended Audience of the *Histories*

We have surveyed Laonikos's conceptions of the "Romans" and the "Greeks," who are both central players in the *Histories* yet difficult to identify, the former because they never really existed, while the latter were, in this very text, being imagined into existence from within the remnants of Byzantine Romanía. To which group did Laonikos address his *Histories*? The question has never been systematically discussed, but it is important, for an author may be presenting events in a particular way, depending on his imagined readers. There are only three contenders: western Europeans (primarily Italians), Greeks, and Turks. Of course, Laonikos may have hoped to find readers among all three, and the linguistic demands of his text would, in any case, have limited his readers to the most educated classes. Any Italians, Greeks, and Turks capable of reading the *Histories* and grasping its Herodotean-Thucydidean matrix would, in terms of their literary and intellectual habits, have had more in common with one another than with less educated members of their own people. Can we be more precise?

I exclude Turks at the outset. Though they are the protagonists of the work, there is no sign in it that it was addressed to them. The hope for a free and powerful Greek people expressed in the preface would not sit well with anyone associated with the Ottoman regime, which would include any Turks and recent Byzantine converts who might actually have been able to read the work. I doubt that there was a significant demographic within Turkish society that could even potentially have formed an audience for this work. Mehmed's vaunted Philhellenism and facility with languages has been exaggerated[41] and would not, in any case, extend

---

41   C. G. Patrinelis, "Mehmed II the Conqueror and his Presumed Knowledge of Greek and Latin," *Viator* 2 (1971): 349–54; cf. Raby, "Mehmed the Conqueror's Greek Scriptorium," 16, 22.

to tolerating such remarks. Laonikos was also, as we saw, highly critical of Mehmed. The notion that he would have written this work to "curry favor" with him can be ruled out.[42]

There is a latent and sometimes implicit tendency to associate Laonikos with the emerging humanism of the Italian Renaissance.[43] Byzantium had just been conquered and the Greeks were about to enter a long dark age. Laonikos's *Histories*, with its imitation of classical historians, neo-Attic prose, ethnography, secular outlook on events, and acceptance of the west's view of who was Roman and who Greek fits well with the intellectual culture of Italy at this time. His teacher Plethon had made an impression on Italian intellectuals at the Council; Laonikos was acquainted with Kyriacus of Ancona; and a number of Plethon's students, most prominently Bessarion, made careers in Italy. The example set by his cousin Demetrios has tended to color the background against which scholars view Laonikos himself; sometimes the two have been confused.[44] The *Histories* was even translated into Latin and French in the sixteenth century.[45] But can we substantiate this vague impression that Laonikos had western readers in mind?

There are only two signs in the text that this may have been the case. The first is that Laonikos feels that he has to justify writing the work in Greek (1.2), which suggests that he is addressing non-Greeks. What he says there may also allude to the presence of Greeks in Italy, possibly also to himself: "the language of the

42   Geanakoplos, *Interaction*, 217, a confusion with Kritoboulos?

43   M. Philippides, "Early Post-Byzantine Historiography," in *The Classics in the Middle Ages*, ed. A. S. Bernardo and S. Levin (Binghamton, 1990), 258, and Moustakas, "Byzantine 'Visions' of the Ottoman Empire," 226, assume that the audience was western.

44   E.g., Bianconi, *Tessalonica*, 138–41, attributed Laonikos's copy of Herodotos to Demetrios.

45   See the Epilogue.

Greeks has spread to many places throughout the world." The second sign is that on two occasions he assumes that the reader knows the names of the days of the week in a Romance language. At 8.18, recounting the final Ottoman assault on Constantinople, he says that it took place on "the day of Ares," i.e., *martedì* (Tuesday); and at 3.15, he says that Muslims pray "on the day of Aphrodite," i.e., *venerdì* (Friday). These mythological references make sense only in the Romance languages. Laonikos does not specify the linguistic framework he is using or supply the equivalent Greek day-names, which may suggest that he took them for granted. We know from Kyriacus that Laonikos was fluent in Latin, and he uses Latin versions for the names of some western cities.[46]

Despite these signs, however, which I will interpret differently below, I believe that Laonikos's intended audience was primarily Greek, and probably almost exclusively so. There are two reasons that lead me to this conclusion. First, if we shift the composition of the work from the 1480s to the 1460s, as we must, the number of Italians capable of reading his prose was vanishingly small. Some of the best Italian scholars (e.g., Valla) had trouble reading Herodotos and Thucydides.[47] Second, the total absence of any ethnographic information about the "Greeks" is striking. They are a major agent in the narrative, but are never "explained" the way all other people are. By contrast, the major powers of Italy are all explained in a way that fills a curious vacuum in Byzantine literature, but that would have been pointless if his intended audience was Italian. It is precisely from what he takes most for granted (i.e., the Greeks) that we can best infer the audience that he imagined.

---

46 Genoa (Ianua) and Strasbourg (Argentina); see H. Ditten, "Die Namen für Venedig und Genua bei den letzten byzantinischen Geschichtsschreiber (15. Jahrhundert)," *Helikon* 6 (1966): 68 n. 117; idem, "Deutschland-Exkurs," 54–55.

47 E. B. Fryde, *Humanism and Renaissance Historiography* (London, 1983), chap. 4.

The offensive way in which he presents the papacy also points away from a western audience. Third, I have proposed that Laonikos was probably in the Ottoman Empire when he researched and wrote the *Histories*, whose earliest surviving manuscript was copied in Constantinople by "Greek" intellectuals only a few years after he stopped writing.

We cannot flesh out here the intellectual contours of the Greek community of post-conquest Constantinople and, besides, too much essential research must be done before we can postulate connections or reconstruct the careers of key individuals. The copyist of the earliest manuscript of the *Histories*, Demetrios Angelos, was a student of medicine, history, and philosophy; he was connected to the philosopher Amiroutzes; and both knew the historian Kritoboulos and the learned patriarch Gennadios. They were also linked across religious divides to Catholic Byzantines in Crete (e.g., Apostoles) and Italy (e.g., Argyropoulos and Bessarion). The two decades after 1453 witnessed a vigorous intellectual scene among the Greek-speaking communities, but we still do not know the extent of the potential audience for the *Histories*; who, after all, could actually read its difficult prose? I do not think at this stage that questions of censorship need to trouble us. Gennadios and Amiroutzes had opposed Plethon in the past, but we should not assume that, like inquisitors, they would have hunted down anyone intellectually affiliated with him. As we have seen, Laonikos was subtle, discreet, and allusive on issues that might have caused offense, including the World Soul, Greek-Roman religious tensions, and papal sexuality; even the crimes of Mehmet II appear only in the last two books of the *Histories*. In addition, Gennadios was only intermittently on the patriarchal throne in the 1450s and 60s, and even when he destroyed Plethon's *Laws* he moved with extreme caution and circumspection. In sum, there was nothing about the intellectual environment of post-conquest Constantinople that need have given Laonikos cause for worry.

If he was writing for Greeks, how can we explain his need to defend using Greek and his allusions to the western names for the days of the week?

The planetary names of the days were an ancient Roman, not Greek, system, and were well established during the early Roman Empire. From that time they became established in the Romance languages, whereas in Greek they were eventually replaced by the numerical system of the Church that is still in use (Monday is the "second" day after the "Lord's Day," Tuesday the "third," etc.; the same was done in medieval Portugal, apparently independently of the Byzantine example).[48] It was, however, possible for any scholar to find out from Greek sources about the ancient names, whether from astronomers, historians of Rome, or Ioannes Lydos (in his own model pagan calendar, however, Laonikos's teacher Plethon eschewed the Roman system). Laonikos's use of that system has rightly, in my view, been labeled an act of antiquarianism on his part.[49] It should not necessarily be taken to indicate a western outlook, though his knowledge of Latin and possibly Italian may have contributed to this antiquarianism. The fifteenth century was generally a time of great interest in the ancient Greek and Roman calendars. Kyriacus himself had dedicated to Konstantinos Palaiologos a brief exposition on the Roman months at the time of his visit to Mistra when he met the young Nikolaos (it does not, however, discuss the names of the days).[50]

---

48 R. Fletcher, *The Barbarian Conversion to Christianity* (Berkeley, 1997), 257.

49 Anastos, "Pletho's Calendar," 221–22 (cites the ancient sources as well).

50 Kyriacus, *On the Order of the Months of the Year*; see P. Botley, "Renaissance Scholarship and the Athenian Calendar," *GRBS* 46 (2006): 395–431.

Moreover, Laonikos deploys planetary names on only two occasions, and in both of them he is probably scoring a point, making their appearance labored rather than "natural." Specifically, he could not avoid pointing out that the City fell on "the day of Ares." As for Friday prayers being on "the day of Aphrodite," I considered above the possibility that Laonikos deliberately used the Roman system here to channel a Byzantine charge against Muslims, namely, that they really venerate Aphrodite.[51] But it is more likely that he had no better way of referring to "Friday," seeing as he had to avoid the Byzantine Christian name (*Paraskeuê*), just as he avoids all Christian vocabulary. His use of the Latin-Romance names was a function of his antiquarianism, which stemmed from the choice to avoid a Christian framework. There was no other system available.

There is one passage where Laonikos does cite what he labels a western view, namely the idea that the fall of Constantinople was Asiatic payback for the fall of Troy: "At any rate, that is how the Romans believe it happened" (8.30). In other words, that interpretation does not come naturally to him nor does he necessarily identify with it or its proponents (even though it is attributed to him by many modern scholars searching for his elusive view of that event).

We come finally to the most interesting point, his *apologia* for the Greek language in the preface. Laonikos's argument has to be understood against a broader context. The early fifteenth century witnessed dramatic upheavals in the relative standing of cultures and languages. Areas of the Byzantine world had long been colonized by Latin powers, but Laonikos was writing in a world in which the Greeks had no state of their own and were everywhere subject to foreign powers that were not likely to become Hellenized, as

51   See p. 119 above.

others had in the past (e.g., the ancient Romans whom Laonikos mentions in the introduction). The Ottoman Turks themselves had only just begun to find their own identity vis-à-vis the Arabic and Persian cultural forms that had dominated Muslim societies until then. In Italy, the vernacular and Latin were trying to define their respective roles, and the study of Greek was a new and controversial element in the mix. All these transformations produced insecurities about language that explain *apologiae* that were made on all sides, not just by Laonikos.

For example, the poet Ashik Pasha felt the need to defend his use of Turkish, which has to be read against his early fourteenth-century Anatolian context,[52] and no Ottoman histories were written in Turkish before the fifteenth century. Kritoboulos, Laonikos's contemporary and a historian of Mehmed, also prefaced his work with a justification for writing in Greek. This way, he argued, the sultan's deeds can become known to the Greeks and to posterity in the same language that commemorated the deeds of the great men of the past. Greek, he adds, is more prestigious than Arabic or Persian, which have limited audiences. Moreover, being written in Greek, Kritoboulos's work will be translated into the western languages, and so the sultan's fame will spread as far as Britain (albeit, as it happened, not until the twentieth century).[53] Thus a defense of Greek does not necessarily imply a western audience. A Turkish audience, or Ottoman context generally, can explain it, even if the work was being addressed to Greeks, as I believe it was. Laonikos's remarks can be seen as bolstering Greek pride in hard times by highlighting cultural assets that the Greeks can build on in the future when they establish independence. Laonikos links his *apologia* directly to his hopes for Greek

52   Kafadar, *Between Two Worlds*, 93; Zachariadou, Ἰστορία καὶ θρύλοι, 32.

53   Kritoboulos, *History* pref. 1–4.

freedom. Greek "is already exceedingly prestigious and will be even more so in the future, when a king who is Greek himself, along with the kings that follow after him, will rule over a substantial kingdom. There the sons of the Greeks may finally be gathered together and govern themselves according to their own customs" (1.2). It would seem, then, that this *apologia* was an internal Greek matter. It was hardly an argument to address to Turkish ears. And it may have indirectly been meant to address western hyperbole about the end of Greek letters after the fall of Constantinople—"I believe Greek letters are finished," "the name of Greece is blotted out," etc.[54]

In a fascinating coincidence, at the very same time that Laonikos stopped working on the *Histories*, his cousin Demetrios was addressing a justification for the study of Greek to his Italian audience that included his employers at Padua-Venice. He emphasized the importance of Greek study, though he was speaking in Latin, of course.[55] It is, as I said above, curious that the two Athenian cousins would both be defending the prestige of the Greek language at around the same time, but we should not read Laonikos against Demetrios just because the latter has enjoyed a more prestigious reception in histories of humanism. Nor should we read either against Kritoboulos. These men were engaged in different projects and contexts. Laonikos was hinting at a project of national Greek renewal whereas Demetrios was making an argument that was fundamentally western-oriented: How can Greek help *you*, the Latin? How is it relevant to *your* needs? We see here already the bifurcation of modern Hellenism into a national project on the

---

54   Hankins, "Renaissance Crusaders," 122; Raby, "Mehmed the Conqueror's Greek Scriptorium," 15; Meserve, *Empires of Islam*, 66–68.

55   Geanakoplos, "The Discourse of Demetrius Chalcondyles," 130–34; idem, *Interaction*, 241–64; in general, see Harris, *Greek Emigres*.

one hand (for Greeks) and a transnational ideal on the other (for the west). In today's terms, Demetrios is a Greek professor of classics abroad explaining the "relevance" of his field to a college Dean to justify funding, whereas Laonikos is addressing Greeks and identifying the grounds on which they might hope for a rebirth after the current "crisis" that was brought upon them by foreign interests and their own incompetent and corrupt leadership. This opens up vistas for further contemplation.

CHAPTER 6

Plethon, Laonikos, and the Birth of Neohellenism

Georgios Gemistos (Plethon), his student Nikolaos (Laonikos) Chalkokondyles, and his enemy Georgios Scholarios (Gennadios) are viewed by historians as belonging either to the dying world of Byzantium or to the origins of modern Neohellenism. In the title of one article written from the perspective of a classicist, Laonikos is alarmingly cast as "the last Athenian historian"—after Dexippos in the third century AD.[1] Modern nationalist historiography, on the other hand, often traces the origin of Neohellenism to 1204 (with dissenting critical voices placing it in the Enlightenment), casting Plethon as its first great theorist and Laonikos as its first historian.[2] Beginnings and ends meet here, but key theoretical terms are used loosely. In the modern debate—a hunt for national origins—we face a tangle of *emic* and *etic* claims of identity, culture, ethnicity, and language, which are evaluated in a framework that has privileged classical and modern constructions of Hellenism, while downplaying Byzantine points of view. How the latter fit into

---

1 W. Miller, "The Last Athenian Historian," *JHS* 42 (1922): 36–49. I am an Athenian too, and a historian.

2 For theories regarding the origin of modern Hellenism, see below.

these long-term narratives is poorly understood, in part because Byzantium is poorly understood, being itself a field colonized by polemical western and nationalist modern Greek claims. In brief, the Byzantines considered themselves to be Romans, not Greeks, but the Latin west, starting in ca. 800, has usually considered them to be Greeks, as its own institutions have laid exclusive claim to the prestige, legacy, and power of Rome. That medieval outlook—that the Byzantines were not really Romans but something else, either Greeks or "Orthodox Christians"—abides and remains normative within the modern discipline of Byzantine Studies, which has rarely validated the study of Byzantine Romanity. That western outlook has also conveniently served the needs of modern Greek scholars, who eagerly look to find Greeks beneath the Byzantine Roman label. The Neohellenism of Plethon and Laonikos has proven especially useful and quotable in validating this nationalist position, but its revolutionary nature in its own context cannot be appreciated when it is simply taken for granted as a historiographical paradigm for modern research on Byzantium.

These are weighty issues, but clarity can be attained. What needs to be stressed is the persistent role played by western interests from start to finish—that is, from when Byzantium began to be perceived as "Greek" in the west around 800 AD to when the west finally authorized the creation of a Greek state in the nineteenth century. It was the rhetorical violence of Latin propaganda that first painted the Byzantines as Greeks and then the physical violence of their colonial regimes that forced Byzantines into that subject position, from which they were "rescued" by the Ottoman conquest. When the revolutionaries in the nineteenth century sought western help against their oppressors, they had again to play the "Greek" in order to obtain it. In the final centuries of Byzantium, which concern us here, the experience of western

colonization left marks on how the Byzantines imagined themselves between Greek and Roman axes of identity. These played
out differently in the spheres of philosophy, language, religion,
and national rhetoric. Plethon and Laonikos took a decisive new
step in this story: they were the first thinkers to emerge within
the Byzantine world who embraced a Greek identity without also
embracing Catholicism; in other words, their Hellenism was not
a function of a western outlook, as was the case with all other late
Palaiologan "Hellenes." They were the first to develop a theory for
how to identify "Greeks" within the otherwise Roman tradition
of Byzantium. Thus they were the first to imagine a "new" Greek
nation. This concept owed nothing to Orthodoxy.

Master and Student: Plethon and Laonikos

The people we call Byzantines were actually Greek-speaking,
Orthodox *Romans*. They did not believe themselves to be Greeks:
they were Christian Romans surrounded by "barbarians," some
of whom were Christians and some not. In the long course of
Byzantine history, there were only two men who argued from
within that this community was, in fact, Greek rather than Roman.
These two men were Plethon and Laonikos, the latter making his
case after the end of Byzantium's existence.

Plethon's famous "let's stop kidding ourselves" moment
occurs in his address to Manuel II Palaiologos regarding the
affairs of the Peloponnese (from the mid- to late 1410s): "We over
whom you rule and reign are Greeks by race [*genos*], as both our
language and ancestral culture [*patrios paideia*] bear witness.
Now, for the Greeks it would not be possible to find any other
land that is more fitting or suited than the Peloponnese and the
regions of Europe by it and the nearby islands. For it seems that

Greeks, the same ones, have inhabited it for as long as human records indicate."[3]

This declaration was revolutionary in scope and context, primarily because for the first time it was not coming from a Latin or a Byzantine convert to Roman Catholicism. Some scholars have maintained that Plethon was not, in fact, rejecting or sidelining the Roman dimension of Byzantine culture,[4] but I believe that was exactly what he was doing and, as we saw, he bequeathed this attitude to Laonikos. The passages in other works where Plethon refers to "the emperors of the Romans" and "the Roman empire" are formulaic, in panegyrical contexts where they could not be avoided. Rather, Plethon "saw in the crisis of Byzantium the realization of a historically necessary transition to a new type of human being inscribed within a proto-nationalistic framework defined by an emerging notion of philosophical Hellenism."[5]

In his declaration of Hellenic identity to Manuel, Plethon's primary goal was not to explain his terms with philosophical clarity, but to give advice on how affairs could be improved. We can quibble about how far his *genos* connotes our "ethnicity" or, in a stronger sense, "race," but it is not much different. He meant a single people inhabiting the same place for thousands of years without much admixture of foreign blood. He was not saying something conventional. Plethon would not go to the trouble to

---

3   Plethon, *Address to Manuel II* 247–48. In his grammatical treatise, Plethon mentions the word "Hellenic" six times in the first paragraph, revealing a strong attachment to the ethnonym, even in a technical grammatical context: M. Scialuga, "Un'inedita grammatica greca alle soglie dell'età moderna: il περὶ παιδείας di Giorgio Gemisto Pletone," *Atti della Accademia delle Scienze di Torino. Classe di scienze morali, storiche e filologiche* 129 (1995): 12.

4   Among others, L. Mavrommatis, "Ῥωμαϊκὴ ταυτότητα, Ἑλληνικὴ ταυτότητα (ΙΓ–ΙΔ αἰ.)," *Σύμμεικτα* 7 (1987): 191.

5   Siniossoglou, *Radical Platonism*, 323.

explain to a king who his subjects "really" were, if he intended to say something banal. His efforts to back up his assertion with evidence, arguments, and "witness" also indicate that he is up to something. To be sure, this was not a claim with which Manuel and his court would have been wholly unfamiliar. As we will see, the Byzantines had by then grown used to being called Greeks in many (conditional) contexts. But it had never before been asserted with such blunt finality by one of their own, taking precedence over—in fact, entirely sidelining—their Roman identity. More importantly, we must not be taken in by Plethon and think that he was saying something natural that made sense at the time, just because a millennium of western prejudice and just over a century of modern Greek nationalist historiography have conditioned us to reject the Roman identity of the Byzantines and see them as Greeks of a sort. Plethon was reconfiguring culture, language, geography, and ethnicity into a new formation.

Laonikos does not exactly give a definition of what made a Greek, though *genos*, language, and customs are his basic categories for distinguishing national groups. He comes close to Plethon's formulation when he defines the empire of Trebizond: "They are Greeks by race and their customs and language too are Greek" (9.27: Ἕλληνάς τε ὄντας τὸ γένος, καὶ τὰ ἤθη τε ἅμα καὶ τὴν φωνὴν προϊεμένους Ἑλληνικήν). After the fall of Trebizond, he sums up regarding the fall of the Greeks everywhere, which was one of the main themes of the *Histories* (1.1):

> This too had been a principality of the Greeks and its customs and way of life were also Greek [ἡγεμονία καὶ αὕτη Ἑλλήνων οὖσα καὶ ἐς τὰ ἤθη τε καὶ δίαιταν τετραμμένη Ἑλλήνων], so that in a short amount of time the Greeks and the rulers of the Greeks had been overturned by this sultan, starting

with the city of Byzantion, after that the Peloponnese, and finally the king and land of Trebizond. [9.78][6]

Plethon and Laonikos viewed ancient Greek and Roman history in the same way, and this, I believe, is because Laonikos learned it from Plethon. The language in which they introduce the Greeks into their narratives is identical.[7] In the previous chapter, moreover, we examined Laonikos's synoptic view of ancient history. He mentions Herakles first, who was preceded by Dionysos and followed by the Athenians and the Spartans, and Alexander the Great. He then cuts to eastern affairs, relying on Diodoros for Arbakes the Mede, who took over from Sardanapalos the Assyrian; then Cyrus, the son of Cambyses, and Alexander, whereupon the Romans become powerful and eventually settle in Byzantium.

Plethon offers historical comparanda for his arguments, rather than history as such, but the same elements recur. For him it was Herakles who established the civilized conditions that allowed Greek culture to develop, followed by the Spartan Lykourgos.[8] We know that one of Plethon's main sources for ancient history

6   This passage was suspected by Darkó to be an interpolation (based solely on its proximity to another passage that *may* be interpolated), but there is no reason to doubt these words: Kaldellis, "Interpolations."

7   Cf. Plethon, *Address to Manuel II* 248: τὰ μέγιστά τε καὶ ἐνδοξότατα Ἕλληνες ἔργα ἀπεδείξαντο, with *Hist.* 1.3: Ἕλληνες μὲν οὖν ὅσα ἀποδεικνύμενοι ἔργα μεγάλα τε καὶ περιφανῆ ἐπὶ μέγα ἀφίκοντο κλέος. This parallel, of course, reflects their common study of Herodotos, possibly from the same manuscript. There is room for further study of how Plethon's prose influenced that of Laonikos. Reading both in tandem, I have noted many affinities. For example, the second half of Plethon, *Address to Manuel II* 249, is basically a template for Laonikos's writing.

8   Plethon, *Advice to Theodoros II regarding the Peloponnese* 116–17, 126–27. For Plethon's view of history, see G. Smarnakes, "Ἀρχαία ιστορία και ερμηνευτικές στρατηγικές στον Πλήθωνα," in *1453: Η Άλωση της Κωνσταντινούπολης και η μετάβαση από τους μεσαιωνικούς στους νεώτερους χρόνους*, ed. T. Kiousopoulou (Heraklion, 2005), 173–81.

was Diodoros, whom he excerpted and commented on.[9] Like Laonikos, he also refers to Sardanapalos's loss of empire to the Medes, and to Cyrus and the Persians' rise to power in Asia.[10] Plethon does not offer many more arguments from history than these, so their overlap with Laonikos's introduction becomes statistically significant. Both refer to the rise of the Romans in similar, synoptic terms.[11] Overall, Plethon and Laonikos have a similar view of history: Herakles and the Greeks; the Spartans, Athenians, and Alexander; a succession of empires in the east, culminating in Cyrus and the Persians. They pay no attention to the Hellenistic kingdoms or early Roman history: the Romans emerge suddenly and establish Constantinople. Both agree that what we call Byzantium was Greek, though they have slightly different theories about why that was so, for they know that the foundation was Roman. Laonikos, as we saw, argues that native Greek elements swamped the Roman (1.5). Plethon instead highlights the pre-Roman, Greek history of the city of Byzantion, which was settled from Greece, and his secondary argument is that the Romans were themselves originally of Greek stock.[12] This idea was most fully developed in the *Roman Antiquities* of Dionysios of Halikarnassos. Plethon's contemporary Ioannes Kanaboutzes discussed it explicitly on the first page of his commentary on Dionysios.[13] But Plethon does not explain how these originally

9   Plethon, *Historical Excepts*; cf. Woodhouse, *Plethon*, 18–19, 221–22.

10   Plethon, *Advice to Theodoros II regarding the Peloponnese* 127–28; *Address to Demetrios Palaiologos*, 207–8.

11   Cf. Plethon, *Advice to Theodoros II*, 117: Ῥωμαῖοί τε ξὺν ἀρετῇ πολιτείας ἐς τὴν μεγάλην ἡγεμονίαν παρῆεσαν, with *Hist.* 1.5: ἐς ὃ δὴ Ῥωμαίους ἐπὶ τὴν τῆς οἰκουμένης μεγίστην ἀρχὴν ἀφικομένους, ἰσοτάλαντον ἔχοντας τύχην τῇ ἀρετῇ.

12   Plethon, *Address to Manuel II* 248–49.

13   Ioannes Kanaboutzes, *Commentary on Dionysios of Halikarnassos* 1, 29; see E. Gabba, *Dionysius and the History of Archaic Rome* (Berkeley, 1991), esp. chap. 4.

Greek Romans lost their Hellenism in antiquity. In one passage, he jumps over the whole of Byzantine history and simply states that all that is left of the once mighty empire of the Romans is the Peloponnese and a few other cities and islands. Neither he nor Laonikos were much interested in Byzantine history. They fixed all their attention on classical antiquity and the present, in this way foreshadowing the imbalanced historical contours of modern Neohellenism, which also jumps over Byzantium.

Both Plethon and Laonikos note that the Peloponnese is effectively an island,[14] and both were unusually interested in the fortification of the Isthmos. Plethon was obsessed with that topic in his memoranda of advice to the despots, while Laonikos gives a brief digression on the history of attempts to wall it off, as well as vivid descriptions of its failures to stop the Ottomans, of which the most dramatic (in 1446) he may have witnessed personally.[15] This is not a matter of textual influence. Laonikos was actually with Plethon at Mistra while many of the events in question unfolded. Through Plethon and at Mistra, Laonikos met or learned about many of the people whose history he would later write.

There are some passages, moreover, which suggest that Laonikos saw the *Histories* as continuing or complementing his teacher's project. Specifically, his enumeration of the territories left to the empire at the time of his birth, which he misleadingly presents as the starting-point for his narrative, seems to be modeled on Plethon's similar statement in a policy memo; in order and emphasis, the two passages are quite similar.[16] But whereas Plethon

---

14   Cf. Plethon, *Address to Manuel II* 249, with *Hist.* 4.19.

15   *Hist.* 4.19, 6.1, 7.17–28, 7.68, 10.51–55.

16   Cf. Plethon, *Advice to Theodoros II regarding the Peloponnese* 129: δύο πόλεε μόνον ἐπὶ Θρᾴκης περιλέλειπται καὶ Πελοπόννησος, οὐδὲ ξύμπασα αὕτη γε, καὶ εἰ δή τι ἔτι νησίδιον σῶν ἐστι, with *Hist.* 1.8: Βυζάντιον καὶ Βυζαντίου τὴν κάτω παραλίαν ἄχρις Ἡρακλείας πόλεως, κατὰ δὲ Εὔξεινον πόντον τὴν ἄνω παραλίαν ἄχρι Μεσημβρίας

proposes new policies to save what is left, Laonikos recounts how that too was lost. In this way, he picks up where Plethon leaves off. Like Polybios, who set out to explain how the Romans so quickly conquered the world, including his own people, the Greeks, Laonikos states that his purpose is to show "how the affairs of the Greeks were quickly ruined, destroyed by the Turks, and how the latter rose to greatness, proceeding during this time always to new peaks of prosperity" (1.8).[17] Specifically, Polybios wanted to show what type of *politeia*, or regime, enabled the Romans to do this. As it happens, Plethon begins one of his memos to Manuel II by claiming that the current weakness of the Peloponnese in the face of barbarian attack was due to its *kakopoliteia*, its bad governance, and that all successful states in the past had succeeded due to the virtue of their *politeia*. He cites the Spartans, Persians, and Romans—the usual list we have found in him and Laonikos. He then adds to it "the barbarians who are now so frightening us, whose *politeia*, if it is not good for anything else at all, is not to be despised when it comes to the annexation of cities and vigor in war."[18] The main theme of Laonikos's *Histories*, accordingly, is to explain the *politeia* that had so crushed any hopes the Greeks had for Plethon's heralded "restoration." In these and other ways, the *Histories* is a Plethonian project.

πόλεως, Πελοπόννησόν τε αὖ ξύμπασαν πλὴν ἢ τριῶν ἢ τεττάρων πόλεων τῶν Ἐνετῶν, ὡσαύτως Λῆμνον, Ἴμβρον καὶ νήσους τὰς αὐτοῦ ταύτῃ ἐν τῷ Αἰγαίῳ ᾠκημένας. Other texts take stock of the territories left to Byzantium at various times, which seems to have been a mini-genre in the Palaiologan period, e.g., Theodoros Metochites, *Moral Essays* 232–43; Demetrios Kydones, *Speech of Advice to the Romans*, in PG 154:964c–965a; Anonymous, *Address to the Council of Florence* 9.

17   Cf. Polybios, *Histories* 1.1.5–6.

18   Plethon, *Address to Ioannes VIII Palaiologos* [actually Manuel II] 309–10. Plethon uses the same words to explain the Arab conquests of the seventh century: *Advice to Theodoros II regarding the Peloponnese* 118.

During the course of this study, we have found many points of resonance between Plethon and Laonikos, and this now extends to their view of the history of the Greeks. Most of Plethon's influence was no doubt exerted in person, but even if we did not have a witness to their personal acquaintance (Kyriacus), we might have suspected it from their texts. In writing the narrative of late Byzantine Neohellenism, it is legitimate to treat them as a pair. Let us now consider their immediate Palaiologan background and revolutionary intentions.

The Colonial Imposition
of a Greek Identity on Byzantium

Laonikos explicitly argued that the people who had called themselves Romans for over a thousand years, those whom we call Byzantines, were really Greeks, not Romans. Plethon seems to have thought the same, though his written declarations on the topic are more implicit. Laonikos dated this Hellenization of the Roman east to the period after the foundation of Constantinople. I happen to believe that he got it exactly wrong. What actually happened at that time was the thorough Romanization of the Greek east. What Laonikos was describing really was a process of Hellenization going on *in his own time*, a process in which he was a major protagonist, only he projected it a thousand years into the past.

This is not the place to discuss what the Byzantines meant when they said they were Romans. I have discussed this elsewhere already and am preparing an expanded treatment.[19] That this is

19   Kaldellis, *Hellenism*, chap. 2; and idem, "From Rome to New Rome, From Empire to Nation-State: Reopening the Question of Byzantium's Roman Identity," in *Two Romes: Rome and Constantinople in Late Antiquity*, ed. L. Grig and G. Kelly (Oxford, 2012), 387–404.

still a problematic area of research stems from prejudices that were built into the modern field of Byzantine Studies, as it gradually became an academic discipline in the modern west. The majority of modern historians have denied that the Byzantines were really Romans, despite what they claimed, and prefer to see them instead as Greek or Orthodox people who were touched by the Roman name only insofar as they were subject to an emperor who used it for reasons of ideology (or propaganda). It is generally not regarded as an identity—which is, however, precisely what it was. Some scholars have been exceptions to this pattern. Hans-Georg Beck and John Bury were emphatic that Byzantium had to be seen as a Roman civilization and proposed some specific ways to do so,[20] though the field has not taken them up. Steven Runciman, who spent more time with the sources than the scholarship, proposed that Byzantium was a Roman nation with its own national culture and proud patriotism.[21] More recently, Chris Wickham has claimed that "Byzantine 'national identity' has not been much considered by historians, for that empire was the ancestor of no modern nation state, but it is arguable that it was the most developed in Europe at the end of our period"—i.e., 1000 AD.[22]

But these are exceptions. The "rule" in the field was expressed by Michael Angold, for whom the Byzantines have no claim to the Roman name.[23] This prejudice is literally medieval. In the

20   E.g., H.-G. Beck, *Res Publica Romana: Vom Staatsdenken der Byzantiner* (Munich, 1970).

21   S. Runciman, *The Emperor Romanus Lecapenus and his Reign* (Cambridge, 1929), 32–33.

22   C. Wickham, *The Inheritance of Rome: Illuminating the Dark Ages, 400–1000* (New York, 2009), 5.

23   M. Angold, *Byzantium: The Bridge from Antiquity in the Middle Ages* (London, 2001), 2. I am preparing a separate study of the reasons historians have given for refusing to see Byzantium as Roman (including—I am not kidding—that it was

early medieval west, Byzantium was unproblematically considered to be, and referred to as, the Roman Empire or the Roman *respublica*. That changed toward the end of the eighth century, with the institution of a self-professed Roman Empire in the west. Henceforth, and for the duration of the Middle Ages and early modernity, the Roman Empire would be called "the empire of the Greeks" or "the empire of Constantinople." Eventually, it would be called "Byzantium," in part because that name also highlighted its Greek past.[24]

I will not survey here the many confrontations that took place over this issue between representatives of the eastern and western Roman powers. Still, it is odd that no study has yet been written of the west's polemical effort to deny the Roman legacy to the Byzantines. We need such a study to understand the political and ideological interests and the historical dynamics that shaped the west's view of Byzantium.[25] Of course, western views were not monolithic. Sometimes the Genoese would recognize the Byzantines as (sort of) Romans in order to spite the Venetians, and Martin Luther did so (again, sort of) to spite the pope. But these were exceptions that prove the rule. The overwhelming trend in western Europe after ca. 800 was to regard the Byzantines as Greeks and to believe that their claim to the Roman name and legacy had lapsed sometime after Justinian—the same picture that we find in Laonikos. As the modern discipline of Byzantine

---

too small, authoritarian, bloodthirsty, Christian, or Greek, etc.). The only thing that these excuses have in common is their purpose: to disqualify Byzantium from being Roman. Otherwise, they are made up *ad hoc*.

24   Cf. C. Rapp, "Hellenic Identity, *Romanitas*, and Christianity in Byzantium," in *Hellenisms: Culture, Identity, and Ethnicity from Antiquity to Modenity*, ed. K. Zacharia (Aldershot, 2008), 129.

25   We have only an old dissertation, full of quaint notions: M. G. Arbagi, "Byzantium in Latin Eyes" (Ph.D. diss., Rutgers University, 1969).

Studies is complicit in this polemical picture, being a direct out-
growth of it, and has not yet made an issue of it (when it is not tacitly or openly endorsing it), we have to emphasize that the west's
Hellenist reading of Byzantium entailed a huge distortion of that
culture's self-definition.[26] Western writers and spokesmen had
no interest in how the Byzantines understood themselves. Their
goal was only to deny them rights to the Roman legacy. Hence it is
still difficult for modern historians to say who the Byzantine were
exactly. I invite the reader to consult any textbook on the subject.

Nor do we have a study of what "Greek" might have meant in
the west. Was the attribution based on language? On a theory
regarding ethnic continuity? Or was it of secondary importance,
coming into use only to fill the void left by the withdrawal of recognition from the Roman identity of the Byzantines? Probably all
these factors were involved. *Graecus*, moreover, encoded negative
characteristics derived from ancient Latin literature that enabled
the west, especially at the time of the Crusades, to play the part
of vigorous and virile ancient Romans in dealing with effeminate,
scholarly Greeks and eventually to conquer them and colonize
their lands.[27] Symbolic "Romans" reconquering putative "Greeks"
was a more presentable narrative than what was really going on.

Therefore, we need a medievalist study with the title (to paraphrase many western spokesmen) "You Are Not Romans!" Part

26   It might even be validly studied as a type of cultural appropriation: B. Ziff and
P. V. Rao, eds., *Borrowed Power: Essays on Cultural Appropriation* (New Brunswick,
1997).

27   There are many studies of how the Byzantines regarded the Latin west,
but few focus on the political aspects of this debate from the western perspective.
For stereotypes and other western perspectives, see H. Hunger, *Graeculus perfidus, Ἰταλὸς ἰταμός: Il senso dell'alterità nei rapporti Greco-Romani ed Italo-Bizantini*
(Rome, 1987); T. Shawcross, "Re-Inventing the Homeland in the Historiography of
Frankish Greece: The Fourth Crusade and the Legend of the Trojan War," *BMGS* 27
(2003): 120–52; Messis, "Lectures sexuées de l'altérité."

of the reason that we do not have such a study must be that the claim has seemed self-evidently true. To acknowledge that it was a politically motivated idea, in fact polemical, would represent a paradigm-shift. All sorts of things that medievalists take for granted would then become quite problematic. To turn the tables for a moment, in the west there were no political communities descended from, and structured according to, the norms of the ancient *respublica*, and no groups with a collective Roman identity.[28] The main bearers of western Roman claims were the emperor, the pope, and the jurists who laid the foundations of European law and the nation-states. But we should not look exclusively to them to find the culprits for the polemical de-Romanization of Byzantium. In a fascinating study, Julia Smith has shown how an abstract and flexible idea of "Rome" became an ordering principle in the west, as paradigm, metaphor, and normative tool for structuring relations of power, culture, law, ancestry, empire, and language.[29] This idea proved to be a useful medium through which a constellation of otherwise disparate groupings in the west came to some kind of understanding among themselves. Smith does not discuss how the Byzantine claim to Rome might have interfered or interfaced with this emerging consensus, but I think that its incommensurate relation to "Rome" was a major reason why Byzantium never joined the western club of nations (in addition to the religious reasons that have received their fair share of attention).

In 1204, the Catholic world set about the conquest and dismemberment of Byzantium and its annexation to western modes. The

28   Except for the people of the city of Rome itself, though their identity was complex and quite often discontinuous. Interestingly, much of the time they were embarassingly in opposition to either the pope or the emperor, the main bearers of western Roman claims—or to both.

29   J. M. H. Smith, *Europe after Rome: A New Cultural History, 500–1000* (Oxford, 2005).

Byzantines now not only had to endure the annoyance of being called Greeks in diplomatic exchanges, but many of them were ruled by racist, colonial lords, who had the power to dictate the terms of all exchanges. It is no accident that at this time Byzantine writers begin to show a heightened interest in what it might mean for them to be Greek and how that might work for or against them. This experimentation with notions of Greek identity was the result of colonial rule, though the potential for the application of modern colonial theory here is still untapped.

In these conditions, previously marginal usages moved to the center.[30] For example, in ecclesiastical debates the Byzantines had previously been able to call Catholics "Romans," as their leader was the bishop of Rome, without infringing upon or jeopardizing their own sense of Roman identity. It was a technical usage for a specific context, but it now acquired a broader significance. Anti-Catholic writers such as Georgios Akropolites, a Roman patriot, could now concede that the Roman east and Latin west had emerged out of the same Roman crucible, though the Latins had deviated from it (this is also what Laonikos implies in his preface).[31] Conversely, some Byzantine thinkers in exile came to terms with the "Greek" subject position in their exchanges with Latins (those under direct Latin rule had no choice). A Greek identity, after all, was not bad in all respects: one could work with

30 For a discussion of thirteenth-century developments, see Kaldellis, *Hellenism*, chap. 6; also D. G. Angelov, *Imperial Ideology and Political Thought in Byzantium, 1204–1330* (Cambridge, 2007), 95–98; G. Page, *Being Byzantine: Greek Identity before the Ottomans* (Cambridge, 2008), chap. 4. There is, unfortunately, no systematic or theoretical survey of Palaiologan Hellenism that reads the texts closely and critically. What we have instead is a set of articles each of which offers or recycles quotations from a handful of texts; many of them are written from a modern Greek nationalist point of view.

31 Georgios Akropolites, *Against the Latins* 2.27 (p. 64); so, too, the patriarch Philotheos Kokkinos, *On the Fall of Herakleia* 240.

it, ameliorate it, even own it. There was much in which a Greek might feel pride. This was a form of stereotype appropriation: "the manifold ways indigenous cultures embrace and act out the stereotypes woven by a colonizing...culture," often to manipulate it to their own advantage.[32] Modern Greek identity is, ultimately, such an act of embracing. We see glimpses of it among Byzantine scholars in Italy who played up their Greek credentials to obtain teaching positions.[33]

To return to the thirteenth century, the philosophical emperor Theodoros II Laskaris made bold and modern-sounding claims on behalf of his people's Hellenism. It is highly revealing that he self-consciously made these claims in order to redeem the prestige of his own culture in the face of western rivals who, he knew, were making great philosophical and economic strides. His was the first articulation of a Neohellenic position and was stimulated by the experience of conquest by the west. Laskaris, however, did not intend to renounce his people's Roman identity, and none of his subjects seems to have been willing to follow him in this thought-experiment.[34] It is a convention in the scholarship to assert that at Nikaia the Byzantines developed a Hellenic consciousness, but there is little evidence for this claim. As far as we can tell, they remained Roman patriots, as did Laskaris. The Hellenizing experiments were not diffused. They do enable us, however, to see Plethon and Laonikos as exponents of an extreme version of these trends, that is, of abandoning the Roman name to the west and appropriating and ameliorating the Greek subject-position. Still, two centuries separated them from

32   D. Frankfurter, *Religion in Roman Egypt* (Princeton, 1998), 225–33.

33   Geanakoplos, *Greek Scholars*, cites examples of this strategy; for Italo-Byzantines, see below.

34   Kaldellis, *Hellenism*, 372–79.

Laskaris, during which the Byzantines became increasingly used to the Greek position—which is not to say that they accepted it.

The recapture of Constantinople in 1261 led to a vigorous reassertion of Roman claims, but the context was forever changed, and the Palaiologan state failed to regain momentum in its dealings with the western powers in its midst. Since the occupation of 1204, "the Greek"—*Graecus, Graikos,* or *Hellene*—was a persona that the Byzantines had to take on regularly, especially in ecclesiastical contexts and in their dealings with the Latin Romans. As the terms Catholic and Orthodox were not then established to distinguish between two Churches (both of them claimed both titles, and still do), *Greek* and *Roman* served that purpose. But the context was usually dictated by the Catholics; when the Byzantines had their way, they tended to assert their right to be the Romans, even ecclesiastically (given that Constantinople was "New Rome"). When they had to use the terms *Graikos* or *Hellene* in narratives, they usually cite them ironically, as the terms of choice of the Catholics, not their own. The Byzantines did not want to be called anything other than Romans. But gone were the imperial days when they could just throw envoys into prison for bearing letters that addressed the emperor as "emperor of the Greeks." Now they had to endure it. Sometimes they protested, even at Church meetings, but those were convened to discuss other matters.[35]

Greek identity-claims begin to make sudden appearances in Byzantine sources, if in incommensurable modes (literary vs. ecclesiastical, self-ascriptive vs. polemical, defensive vs. ameliorative, etc.). It is hard to align them into any kind of coherent theory. This Hellenism, moreover, is allusive, in that its precise meaning in the Byzantine Roman context is always deferred: no "theory" of

---

35 Mavrommatis, "Ῥωμαϊκὴ ταυτότητα," cites examples. Many thirteenth-century examples are cited in Kaldellis, *Hellenism,* chap. 6.

Greek ethnicity or nationality is developed by any thinker before Plethon, and no real attempt to coordinate "Roman" and "Greek" before Laonikos. And that was more or less how matters stood until the early fifteenth century—with two significant exceptions, neither of which has received much attention.

The first are the writings of the early fourteenth-century philosopher and statesman Theodoros Metochites, who wrote many essays engaging with ancient writers and reflecting critically on Greek history and culture. He displays an unresolved mixture of identification with and detachment from the Greeks. Echoing Theodoros II Laskaris, he could claim that "we share in their *genos* and language, and are their successors."[36] He was clearly a Roman patriot, however, though he declined to explain how the two interfaced. Were his people a branch of the Romans descended from the Greeks? Metochites usually regarded the Greeks as a different people, one among many who had lived in the past, and he identified personally with ancient Roman history, on which he wrote several essays. In any case, he should not be taken as speaking for anyone but himself, and he is a notoriously difficult writer. He did not stimulate a rush of Hellenist claims in later Byzantium.

36   Theodoros Metochites, *Moral Essays* 595. The standard works on Metochites are H.-G. Beck, *Theodoros Metochites: Die Krise des byzantinischen Weltbildes im 14. Jahrhundert* (Munich, 1952); I. Ševčenko, *La vie intellectuelle et politique à Byzance sous les premiers Paléologues: Études sur la polémique entre Théodore Métochite et Nicéphore Choumnos* (Brussels, 1962); and E. de Vries-van der Velden, *Théodore Métochite: Un réévaluation* (Amsterdam, 1987). Also J. M. Featherstone, "Theodore Metochites's *Semeioseis Gnomikai*: Personal Encyclopedism," in *Encyclopedic Trends in Byzantium?* ed. P. van Deun and C. Macé (Leuven, 2011), 333–44; but we have no systematic study of his Hellenism (i.e., his notion of what it meant to be Greek, rather than his view of *paideia*); cf. A. Garzya, "Byzantium," in *Perceptions of the Ancient Greeks*, ed. K. J. Dover (Cambridge, MA, 1992), 33–35 and 50 n. 22; for his *Byzantios*, see P. Magdalino, "The Beauty of Antiquity in Late Byzantine Praises of Constantinople," in Odorico and Messis, eds., *Villes de toute beauté*, 101–15.

The second development is even trickier than Metochites's prose. There are a number of Greek texts from the late fourteenth century on that reveal a conflicted idea of who the *Romans* are— are they Byzantines, Catholics, both?—or that flatly call the Byzantines *Greeks*. These are often cited by scholars as proof of a rising Hellenic self-consciousness of the Byzantines, but it goes routinely unmentioned that almost all of these were written by Byzantine converts to Catholicism, who had adopted a western outlook when it came to many issues, including the "Roman" question.[37] I am referring to the likes of Demetrios Kydones, Manuel Chrysoloras, Ioannes Argyropoulos, Bessarion, and Michael Apostoles.[38] To read them, one could easily conclude

37 This is not mentioned, for instance, by S. Runciman, *The Last Byzantine Renaissance* (Cambridge, 1970), 21–22; Woodhouse, *Plethon*, 109; G. Pitsakis, "Universalité et nationalisme: La Nouvelle Rome. Quelques points de repère à travers les textes grecs," in *Umanità e Nazioni nel Diritto e nella Spiritualità da Roma a Costantinopoli a Mosca* (*Rendiconti del XII Seminario Internazionale di Studi Storici "Da Roma alla terza Roma"*) (Rome, 1995), 34; C. Maltezou, "Still More on the Political Views of Bessarion," in *Der Beitrag der byzantinischen Gelehrten zur afendländischen Renaissance des 14. und 15. Jahrhunderts*, ed. E. Konstantinou (Frankfurt and Main, 2006), 100; T. Kiousopoulou, "Η έννοια της πατρίδας κατά τον 15° αιώνα," in *1453: Η Άλωση της Κωνσταντινούπολης και η μετάβαση από τους μεσαιωνικούς στους νεώτερους χρόνους*, ed. T. Kiousopoulou (Heraklion, 2005), 147–60; and eadem, *Βασιλεύς ή οικονόμος: Πολιτική εξουσία και ιδεολογία πριν την άλωση* (Athens, 2007), 217–34.

38 Kydones refers to the Byzantines alternately as Romans or Greeks, the latter mostly in connection with their language and literature, or as possessors of ancient Greek wisdom and so shaped by it, but these are not formal or comprehensive definitions of what it may have meant "to be Greek" for him. As for Catholics, he calls them Romans, Latins, or westerners in his *Letters*; *Apology for his Faith* 359–403; and the *Speech of Advice to the Romans* in PG 154, esp. 977d: "Who but the Romans would make the best allies for the Romans?" He produces no theory to govern his use of these terms. Like Akropolites, he seems to have thought that Latin and Byzantine Romans had the same origin "but later, I don't know how, we separated from each other": *Apology for his Faith* 401; cf. Siniossoglou, *Radical Platonism*, 349. For Manuel Chrysoloras, see below. Ioannes Argyropoulos sounds in Greek like a normal Byzantine, except he refers consistently and even insistently to the

that "the Byzantines" thought that they were Hellenes. But what we are witnessing is largely the extension of western colonization from economies and lands to minds and hearts. We are hearing the same western narrative about the *Graeci*, only in Greek and by Greeks themselves, as proud but humbled *Hellenes* now.

I do not doubt these writers' sincerity. Their choices placed them in an ambiguous position with regard to their native culture and people, and they were making the best of it. They were proud of who they were but in Italy, where most of them moved, they could only be Greeks. So they cultivated Hellenic pride (though at times they could let their Roman colors show).[39] In fact, these Italo-Byzantines and their intellectual heirs were to play a key role in the construction and dissemination in the west of a *positive* Greek national identity, which would harbor refugees from the collapse of Byzantium by presenting them with an identity that their western hosts could recognize. Crucially for the long term, it would provide the rubric under which western powers understood the Greek-speaking population of the Ottoman empire, even if that population still did not regard itself as Greek (but as Roman, down to the nineteenth and, in places, into the early twentieth century). This construction of a modern Greek national identity in the post-Byzantine west is a fascinating, albeit long-neglected, topic. We will touch on it the following section; our main concern here is with what was happening in Byzantium in the early fifteenth century.

Byzantines as Greeks, *never* as Romans—for example, in his *Monodia for Ioannes VIII Palaiologos*. For the Hellenism of Bessarion, see Lamers, *Reinventing the Ancient Greeks*, chap. 3. After his move to Italy, he presents his people consistently and exclusively as Greek, even when addressing the Palaiologoi, e.g., in his *Address to the despot Konstantinos*, except at 38, where he says that "our laws are both Roman and Greek." For the Hellenism of this work, see Maltezou, "Still More on the Political Views of Bessarion."

39 E.g., Geanakoplos, *Greek Scholars*, 205.

Neither the philosophizing experiments of Laskaris and Metochites nor the Hellenist rhetoric of the Catholic converts moved the majority of Byzantines from their Orthodox and Roman positions.[40] In what remained of Byzantium, the *Romaioi* knew by now that they had a Greek alter-ego in the eyes of the west, and they had to play that role more often than ever in their diplomatic, commercial, and local exchanges. Still, it was internalized as a purely situational identity, contingent on the facts of power. The latter were both local and imperial. The empire was contracting, gobbled up by Turks and Latins. Catholic converts were increasingly prominent at the court and in intellectual life, and some of the emperors presented themselves as Catholics too (though without renouncing their Roman claims). They also had to accept the Greek subject-position, in not only western diplomatic texts but also their own court literature. The labels, dynamics, and politics of identity were shifting dramatically when Plethon was formulating his Hellenist thesis and passing it on to Laonikos. In fact, we should not overlook Plethon's role as Bessarion's teacher, and it has been suggested that he may also have been the teacher of Argyropoulos and Apostoles.[41] It is possible, then, that what we are seeing in the texts that I mentioned above is a convergence of Plethonian and Catholic Hellenism.

This confusing context generated novel formulations, including Plethon's theory, which would have puzzled past Byzantines. Laonikos's contemporary Ioannes Kanaboutzes wrote a commentary on the *Roman Antiquities* of Dionysios of Halikarnassos for the benefit of Palamede Gattilusio, lord of Ainos, in which he usually refers to the Romans in the transliterated Latin form, *Romanoi*.

---

40   I agree with Reinsch, "Η θεώρηση," especially 72, 75 (against Vryonis), who points to Sphrantzes as expressing the prevailing Roman Orthodox standard.

41   Woodhouse, *Plethon*, 40–41.

Is this because he wanted to keep *Romaioi* for his own people and their past? In his panegyric for Manuel II and Ioannes VIII, Isidoros of Kiev recounts the history of Constantinople. First in his schema is the Greek city, then the best of the Romans come and mingle with the best of the Hellenes, producing a single, most noble *genos* "that one might call *Romellenes*."[42] This theory was expounded also by Scholarios.[43] Laonikos, then, was not alone in revisiting the foundation of Constantinople in light of the newly discovered role of the Hellenes, of which prior Byzantines had been unaware. Manuel Chrysoloras, in the comparison of Rome and Constantinople that he wrote for Manuel II, proposed that the latter had been built jointly by Romans and Greeks.[44] These thinkers were literally reinventing the foundations of Byzantium and making them seem more Greek.

Laonikos's Neohellenism makes more sense against this revisionist context, except he and Plethon should be seen as exponents of a distinctive outlook. They seem to be closest to the Catholic-Byzantine "Greeks" such as Argyropoulos and Bessarion, but this

---

42   Isidoros, *Panegyric for Manuel II and Ioannes VIII* 152; for the Greek foundation, see 149.

43   C. Livanos, *Greek Tradition and Latin Influence in the Work of George Scholarios: "Alone against All Europe"* (Piscataway, 2006), 117–18.

44   Manuel Chrysoloras, *Letter to Manuel II with a Comparison of Elder and New Rome*, in PG 156:40d; and for contemporary Greeks, 25d; for the double descent from Romans and Greeks, see his *Address to Manuel II* 117. For the *Comparison*, see H. Homeyer, "Zur Synkrysis des Manuel Chrysoloras, einem Vergleich zwischen Rom und Konstantinopel: Ein Beitrag zum italienischen Frühhumanismus," *Klio* 62 (1980): 525–34; H. Saradi-Mendelovici, "Christian Attitudes toward Pagan Monuments in Late Antiquity and their Legacy in Later Byzantine Centuries," *DOP* 44 (1990): 59, sees "national pride" in his reference to the Greek inscriptions at Rome; R. Webb, "Describing Rome in Greek: Manuel Chrysoloras's Comparison of Old and New Rome," in Odorico and Messis, eds., *Villes de toute beauté*, 123–33. For the correct addressee, see L. Thorn, "Das Briefcorpus des Manuel Chrysoloras: eine Blütenlese," in *Der Beitrag der byzantinischen Gelehrten*, ed. Konstantinou, 21.

similarity is superficial. Plethon adamantly opposed Union at Florence, while Laonikos mocked the papacy in a way that would have tickled Orthodox Byzantines. Plethon's and Laonikos's Hellenism was not primarily about the question of ecclesiastical Union. Plethon was a pagan Platonist who preferred Orthodoxy, only because its tradition offered the best prospects for his non- and anti-Christian project,[45] and I believe that Laonikos was largely with him in this. In one sense, their Hellenism was the ultimate result of the Greek position into which the west had pushed Byzantium over the course of centuries. Were it not for 1204, there might not have been a Plethon. But the Platonists differed in both form and content from the Hellenism of the Byzantine Catholics. The latter had to accept the position that their new masters had defined for them and make the best of it. Plethon and Laonikos, by contrast, had no claim or interest in either the Roman or Orthodox legacies. Theirs was a positive and autonomous Greek identity that drew on Hellenic texts and ideals that had survived the millennium of Byzantine Orthodoxy. Plethon took Hellenism the whole way, fusing what the Byzantines regarded as its positive cultural and its negative religious aspects into a single program. This was a radical departure, and if the Catholic Church was ultimately responsible for creating the *Graeci* of late Byzantium, this version was beyond its control.

The Modern Legacy of Late Byzantine Neohellenism

Plethon and Laonikos may have had a coherent and consistent Hellenic identity that embraced culture, language, history, and possibly religion, but they were unusual in this regard. Most late and post-Byzantines had to navigate a number of situational

---

45 Siniossoglou, *Radical Platonism.*

appellations, as we see in the case of Scholarios, who had vacillated regarding Union and many other matters. His use of identity labels was dependent on context, and the only one he took as unconditional was probably "Christian"—assuming that his own brand of Christianity was meant! It is hard and possibly futile to try to systematize his usage and find the "truth" about his identity.[46] He was not alone in this. Categories were mixed, and incommensurate paradigms were deployed in the same contexts. One of Plethon's eulogists divided his admirers into Greeks and barbarians (including the Latins), another into Greeks and Romans (meaning the Latins).[47]

The Ottoman liquidation of Romanía also produced some uncertainty, at least at first, regarding whether the sultans should be seen as the new rulers of the Romans or of the Greeks, and as to what Ottoman policy would be toward the conquered Byzantines. Two leading intellectuals favored by Mehmed in the 1460s, Kritoboulos and Georgios Amiroutzes, hedged their bets by authorizing Mehmed to regard himself as the conqueror of both the Greeks and the Romans (in this context, the latter did not mean the Latins).[48] But this situation resolved itself

46   For discussions, see S. Vryonis, "Byzantine Cultural Self-Consciousness in the Fifteenth Century," in *The Twilight of Byzantium: Aspects of Cultural and Religious History in the Late Byzantine Empire*, ed. S. Ćurčić and D. Mouriki (Princeton, 1991), 9–11, who has a national Greek agenda; A. D. Angelou, "'Who am I?' Scholarios's Answers and the Hellenic Identity," in *Φιλέλλην: Studies in Honour of Robert Browning*, ed. C. N. Constantides (Venice, 1996), 1–19; Livanos, "Conflict between Scholarios and Plethon"; idem, *Greek Tradition and Latin Influence*, 89–92.

47   Hieronymos Charitonymos in PG 160:807c–d and Gregorios in ibid. 813d; see Woodhouse, *Plethon*, 11–12.

48   In his *History* of Mehmed, Kritoboulos calls the Byzantines Romans, but he also authorizes Hellenist readings of their culture and of the events of the conquest, especially in the preface and in having Mehmed present himself as the avenger of the Trojans against the descendants of their former Greek enemies (at 4.11.6). In his poems, Amiroutzes praised Mehmed as the leader of both Romans and Greeks:

quickly. Whatever classicism or Philhellenism was at first associated with Mehmed proved transitory. The post-Byzantine population retained its Roman Orthodox identity, even if now it was deprived of its national state and was reconstituted as a primarily religious community under the leadership of the patriarch of Constantinople. This was not at all the same as the Roman national community of Byzantium, but the Ottomans regarded their Orthodox subjects as Romans, or *Rum*, which is what they remained until the nineteenth century.

Western powers, however, continued to regard them as *Graeci*, and they held dominion over some of them, educated some of their intellectual class, and wielded influence within the Ottoman Empire. The history of the Greek-speaking population caught in the middle was determined by the push and pull of these two forces. Had they been fully conquered and absorbed by the west—that is, had the *Frangokratia* not been rolled back by the *Tourkokratia*—they might have come to accept a Greek identity sooner; as it was, that was not to happen until the nineteenth century, when the hold of the Ottomans over a portion of them yielded to the leading western powers.

This brings us to the complex and controversial question of the origin of modern Greek identity. There are two schools of thought, one that regards it as originating in the thirteenth century and after, in the Hellenism of thinkers such as Laskaris, Plethon, and Laonikos, and another that regards it as the product of developments immediately prior to the Revolution.[49] The first

Janssens and Van Deun, "George Amiroutzes and his Poetical Oeuvre," 314–15, 318. Amiroutzes calls Mehmed the emperor of both Greeks and Romans in his letter to Bessarion on the fall of Trebizond: PG 161:724c. Amiroutzes and Kritoboulos were on close terms.

49   Cf. A. E. Bakalopoulos, Ἱστορία τοῦ Νέου Ἑλληνισμοῦ, vol. 1, Ἀρχὲς καὶ διαμόρφωσή του, rev. ed. (Thessalonike, 1974); and G. Karabelias, Τὸ 1204 καὶ ἡ διαμόρφωση

stresses national continuity, the second fluidity and the historical construction of modern national identities. The first is untheoretical and draws predictable nationalist conclusions from a small number of elite sources, while the second is highly theoretical and in tune with current thinking in the social sciences. Certainly, the nationalism of ca. 1800 needs to be understood in terms of its specific context, but that does not mean that long-term processes had not already set the stage. The first theory ignores and wants to suppress the dominant Roman identity that the Byzantines and post-Byzantines held long after Laskaris and Plethon. Those intellectuals, especially Laskaris, spoke only for themselves or small circles. As for the second school, it has a modernist bias and ignores the construction and circulation of a national Hellenic identity for centuries before the Revolution. That identity, as we have seen, originated in the west's ideological and military attack on Byzantium and was then modified and ameliorated by post-Byzantine thinkers operating in an Italo-Byzantine context.[50] Ultimately, it was this diasporic construct that took over

---

του νεώτερου Ελληνισμού, 3rd ed. (Athens, 2007), with P. M. Kitromilides, "'Imagined Communities' and the Origins of the National Question in the Balkans," *European History Quarterly* 19 (1989): 149–94; and idem, "On the Intellectual Content of Greek Nationalism: Paparrigopoulos, Byzantium and the Great Idea," in *Byzantium and the Modern Greek Identity*, ed. D. Ricks and P. Magdalino (Aldershot, 1998), 25–33.

50   This needs more study; see Geanakoplos, *Interaction*, 172–99 (who takes the Greek identity of his subjects for granted); Harris, *Greek Emigres* and "Being a Byzantine after Byzantium: Hellenic Identity in Renaissance Italy," *Kambos: Cambridge Papers in Modern Greek* 8 (2000): 25–44; T. Glaser, "The Remnants of the Hellenes: Problems of Greek Identity after the Fall of Constantinople," in Konstantinou, ed., *Beitrag der byzantinischen Gelehrten*, 199–209; L. Bargeliotis, "The Enlightenment and the Hellenic 'Genos': From Plethon to Vulgaris," *Skepsis* 20 (2009): 44–61 (who makes problematic philosophical assumptions); H. Lamers, "A Byzantine Poet in Italian Exile: Manilius Cabacius Rallus's Self-Presentation in the Context of Leo X's Philhellenism," in *Acta Conventus Neo-Latini Uppsaliensis: Proceedings of the Fourteenth International Congress of Neo-Latin Studies, Uppsala,*

the homeland in the nineteenth century, when rebels against the Ottomans sought western support against the Turks and, again, had to play the role of the Greeks, which was the only label under which the "Romans" of the east could be recognized in the west. This is a substantially different picture of the long-term history of modern Hellenism than any found in print. The west and the western diaspora played a greater role in it than either of the two leading theories has recognized. Modern Neo-Hellenism began as a western colonial imposition and became a diasporic construct that returned to Greece in the late Ottoman period.

Laonikos has played an interesting role in the retroactive Hellenization and de-Romanization of Byzantium that has preoccupied Greek historiography since the later nineteenth century. This is understandable, as he was the first Greek thinker to propose such a project. In many studies, he is quoted as an authentic voice authorizing a thorough Hellenist reinterpretation of Byzantium. He even provided a framework for the historical encounter of Greeks and Romans that purported to explain how the Byzantines were "really" Greeks. But the modern continuation, or revival, of his project must itself be historicized. It is now well understood that the first theorists of the new Greek nation after the Revolution emphasized primarily the links between themselves and the *ancient* Greeks, the only Greeks that the west deemed worthy of rescue from Ottoman barbarism. But in the second half of the nineteenth century, the embarrassingly massive gap between ancient and modern Greeks was bridged by a wholesale acceptance of the western view that the Byzantines were really "medieval

2–9 August 2009, ed. A. Steiner-Weber (Leiden, 2012), 593–604; and idem, "The Imperial Diadem of Greece: Giovanni Gemisto's Strategic Representation of 'Graecia' (1516)," in *Discourses of Power: Ideology and Politics in Neo-Latin Literature*, ed. K. Enenkel (Hildesheim, 2012), 65–95.

Greeks," after all. The official national historian Konstantinos Paparrigopoulos, who was born in Istanbul and died in Athens (1815–91), is usually credited with the invention, on the Greek side, of medieval Hellenism. The entire theory is only a restatement of Laonikos's preface: "Roman" was just a name for the Byzantines, not a reality; it was but a title misleadingly used by the emperors, and Paparrigopoulos duly trots out Laonikos in support.[51]

While some scholars correctly observe that Laonikos sounds a lot like a modern Greek national historian,[52] actual modern Greek national historians cite him as proof that their view of the past is grounded in the sources.[53] Speros Vryonis has repeatedly emphasized that it does not matter what the Byzantines called themselves, for we know that they "really" were Greeks. For him Laonikos was not a revisionist historian or a student of the most revolutionary dissident thinker that Byzantium ever produced, but someone who understood the truth about the Byzantines better than they themselves had: he "grasped" this insight and "is essentially correct, but his is the first historical statement of this political, cultural, and demographic reality" ("demographic" is code for "racial"). Vryonis adduces as evidence for his thesis what medieval *western* authors called the Byzantines, as if their usage was apolitical.[54] Another scholar has hinted that Laonikos could

51   K. Paparrigopoulos, Ἱστορία τοῦ Ἑλληνικοῦ Ἔθνους, vol. 3 (Athens, 1902), 21–22, esp. 26–27.

52   E.g., Ditten, "Bemerkungen," 246; M. Mantouvalou, "Romaios—Romios—Romiossyni: La notion de 'Romain' avant et après la chute de Constantinople," Ἐπιστημονικὴ Ἐπετηρὶς τῆς Φιλοσοφικῆς Σχολῆς τοῦ Πανεπιστημίου Ἀθηνῶν 28 (1979–85): 188.

53   E.g., D. Missiou, "The Importance of Macedonia during the Byzantine Era," in *Byzantine Macedonia: Identity, Image and History*, ed. J. Burke and R. Scott (Melbourne, 2000), 108.

54   S. Vryonis, "Greek Identity in the Middle Ages," *Études balkaniques* 6 (1991): 27 (against names), 33 (western evidence), and 35 (Laonikos); and idem, "Introductory

say what he said only because there was no longer any political establishment to prevent him from doing so, implying that previous Byzantines had somehow been censored from expressing their Hellenic identity (i.e., the absence of prior evidence is proof of its suppression). The Roman name was merely "a false identity, an inexplicable label."[55] This is wishful thinking.

When Laonikos misrepresents the "essence" of Byzantium, we can call it a revolutionary agenda. When modern historians do it, it is a travesty. To be fair, it is not only Greek historians who have produced such travesties. In fact, their view is basically authorized and enabled by centuries of western writing about Byzantium and is but a sidenote to it. The real obstacle that we face not only in grasping Laonikos's innovative thesis, but in understanding Byzantium to begin with, is the medieval (but ongoing) polemical agenda to deny that Byzantium was Roman in a meaningful way. It was not Greek scholars who invented terms such as "empire of the Greeks," "empire of Constantinople," and "Byzantium." All of these were coined by courts and scholars in the west precisely in order to avoid calling it what it was. In fact, it has been proposed that the term *byzantinus* was coined for Hieronymus Wolf's 1562 edition of four historians (the *Corpus universae historiae byzantinae* that included Zonaras, Choniates, Gregoras, and Chalkokondyles), precisely on the basis of Laonikos's preface.[56] Laonikos, then, is important not only for western knowledge of

Remarks on Byzantine Intellectuals and Humanism," *Skepsis* 2 (1991): 113, 117. Elsewhere, however, Vryonis recognizes that Plethon's project was utterly radical in its context: "Crises and Anxieties," 120–22.

55 P. Gounaridis, "Η εξέλιξη της ταυτότητας των Ελλήνων στη Βυζαντινή αυτοκρατορία," *Études balkaniques* 6 (1991): 62, 66.

56 A. Ben-Tov, *Lutheran Humanists and Greek Antiquity: Melanchthonian Scholarship between Universal History and Pedagogy* (Leiden, 2009), 109.

the early Ottomans, but also for the very constitution and ideology of the modern discipline of Byzantine Studies.

Before there was a modern Greece, Gibbon too had seized on Laonikos's declarations as proof that "the Franks and Latins . . . asserted, with some justice, their superior claim to the language and dominion of Rome. They insulted the aliens of the east who had renounced the dress [*sic*] and idiom of Romans; and their reasonable practice will justify the frequent appellation of Greeks" [i.e., by Gibbon in his narrative].[57] There can be no clearer statement of the link between medieval polemics and modern scholarship on Byzantium, a field that has its origin in an "insult." In Gibbon's eyes, Laonikos, standing in for all Byzantines here, could finally accept this insult the way a properly conquered subject should, for "all pride was extinct in the bosom of Chalcondyles; and he describes the Byzantine prince, and his subjects, by the proper, though humble names of Ἕλληνες."[58] It was left to Greek national historians of the nineteenth century to prettify this story, but its origins were humiliating. Laonikos, after all, was a historian of defeat, of the last Decline and Fall of the Roman Empire.

---

57 E. Gibbon, *The History of the Decline and Fall of the Roman Empire*, ed. D. Womersley (London, 1994), 3:416.

58 Ibid., 3:874 n. 24.

Epilogue

Laonikos's hope that the Greeks would one day establish a kingdom of their own came to pass four centuries after he finished writing the *Histories*. That kingdom was initially based in his own corner of the Greek world, the Peloponnese and Athens, and its politics were just as much a function of the tense relationship between the west and the Ottomans as were those of the Byzantines of his day. Like Laonikos, the New Greeks generated a bipolar view of history that reached past the Roman and Byzantine millennium to link the present to the prestigious, legitimating antiquity of classical Greece. It was to be a few more decades before the Greeks "rediscovered" Byzantium, but by then most of the Byzantine remains of Athens had been cleared away in the name of modernization. Athens today is a city that is all ancient and modern, with vanishingly little in between, just like Laonikos's view of history. Byzantine Romanía and the experience of Latin rule sit awkwardly still within the Greek consciousness, just as their physical remains were regarded as a nuisance and an eyesore when it came to constructing a modern capital. There is no "medieval Athens" left. Greeks in general have an antiquity but little to link them personally, materially, or genealogically to the more proximate past—that is, to anything before the 1850s. In this, they are much like Laonikos in his direct reengagement with Herodotos and avoidance of Byzantine historiography. There are few Athenian families that pretend to have a pedigree and among them, amusingly, are people who have his last name. For all of his classicism, his name today ironically invokes a vague sense of continuity from a less antique and more Byzantine past.

We do not know whether Laonikos had any direct descendants, but his *Histories* soon entered the historiographical gene-pool, especially in the west. It survives in about thirty manuscripts, far outpacing his potential Greek rivals. Kritoboulos's *History*, which is ostensibly pro-Ottoman, but says nothing about religion (Kritoboulos evidently found it impossible to describe or even mention Islam), survived in one copy in the sultan's private library. Doukas, who was anti-Ottoman and anti-anti-Union (more than he was pro-Union), survives (effectively) in one copy too. Thus, the Greek view of the rise of the Ottomans, at least in the eyes of the western reading public, was Laonikos's, and we have seen that his view incorporated Ottoman traditions.

We have few studies of the individual manuscripts of the *Histories*.[1] Their travels, copyists, annotators, and readers will form a key chapter in the history of his reception, if and when that is written. The *Histories* was translated into Latin and French already in the sixteenth century. The French translation, incidentaly, was made by the cryptographer Blaise de Vigenère (published

---

1   Exceptions are Mondrain, "Éparque," 158–59, and idem, "Argyropoulos," for Par. gr. 1780 and 1781; H. Wurm, "Der Codex Monacensis gr. 307a: Ein Beitrag zur Überlieferungsgeschichte des Laonikos Chalkokondyles," *JÖB* 44 (1994): 455–62, and idem, "Handschriftliche Überlieferung."

in 1577 and now available online).[2] One can appreciate how cryptographic skills came in handy. His translation is sometimes loose, and he elaborates on topics that he did not believe Laonikos covered adequately. Laonikos's narrative was extended down to 1612 by Artus Thomas in 1662. The Latin translation published by Conrad Clauser in 1556 accompanied the text into its Bonn Corpus (1843) and PG v. 159 (1866) editions, but it is often evasive and periphrastic. Clauser's translation quickly became popular, and was read and absorbed by many scholars, including, for example, Melanchthon.[3] Han Lamers informs me that he has found in Rome, in the Biblioteca Angelica, a manuscript with a Tuscan translation of parts of the work: "It includes passages from books 4, 5 and 9, dates from about 1542, and was composed by Donato di Ruberto Acciaiuoli, so related to the Florentine dukes of Athens. Not surprisingly, he translated those parts on the history of the House of Acciaiuoli, and on the spine it says: 'Storia della Casa Acciaiuoli.' As far as I have seen, the passages were rendered quite literally, sometimes in extremis, e.g., including back references to untranslated passages" (pers. comm.).

These translations are signs of a vigorous interest in Laonikos's *Histories* in the century after it was written. In fact, it appears to have been used as a source already by Sabellico (Marcantonio Coccio) for the Turkish digression in his world history, the *Enneades* (1498).[4] The *Histories* eventually entered the mainstream

2   J. Balsamo, "Byzance à Paris: Chalcondyle, Vigenère, L'Angelier," in *Sauver Byzance de la barbarie du monde*, ed. L. Nissim and S. Riva (Milan, 2004), 197–212; cf. above, 145 n. 104.

3   Ben-Tov, *Lutheran Humanists*, 93–95, 99; for other sixteenth-century historians who used Laonikos, see Pippidi, *Visions of the Ottoman World*, 45–46, 78–79, 94.

4   Cochrane, *Historians*, 85, 329, who reports that he lent it to Giovan Battista Egnazio, though the latter did not use it in his *De Origine Turcarum.*

of western inquiries regarding the Turks, through Sansovino (1564) and Belleforest (1575) to Leunclavius (1591).[5] But the work also continued to resonate among Greeks.

It is unclear to what extent Laonikos was used by Theodoros Spandounes (Spandugnino) who, in the early sixteenth century, wrote a brief and influential account of Ottoman history in Italian that he later expanded (the final version was in 1538). A second-generation Greek probably born in Venice, Spandounes claimed to be descended from the Kantakouzenoi and had family connections in many places of the empire. No specific debts to Laonikos have been identified, but in his conclusion on sources he mentions "Laonico Atheniense," whom he identifies as a secretary of Murad II. This was a false deduction probably made on the basis of the vividness of Laonikos's account of the sultan's battles. It is Spandounes who reports that Sigismondo Malatesta removed the remains of Plethon from Mistra to Rimini in 1464.[6]

Nikandros (Andronikos) of Kerkyra wrote a lively account of northwest Europe in the late 1540s that relayed much contemporary information, among it the wives of Henry VIII. But it is also likely that he borrowed some of Laonikos's terminology, categories of ethnographic and geographic analysis, and reports. Their relationship should be further investigated.[7]

Antonios Kalosynas, a doctor and scholar active in Toledo in the second half of the sixteenth century, is said to have written a

5   Cochrane, *Historians*, 335, and Zachariadou, Χρονικό, 22–26, for Sansovino; Heath, "Renaissance Scholars," 467, for Belleforest and Leunclavius; in general, C. Göllner, *Turcica: Die europäischen Turkendrücke des XVI. Jahrhunderts*, 2 vols. (Bucharest, 1961–68).

6   D. M. Nicol, *Theodore Spandounes: On the Origin of the Ottoman Emperors* (Cambridge, 1997); Laonikos is mentioned at 261 (Sathas) = 145 (Nicol); Plethon at 160 (Sathas) = 41 (Nicol).

7   See p. 70 above.

brief notice in Greek on the contribution to Greek letters made by the two Chalkokondylai brothers (or so he deems them), Nikolaos and Demetrios.[8] It is clear that he had no biographical information about the former (unlike the latter) beyond what one can infer from the *Histories*. Kalosynas assumed that Nikolaos had left Greece for the west, to escape Ottoman tyranny. As for the *Histories*, he comments that it was written in a Greek no less Attic than that of Thucydides (but the authorship of this note is in doubt; it may not be by Kalosynas at all).[9]

In the later sixteenth century, material from the *Histories* was recycled into two distinctive works of Greek historiography, both written in Italy (or in Italian-controlled lands). The first was a vernacular history of the sultans down to 1520, conventionally called the *Barberini Codex 111*. This relied on some of the Italian compilations mentioned above, especially the second edition of Sansovino (1571), through which it gained access to Laonikos.[10] The second is the expansion and elaboration of Sphrantzes's *Chronicle* by Makarios Melissourgos (aka Melissenos). Makarios was from the

8   The text is in C. Hopf, *Chroniques gréco-romaines inédites ou peu connues* (Berlin, 1873), 243–45; for Kalosynas, see Geanakoplos, *Greek Scholars*, 255.

9   According to Hopf, *Chroniques*, the text was copied by Darmarios, who, M. Philippides tells me, was associated with that family of industrious forgers, the Melissourgoi/Melissenoi. Moreover, Kampouroglous, *Οἱ Χαλκοκονδύλαι*, 112, notes that the manuscript actually attributes this *vita* of the Chalkokondylai to a certain "Ioannes of Kyzikos." The issue is not worth pursuing here, as the text has little of direct value anyway.

10   The major study is Zachariadou, *Χρονικό*, esp. 35–39; M. Philippides, *Byzantium, Europe, and the Early Ottoman Sultans, 1373–1513: An Anonymous Greek Chronicle of the Seveneenth Century (Codex Barberinus Graecus 111)* (New York, 1990), 14, suggests possible indirect use, either through a paraphrase (which is, however, not attested) or the material in Sansovino; for the complexity of the tradition, see D. Sakel, "A Probable Solution to the Problem of the Chronicle of the Turkish Sultans," in *Byzantine Narrative: Papers in Honour of Roger Scott*, ed. J. Burke et al. (Melbourne, 2006), 204–20.

Peloponnese, but fled after the battle of Lepanto to avoid arrest by the Ottoman authorities, because he had worked for the Spaniards; he wrote up his enhanced version of Sphrantzes at Naples.[11] This was long believed to be the original, allegedly fuller, version, but has since been exposed for what it was. Melissourgos invented a great deal of history and prosopographical connections in it, which have since had to be methodically undone (and he has been convicted of forging other documents).[12] If Laonikos, then, was the Father of (Neo-Herodotean) History, Melissenos was his counterpart Father of Lies. Among his inventions was the last name of the widow of Antonio I Acciaiuoli of Athens, who, Laonikos tells us, was a distant kinswoman who wanted to marry his father Georgios and rule Athens jointly with him. Well, Melissourgos endows her with a last name ... Melissene, thereby nicely linking his own family to that of the historian whose work he was cribbing.[13] Interestingly, it is now being proposed that he should be seen more as "a literary figure of the sixteenth century, rather than as an incorrigible counterfeiter" and his chronicle should be seen as "one of the most important Greek literary works of that dark era."[14]

The present study has aimed to shed light on the *Histories* of Laonikos as a narrative and work of scholarship. Now that it has been translated and we know the dates of its composition, we can begin to trace its influence on later views of the origins of the Ottoman Empire and the fall of "the empire of the Greeks."

11 I thank Marios Philippides for this information.

12 For his use of Laonikos, see R.-J. Loenertz, "Autour du *Chronicon maius* attribute à Georges Phrantzès," in *Byzantina et Franco-Graeca*, ed. R.-J. Loenertz and P. Schreiner (Rome, 1970), 18–26.

13 See p. 3 above.

14 Philippides and Hanak, *Siege and the Fall*, 152.

APPENDIX 1:
Laonikos of Athens was not Laonikos of Chania

Only one attempt with *prima facie* plausibility has been made to identify Laonikos with a person known from external sources (beyond Kyriacus's diary, that is). In 1927, E. Darkó, Laonikos's editor, reproposed that he was the same man as the priest Laonikos of Kydonia (i.e., Chania) who corresponded with the scribe, teacher, and pamphleteer Michael Apostoles, who was then based in "Gortyn" (i.e., Herakleion). This Cretan Laonikos seems to have been a former pupil of Apostoles and was the same priest Laonikos who pioneered Greek printing in Venice by publishing the *Batrachomyomachia* in 1486.[1] The second identification—that is, between Apostoles's Laonikos the priest and the scholar in Venice—may be sound, but the first is extremely circumstantial and faces formidable problems when the evidence is examined more closely. It is based on three weak associations (and some worthless ones that I will mention only in a note). First, the two men had the same name (assuming that it was the real name of either). Second, in one of the letters Apostoles discusses some philosophical problems associated with motion, which is a topic that

---

1 Darkó, "Neue Beiträge." Apostoles's letters to Laonikos are *epp.* 3, 16, 22 (Legrand) and *epp.* 51, 94, 95, 104 (Noiret; and he is mentioned in 99). For Laonikos the editor of the *Batrachomyomachia*, see Geanakoplos, *Greek Scholars*, 58–59, 107–8; the standard work on Apostoles is ibid. chap. 4; but see now R. Stefec, "Aus der literarischen Werkstatt des Michael Apostoles," *JÖB* 60 (2010): 129–48.

Laonikos the historian discusses in connection with the tides in England.[2] Third, Laonikos the priest of Chania may have been the same man who received Apostoles's letter "to Chalkokandeles."[3] I will discuss points two and three in order.

The philosophical problems of motion, generation, and corruption were extensively debated in the mid-fifteenth century. Plethon, Bessarion, and their many critics and interlocutors touched on this debate in their heated contentions over Plato and Aristotle. Indeed, just about every intellectual of this era had something to say about these issues, so it hardly narrows the field to our historian, who makes some comments in passing in a digression on the tides. The lecture-notes of Georgios Amiroutzes that have now been published are full of arguments on precisely the concepts that Apostoles raises in his "philosophical" letter to Laonikos the priest (and we know that Apostoles was on intimate terms with Amiroutzes).[4] But the main problem with Darkó's argument is that he disregarded the entire context of Apostoles's letter. Apostoles was not discussing the philosophical issues for the benefit of Laonikos the priest in the first place. If I have read his obscure prose correctly, what actually happened was that, along with a letter by Laonikos the priest, Apostoles had received an anonymous letter that contained thoughts on the issue of generation and corruption. Apostoles suspected that the letter was by

2   Apostoles, *ep.* 94 (Noiret); cf. *Hist.* 2.41–43.

3   Apostoles, *ep.* 40 (Legrand). Worthless associations include that Laonikos the historian took Thucydides as a model, while Apostoles, *ep.* 106 (Noiret), cites Demosthenes and Thucydides as models of style in writing to a certain Manuel of Adramyttion: Darkó, "Neue Beiträge," 279–80; also, that living on Crete helped Laonikos the historian gather information on Venice and infused his work with a "Renaissance" spirit: Nicoloudis, *Laonikos*, 54–55.

4   Monfasani, *George Amiroutzes*, for the "tractates." A. Frangedaki, "On Fifteenth-Century Cryptochristianity: A Letter to George Amoiroutzes from Michael Apostolis," *BMGS* 9 (1984–85): 221–24, for Apostoles and Amiroutzes.

a mutual friend, Troïlos, but because he disagreed with its contents he decided to treat it as if it were really by someone else who
was pretending, albeit poorly, to be Troïlos, in order to win praise
from Apostoles. Apostoles refuted the thesis of this anonymous
writer, presumably expecting that Laonikos would know him and
pass his response along. In other words, the "philosophy" in question was not primarily (or at all) addressed to Laonikos. Apostoles
does not impute views on this topic to Laonikos the priest, only to
the anonymous third party. In a follow-up letter, Apostoles asked
Laonikos to tell that person to stop taking on matters that were
beyond his ability.[5]

It must also be noted that the philosophical question at issue
in Apostoles's correspondence was not the same as in Laonikos
the historian's digression. The motions debated by Apostoles and
his correspondent were those from non-being into being and the
reverse, and the identity of "corruption" (*alloiôsis*) within that
dynamic. While Laonikos the historian mentions the comple-
mentary processes of "birth and growth" versus "decline and fall"
at the end of his digression, the two types of motion that he mostly
discusses concern physical bodies—water, in this case. He never
raises the question of coming-into- and going-out-of-being. His
discussion is explicitly about things already "in being" (τοῖς τῇδε
οὖσι). All this, I believe, removes the second association between
the two Laonikoi, which was weak to begin with.

Moving to the third pillar of Darkó's argument, there is no
reason to identify Apostoles's "Laonikos" with his correspondent Chalkokondyles. There is no thematic relationship between
the one letter to him and the seven to Laonikos. Darkó regarded
the identification as obvious, because Apostoles would not have
sent a friendly letter to Demetrios Chalkokondyles (given their

5   Apostoles, *ep.* 95 (Noiret).

clash in debate about Plato), and allegedly we know no other Chalkokondylai.[6] But Apostoles's attack on Demetrios took place in 1467,[7] and his letter to this Chalkokondyles, which is about Hermes and friendship, may have been sent before or after. They could have patched things up, or Apostoles might have been trying to do so (he may have lived into the 1480s; Demetrios died in 1511).[8] Moreover, *pace* Darkó, Apostoles's letter to Chalkokondyles does not make it obvious that the recipient had briefly been a student of Apostoles (which, if true, would rule out Demetrios Chalkokondyles as its recipient). Finally, it is important that Apostoles addressed the two men by different names. His Laonikos was apparently not a Chalkokondyles, and vice versa. This cuts against Darkó's theory.

Rudolf Stefec, who has written a series of studies on Apostoles, has recently shown that this letter was, in fact, sent to Demetrios Chalkokondyles, and he also rejects Darkó's identification of the two Laonikoi.[9] (He has also kindly informed me that he intends to argue in a future publication that Apostoles's Laonikos was the protopappas Nikolaos Kabbadatos, who had nothing to do with Laonikos the historian.)

Conversely, Darkó's thesis faces many problems. Laonikos the historian was the scion of the most illustrious Greek family of Athens, the most illustrious city in the humanist circles in which Apostoles moved. One would have expected Apostoles to allude to that fame in the seven letters in question, or call him by his full name. But let us not rely on arguments from silence. In a

---

6 In fact, we do: see Necipoğlu, *Byzantium*, 229.

7 Geanakoplos, *Greek Scholars*, 91–92.

8 So G. Cammelli, *Demetrio Calcondila*, vol. 2 of *I dotti bizantini e le origini dell'umanesimo* (Florence, 1954), 24–25.

9 Stefec, "Aus der literarischen Werkstatt," 134 and n. 36.

passage that has been swept under the rug by proponents of the
Cretan thesis, Apostoles states directly and unambiguously that
the πατρὶς of Laonikos the priest was Kydonia,[10] hardly the thing
to say to Laonikos the historian of Athens, in a letter negotiating
over a salary at that. For example, Demetrios was always regarded
as "the Athenian" in Italian humanist circles, even though he had
left Athens when he was twelve (at the latest). That origin simply had too much cachet. Our historian Laonikos called himself
"the Athenian" in the only two places where we know he wrote
his name, at the beginning of his *Histories* and in his copy of
Herodotos. Surely Apostoles would not have transferred his *patris*
to Kydonia when he was trying to ask a favor from him.

In another letter (also a plaintive effort to improve his lot),
Apostoles pleads that his own πατρὶς had been taken by the Turks,
i.e., Constantinople.[11] This indicates that for him a *patris* was the
place of one's origin, rather than where one was making a living.
But it would have been a strange argument to make to Laonikos
the historian, especially after 1456, when Athens had also been
taken by the Turks. Given that Apostoles's Laonikos was publishing in Venice in 1486, this correspondence is certainly to be dated
after 1456, after the loss of Laonikos the historian's *patris* (Noiret
dated this correspondence to 1461–71, and Apostoles did not settle
at Herakleion long before 1455, anyway).[12] Why would Apostoles
not seek to evoke sympathy for himself by saying that Laonikos's
own *patris* had also suffered the same fate? Instead, he is writing in

10   Apostoles, *ep.* 3 (Legrand). Scholars who maintain that Apostoles's Laonikos
was not originally from Crete are extending to him the implications of the invoca-
tion of Zeus Xenios in Apostoles's *Letter to Chalkokondyles*, without even realizing
that they are doing so: Nicoloudis, *Laonikos*, 53; Zographopoulos, *Λαόνικος*, 43. See
below for what Apostoles meant by *patris*.

11   Apostoles, *ep.* 16 (Legrand).

12   Darkó, "Neue Beiträge," 281; Geanakoplos, *Greek Scholars*, 82.

this letter as if his addressee were a local who had not experienced such things.

Finally, if Laonikos the historian had became a priest on Crete, he would have done so under his Christian name, Nikolaos.

One more work remains to be discussed. Aslihan Akışık, who supports the identification of the two Laonikoi, has kindly alerted me to a short dialogue by Apostoles called *Menexenos* on the topic of the Trinity. One of its interlocutors is named Laonikos; in fact, he is the learned star of the piece, and the other two men, Menexenos and Diophanes, consult him to resolve their doubts on the question of the Trinity in favor of Christianity and against Islam. Other than its first line, the dialogue has nothing in common with Plato's *Menexenos*. The fictionalized format makes it hard to identify the interlocutors with historical individuals, but Laourdas, its editor, makes a good case that "Laonikos" is really Apostoles himself. He is said to be a learned Constantinopolitan who came to Crete from Thessaly in poverty after suffering captivity, facts that fit the life of Apostoles exactly and preclude an identification with Laonikos the historian, who was not a Constantinopolitan and twice proudly described himself as an Athenian. Laourdas also argues that the Laonikos of the dialogue is described in terms that Apostoles sometimes uses for himself in his letters. Moreover, the dialogue concerns a question that was widely debated at the time, and its pro-Christian and anti-Muslim stance does not correspond to the outlook of Laonikos the Athenian historian. We do not know why Apostoles chose to cast himself as Laonikos in this dialogue, or whether it was meant to allude also to his acquaintance of Chania, but there is no reason to think it had anything to do with our historian.

In sum, there is no good reason to identify Laonikos the Athenian with Laonikos of Chania.

APPENDIX 2:
Laonikos's Knowledge
of Fourteenth-Century Athenian History

On 15 March 1311, the Catalan Grand Company defeated Gautier de Brienne, Duke of Athens, at the battle of the Kephissos near Thebes, and took his duchy.[1] Laonikos, who describes the attacking force correctly as consisting of elements from both Spain and Italy, recounts the battle and concludes: "later each of them crossed over to Italy and returned home" (1.20: οὗτος μὲν οὖν ὕστερον ἐς Ἰταλίαν περαιούμενος ἐπ᾽ οἴκου ἐτράποντο ἕκαστος). Did he not know about the Catalan domination of his native city, which lasted to 1388? This "ignorance" has been imputed to him and called "quite puzzling . . . His error should be seen in the context of his apparently incomplete knowledge of the history of Athens."[2]

While Laonikos makes many errors and garbles chronology, especially in Book 1, I believe it is going too far to say that he did not know that the Catalans took over Athens in 1311. As it happens, he later explains that Nerio I had taken Athens "from the Celtiberians of Navarre, for the Iberians had held this city too after they conquered it" (4.56). This sentence simplifies a complicated

---

1 Some historians, following K. Setton, *The Papacy and the Levant, 1204–1571,* 4 vols. (Philadelphia, 1976–84), 1:441–42, believe that the battle should be relocated to Halmyros in Thessaly: D. M. Nicol, *Last Centuries of Byzantium 1261–1453* (Cambridge, 1993), 135.

2 Nicoloudis, *Laonikos,* 162 n. 41.

sequence of events. First, we must note that Laonikos's terminology for Spain is not always as precise as we would like.[3] He never uses the word Catalan, calling the Grand Company "Aragonese" instead, as Catalonia was under the crown of Aragon. By "Iberia" he means both the Iberian peninsula and the kingdom of Castile, so that there is some ambiguity as to whether Celtiberia (including Navarre) is a part of Iberia; usually it is not (2.32, 5.72; cf. 2.33). "Celtiberians" in Laonikos translates as "the French Spaniards," i.e., those who live between Castile and France. It is likely, then, that in the sentence quoted above about Nerio's conquest of Athens, the Celtiberians (Navarrese) are to be distinguished from the Iberians (Catalans; cf. 5.64 where Barcelona is a part of Iberia), but the matter remains unclear.

When Nerio intervened north of the Peloponnese, the Navarrese had taken Thebes from the Catalans and were at war with them. Nerio managed to acquire Thebes from the Navarrese and eventually took the lower city of Athens (ca. 1387) and its acropolis (1388) from the Catalans. Some historians suspect that Nerio had actually employed the Navarrese to displace the Catalans, but after his capture of Athens he fought against them (or their brethren) in the Peloponnese, where he was captured and eventually ransomed from them.[4] Laonikos's statement is, then, not fully accurate, but it is within the acceptable range of confusion that his knowledge of "distant" history permits, known as it was through oral sources.

Let us return to the problematic statement with which we began, namely that the Aragonese "later" returned home to (or via) Italy. The question is, how much later does Laonikos mean? At

3   Ditten, "Spanien und die Spanier"; Ducellier, "Peninsule ibérique"; Morfakidis, "Península ibérica."

4   K. M. Setton, *Athens in the Middle Ages* (London, 1975), IV 218–19, VI 233, 240–45; D. K. Giannakopoulos, Δουκάτο των Αθηνών: Η κυριαρχία των Acciaiuoli (Thessalonike, 2006), 80–83.

2.12, discussing the background of Louis Fadrique (vicar-general of the Aragonese king for the duchies of Athens and Neopatras, 1375–1382), Laonikos makes a similar statement. These Aragonese came from Italy to govern lands in Greece but "lost their rule not long thereafter (ὕστερον χρόνῳ οὐ πολλῷ διελθόντι), whereupon some of them went back to Italy, while others stayed there until they died." Laonikos's temporal designations are usually vague. I believe that in both passages (1.20 and 2.12) he is referring to the same event, namely, the departure of the surviving Catalans to their lands in Italy (and beyond) upon the collapse of their rule in Greece, in the 1370s and 80s. It is preferable to conclude that he awkwardly jumps ahead many decades at the end of 1.20 than that he did not know that the Catalans had ruled Athens.

APPENDIX 3:
Herodotean Expressions in Laonikos

The following list is not comprehensive. For a list of Thucydidean parallels, see F. Rödel, "Zur Sprache des Laonikos Chalkondyles und des Kritobulos aus Imbros," *Programm des königlichen humanistischen Gymnansiums Ingolstadt 1904–1905* (Munich, 1905), 12–34.

1. Military Narrative

Much of Laonikos's language for describing military conflicts is taken directly from Herodotos. The following sample passages contain most of the vocabulary and narrative templates that he uses:

Hdt. 1.127: Ἀστυάγης δὲ ὡς ἐπύθετο Κῦρον ταῦτα πρήσσοντα, πέμψας ἄγγελον ἐκάλεε αὐτόν... Ὡς δὲ οἱ Μῆδοι στρατευσάμενοι τοῖσι Πέρσῃσι συνέμισγον, οἱ μέν τινες αὐτῶν ἐμάχοντο.

Hdt. 1.68: ἤδη δέ σφι καὶ ἡ πολλὴ τῆς Πελοποννήσου ἦν κατεστραμμένη.

Hdt. 1.76: Kroisos εἷλε μὲν τῶν Πτερίων τὴν πόλιν καὶ ἠνδραποδίσατο, εἷλε δὲ τὰς περιοικίδας αὐτῆς πάσας (Laonikos uses this classical meaning of *perioikos*).

Hdt. 1.76: Κῦρος δὲ ἀγείρας τὸν ἑωυτοῦ στρατὸν καὶ παραλαβὼν τοὺς μεταξὺ οἰκέοντας πάντας ἠντιοῦτο Κροίσῳ. Πρὶν δὲ ἐξελαύνειν ὁρμῆσαι τὸν στρατόν, πέμψας κήρυκας ἐς τοὺς Ἴωνας ἐπειρᾶτό σφεας ἀπὸ Κροίσου ἀπιστάναι. Ἴωνες μέν νυν οὐκ ἐπείθοντο.

Hdt. 1.154: Ἐλάσας δὲ ἐπὶ τὰς Σάρδις ἐπολιόρκεε.

Hdt. 3.54: ἐπεξῆλθον οἵ τε ἐπίκουροι καὶ αὐτῶν Σαμίων συχνοί, δεξάμενοι δὲ τοὺς Λακεδαιμονίους ἐπ᾽ ὀλίγον χρόνον ἔφευγον ὀπίσω· οἱ δὲ ἐπισπόμενοι ἔκτεινον.

Hdt. 4.204: Τοὺς δὲ ἠνδραποδίσαντο [i.e., the Persians] τῶν Βαρκαίων, τούτους δὲ ἐκ τῆς Αἰγύπτου ἀνασπάστους ἐποίησαν παρὰ βασιλέα· βασιλεὺς δέ σφι Δαρεῖος ἔδωκε τῆς Βακτρίης χώρης κώμην ἐγκατοικῆσαι.

2. Laonikos as a Historian

His title is ἀποδείξεις ἱστοριῶν; cf. Hdt. 1.1: ἱστορίης ἀπόδεξις ἥδε.

πυνθάνομαι and ἀναπυνθάνομαι are common to both authors: cf. esp. *Hist.* 5.54: ἀναπυνθανόμενος εὗρον with Hdt. 5.57 ἀναπυνθανόμενος εὑρίσκω.

Uncertainty: *Hist.* 1.10: ὡς μὲν οὖν τούτων ἕκαστα ἔχει ἀληθείας, καὶ ἐφ᾽ ἃ δέῃ τούτων χωροῦντας πείθεσθαι ἄμεινον, οὐκ ἔχω ξυμβαλέσθαι ὡς ἀσφαλέστατα; 1.38: οὐκ ἂν δὴ ἔχω διεξιέναι; 2.46: οὐκ ἔχω δὲ τοῦτο συμβάλλεσθαι, ὡς εἴη ἀληθές, οὐ δυνάμενος ἐξευρεῖν διαπυνθανομένῳ; 5.15: οὐκ ἂν εἰδείην σαφῶς ἰσχυρίζεσθαι; 5.50: οὐκ ἔχω δέ, ὅπῃ τοῦτο ἀληθὲς εἶναι συμβάλλωμαι (the same expressions also in 1.29, 6.18, etc.). As for Herodotos, his most common phrases are οὐκ ἔχω εἰπεῖν (1.49, 7.153), οὐκ ἔχω ἀτρεκέως εἰπεῖν (1.57, 1.172, 2.103, 7.60, etc.), or οὐκ ἔχω φράσαι (7.26). It seems that Laonikos has kept the verbs and switched ἀτρεκέως with ἀσφαλῶς or the like. As for συμβάλλομαι, see Hdt. 7.10: ἐγὼ δὲ οὐδεμιῇ σοφίῃ οἰκηίῃ αὐτὸς ταῦτα συμβάλλομαι, and 7.184: ὡς ἐγὼ συμβαλλόμενος εὑρίσκω (also 7.187, 8.30).

At *Hist.* 3.31 (οὔτε ἄλλου τινὸς ἐπυθόμην τῶν παλαιοτέρων διεξιόντος, οὔτ᾽ ἂν ἔχοιμι πάντῃ ὡς ἀληθῆ διασημήνασθαι), Laonikos combines the above language with that of Hdt. 2.29: ἄλλου δὲ οὐδενὸς οὐδὲν ἐδυνάμην πυθέσθαι (cf. 7.60).

Enough said about that: Hist. 3.29: καὶ περὶ μὲν τούτων ταύτῃ ἐπὶ τοσοῦτον εἰρήσθω; Hdt. 6.55: καὶ ταῦτα μέν νυν περὶ τούτων εἰρήσθω (also 1.92, 2.34, 2.76, 3.113, 4.15, 4.36, 4.45, 4.127, 4.199, 6.55).

Refusal to divulge information. Hist. 5.54: ὧν δὴ ἕνα τε καὶ δύο ἀναπυνθανόμενος εὗρον, καὶ ἐξέμαθον τό τε γένος αὐτῶν καὶ τοὺς πατέρας· ἀλλ᾽ οὐκ ἐξοίσω ἐς τοὺς πολλοὺς τοὔνομα διασημήνας; 10.43: διενεχθέντα ἐπὶ τρόπῳ, ὃν παραλιπεῖν ἄξιον; Hdt. 1.51: τοῦ ἐπιστάμενος τὸ οὔνομα οὐκ ἐπιμνήσομαι; 2.47: ἐμοὶ μέντοι ἐπισταμένῳ οὐκ εὐπρεπέστερός ἐστι λέγεσθαι. 2.123: τῶν ἐγὼ εἰδὼς τὰ οὐνόματα οὐ γράφω; cf. also 2.171, 4.43.

Let us return to where we left off. Hist. 1.22: ἐπάνειμι δὲ ἐπ᾽ ἐκεῖνο τοῦ λόγου, ὅθεν μοι ἐξέλιπε; 2.43: ἐπάνειμι δὲ ἐπ᾽ ἐκεῖνα τῆς ἀφηγήσεως, ὅθεν ταύτῃ ἀπετραπόμεθα; 4.60: τούτων μὲν πέρι ἐς τοσοῦτον ἐπιμνησάμενος, ἐπάνειμι δή . . . ; 5.79: ἐπάνειμι δέ, ὅθεν τὴν ἐκβολὴν τοῦ λόγου ἐποιησάμην, ἄχρι τοσοῦτον διενεχθείς; 6.30: ἐπάνειμι δὲ ἐπὶ τὸν πρότερον λόγον; 8.34: μέτειμι δὲ ἐφ᾽ οὗ ἦια λέξων ἐφεξῆς λόγου; 8.65: εἶμι δὲ ἐπ᾽ ἐκεῖνο τοῦ λόγου, ὅθεν ἐπὶ τοσοῦτον ἐτραπόμην, ἐς τοσοῦτον διεξιὼν τὸν λόγον; 10.32 ἐπάνειμι δὲ ἐπ᾽ ἐκεῖνο τοῦ λόγου, ᾗ πρότερόν μοι ἐδεδήλωτο; Hdt. 7.137: ἐπάνειμι δὲ ἐπὶ τὸν πρότερον λόγον; 4.82 τοῦτο μέν νυν τοιοῦτό ἐστι, ἀναβήσομαι δὲ ἐς τὸν κατ᾽ ἀρχὰς ἦια λέξων λόγον.

"Fatalism": Hist. 8.43: ἀλλ᾽ ἐχρῆν μὲν ταῦτα, τύχῃ οὐκ ἀγαθῇ φερόμενα, ταῦτ᾽ ἄρα ἴσχειν σφίσι τὴν τελευτήν, καὶ οὕτω ἀποβήσεσθαι ἐς τὸ μηδὲν εἶναι γενόμενα; Hdt. 2.161: ἐπεὶ δέ οἱ ἔδεε κακῶς γενέσθαι (also 4.79, 5.92, 6.64, 9.109), and χρῆ / δεῖ γενέσθαι constructions: Hdt. 1.8, 1.161, 6.135.

3. Ethnography and Geography

The following citations include both exact parallels and loose comparisons, which show that Laonikos relied on Herodotos's terminology, not necessarily a specific passage in each instance. Ditten,

"Laonikos Chalkokondyles und die Sprache der Rumänen," 101–4, has shown that Laonikos's vocabulary for discussing foreign lanaguages is from Herodotos.

Hist. 1.34 (and passim): οἱ κατὰ τὴν Ἀσίαν Σκύθαι τε οἱ νομάδες; Hdt. 4.11: Σκύθας τοὺς νομάδας οἰκέοντας ἐν τῇ Ἀσίῃ.

Hist. 1.29 on the Slavs: γένος δὲ ἐκεῖνο τῶν Ἰλλυριῶν μέγα τε καὶ ἐπὶ πλεῖστον διῆκον τοῦ Ἰονίου πελάγους ἔστε ἐπὶ Ἐνετούς; and 2.38 on the British: γένος δὲ ἐνοικεῖ τὴν νῆσον πολύ τε καὶ ἄλκιμον; Hdt. 1.201 on the Massagetai: τὸ δὲ ἔθνος τοῦτο καὶ μέγα λέγεται εἶναι καὶ ἄλκιμον, οἰκημένον δὲ πρὸς ἠῶ τε καὶ ἡλίου ἀνατολάς.

Hist. 1.29 on the Slavic nations: φωνῇ τε γὰρ ἀμφότεροι τῇ αὐτῇ χρῶνται ἔτι καὶ νῦν, καὶ ἤθεσι τοῖς αὐτοῖς καὶ διαίτῃ; Hdt. 4.109: Βουδῖνοι δὲ οὐ τῇ αὐτῇ γλώσσῃ χρέωνται καὶ Γελωνοί, οὐδὲ δίαιτα ἡ αὐτή. See also the terms of the debate that follows each statement.

Hist. 1.29: οἶδά τε αὐτὸς ἐπιστάμενος, ἀπὸ πολλῶν τεκμαιρόμενος, καὶ πολλῶν δὴ ἀκήκοα; Hdt. 2.52: ὡς ἐγὼ ἐν Δωδώνῃ οἶδα ἀκούσας.

Hist. 1.38 on the question of whether two people are in fact the same: εἰ δέοι ταύτῃ τεκμαιρόμενον λέγειν; Hdt. 1.57: εἰ δὲ χρεόν ἐστι τεκμαιρόμενον λέγειν (used twice), in connection with the same type of question.

Hist. 1.38–39 on the extreme north: ἔστε ἐπὶ χώραν τὴν διὰ τὸ ψῦχος ἀοίκητον … τὰ ἐκεῖ τῆς οἰκουμένης σχεδόν τι ἀοίκητα ἀφικέσθαι; Hdt. 4.31 on the same parts of the world: διὰ τὸν χειμῶνα τοῦτον ἐόντα τοιοῦτον ἀνοίκητα τὰ πρὸς βορέην ἐστὶ τῆς ἠπείρου ταύτης. But Laonikos's proximate source is likely to be pseudo-Aristotle's *Meteorology* or Plethon; see the second section of chap. 3.

Hist. 2.16 on the Germans: ὡς εἰ ταὐτὸ φρονοίη, καὶ ὑφ᾽ ἑνὶ ἄρχοντι ἡγεμόνι, ἀμάχητόν τε ἂν εἴη καὶ πολλῷ κράτιστον; Hdt.

5.3 on the Thracians: εἰ δὲ ὑπ' ἑνὸς ἄρχοιτο ἢ φρονέοι κατὰ τὠυτό, ἄμαχόν τ' ἂν εἴη καὶ πολλῷ κράτιστον πάντων ἐθνέων.

Hist. 2.16 on the Germans: ὑγιεινότατον δὲ ὄν; Hdt. 4.187 on the Libyans: εἰσὶ γὰρ ὡς ἀληθέως οἱ Λίβυες ἀνθρώπων πάντων ὑγιηρότατοι τῶν ἡμεῖς ἴδμεν.

Hist. 2.17 on the language of the Hungarians: φωνῇ δὲ χρῶνται οὐδαμῇ παραπλησίᾳ ἑτέρῳ τινὶ τῶν γενῶν; Hdt. 4.183: γλῶσσαν δὲ οὐδεμιῇ ἄλλῃ παρομοίην νενομίκασι.

Hist. 2.17 on the Hungarians: οἴονται δέ τινες τούτους οἱ μὲν Γέτας γενέσθαι τὸ παλαιόν; Hdt. 1.201: εἰσὶ δὲ οἵτινες καὶ Σκυθικὸν λέγουσι τοῦτο τὸ ἔθνος εἶναι.

Hist. 2.33 on the Muslims of Granada: τὸ δὲ γένος τοῦτο Λιβύων γλώττῃ μὲν διαχρῆται τῇ Ἀραβικῇ, καὶ ἤθεσι δὲ καὶ θρησκείᾳ τῇ Μεχμέτεω, ἐσθῆτι δὲ τοῦτο μὲν βαρβαρικῇ, τοῦτο δ' αὖ καὶ Ἰβηρικῇ; Hdt. 4.108: εἰσὶ γὰρ οἱ Γελωνοὶ τὸ ἀρχαῖον Ἕλληνες ... καὶ γλώσσῃ τὰ μὲν Σκυθικῇ, τὰ δὲ Ἑλληνικῇ χρέωνται.

Hist. 3.11 on the people of the Caspian Sea region, after a description of that Sea: ἔθνη πολλά τε καὶ ἄλκιμα; Hdt. 1.203 on the people of the Caucasus after a description of the Caspian Sea: ἔθνεα δὲ ἀνθρώπων πολλὰ καὶ παντοῖα.

4. Other Borrowed Expressions

Hist. 1.1: μηδὲν αὐτῶν ἀκλεῶς ἔχειν; Hdt. 1.1: μήτε ἀκλεᾶ γένηται.

1.4: ἐπὶ τὸ μνήμης μακρότατον; Hdt. 4.16.

1.7: ἐπὶ ξυροῦ ἀκμῆς; Hdt. 6.11.

1.34: ὡς ἤδη ἡ ἠὼς ὑπέφαινε (and passim); Hdt. 9.47.

1.45: ἀλλὰ καὶ τὸν παῖδα συνέπαινον γενέσθαι ἐς ταῦτα; Hdt. 3.119, a similar expression, in a similar context, i.e., a plot.

2.14, 3.13: ἀνδρὶ εὐζώνῳ as a unit of travel; Hdt. 1.72, 1.104, and 2.34.

2.28: μεγάλη χειρί, a large army (also 3.64, 6.34, 9.96; cf. 3.54 for ὀλίγη χειρί); Hdt. 1.74, 5.72, 7.157.

2.35: ὑφίεντο μέντοι τῆς ἀγνωμοσύνης; Hdt. 9.4.

2.35: τοῖς ἐν τῇ πόλει προδοσίαν συνθέμενος, εἷλεν ἐπιβουλῇ; Hdt. 6.88.

2.36: ἐς τὸ ἔσχατον τοῦ κακοῦ ἀφιγμένοι; Hdt. 1.22.

5.15: for the three half-talents as a unit for weight, cf. Hdt. 1.50.

5.69: ὑπεξέσχεν is from Hdt 5.72, 6.74, 8.132.

7.55: περὶ πλήθουσαν ἀγορὰν for late in the morning (also 8.22); Hdt. 1.173: μέχρι ὅτεο πληθώρης ἀγορῆς.

8.43: ἐς τὸ μηδέν ("comes to nothing"); Hdt. 1.32 ("counts for nothing").

8.58: τὰ στρατεύματα αὐτῷ δρασμῷ τε ἐπεχείρει; Hdt. 6.70.

8.65: for ἀπέχρη . . . ἡσυχίαν ἄγειν; Hdt. 1.66, 6.137, 9.79.

9.7: ἐκλελοιπότες γὰρ οἱ ἐν τῇ πόλει; Hdt. 8.50.

9.85: συμπροπέμποντι; Hdt. 9.1.

9.104: ἐν θαύματι ἐνσχεθείς; Hdt. 7.128, 9.37.

10.30: χαλεπῶς ἐλαμβάνετο; Hdt. 2.121δ.

APPENDIX 4:

The Known History of Laur. 70.6
between 1318 and 1480

I include here only facts (or what are asserted by scholars as facts) about the manuscript's locations, owners, and readers between 1318–1480, not hypotheses about how it moved from place to place, all of which are conjectural, as far as I can tell.[1] Not all of these facts may withstand further scrutiny by paleographers (which I am not). The manuscript tradition of Herodotos is famously complex.

1318, MARCH (THESSALONIKE): Laur. 70.6, containing the whole of Herodotos and nothing else, is produced by Nikolaos Triklines. The name is a demotic way of spelling Triklinios,[2] so he is assumed to be a relative of Demetrios Triklinios, possibly his brother.[3] We do not know with certainty where he copied this manuscript, but Thessalonike is most likely.

---

1   The standard citation is A. Turyn, *The Dated Greek Manuscripts of the Thirteenth and Fourteenth Centuries in the Libraries of Italy* (Urbana, 1972), 1:132–33, which, however, contains only a fraction of the following historical information.

2   Hemmerdinger, *Manuscrits d'Hérodote*, 106. Nikolaos's subscription is in H. Stein, *Herodoti Historiae* (Berlin, 1869), 1:xii.

3   O. Smith, "Tricliniana II," *ClMed* 43 (1992): 188–89. For some of his other productions, see Bianconi, *Tessalonica*, 122–41, 251.

1372, JUNE (ASTROS, BY NAUPLION, PELOPONNESE): Laur. 70.6 is the original from which Par. gr. 1634, also containing only Herodotos, is copied by the priest Konstantinos of Olympia.[4]

1420S (CONSTANTINOPLE): De Gregorio has hypothesized that Laur. 70.6 was used by Georgios Chrysokokkes.[5]

1436, MAY (MISTRA, PELOPONNESE): Laur. 70.6 is the original from which Marc. gr. 365 is copied by Bessarion himself (it also contains Thucydides, Xenophon, and a bit of Diogenes Laertios).[6]

?–1452? (MISTRA, PELOPONNESE): Bianconi has demonstrated that folios 164r–165v were restored by the hand of Plethon himself.[7] Hemmerdinger had confused the issue by attributing *all* corrections in Laur. 70.6, including 164r–165v and others, to Laonikos Chalkokondyles, based on his subscription at 340v. He dated these corrections to 1447, because that was when Kyriacus met Laonikos at Mistra (though he knew that Laonikos was a teenager then). Hemmerdinger thereby contradicted himself, because he also found that some of the corrections made by "Laonikos" were copied into Marc. gr. 365, made in 1436 by Bessarion.[8] But it is likely that many hands altered or corrected Laur. 70.6 in different ways. We need a complete list of these corrections and alterations and separate arguments about each type. In responding to Hemmerdinger, Bianconi confused Laonikos with his cousin

4   His subscription in Stein, *Herodoti Historiae*, 1:xvii.

5   G. De Gregorio, "L'Erodoto di Palla Strozzi (cod. Vat. Urb. gr. 88)," *BollClass* 23 (2002): 47–49; see Bianconi, *Tessalonica*, 140–41.

6   Hemmerdinger, *Les manuscrits d'Hérodote*, 109; for the creation of Bessarion's library over the years, see E. Mioni, "La formazione della biblioteca greca di Bessarione," in *Bessarione e l'umanesimo* (Naples, 1994), 231.

7   Bianconi, *Tessalonica*, 138–39; and idem, "La biblioteca di Cora tra Massimo Planude e Niceforo Gregora: Una questione di mani," *Segno e Testo* 3 (2005): 403–5.

8   Hemmerdinger, *Manuscrits d'Hérodote*, 119. Hemmerdinger made it especially difficult to follow his arguments in the ms. by citing the corrections not by folio number but by passage in Herodotos.

Demetrios, who was not, as far as we know, associated with this book. Pagani has recently argued that Plethon made alterations to his texts of Plato in order to bring the philosophy in line with his own thinking and has suggested that Plethon may have made similar erasures to Laur. 70.6, for example at 33r.[9]

CA. 1450–? (MISTRA? AND?): Laonikos Chalkokondyles comes into possession of Laur. 70.6; he was almost certainly given it by Plethon. He adds his subscription at 340v.[10] If this book was used by Valla in Rome (see below), then Laonikos did not have it for long; otherwise, which is more likely (as argued above), Laonikos had it while he was composing his *Histories* in the 1450s and 60s, at most until 1480, when it appears in Rome (see also below).

1450S (ROME?): Alberti hypothesized that Laur. 70.6 was used by Lorenzo Valla, when he made his Latin translation of Herodotos. Valla primarily relied on other mss. and it is not absolutely certain that he used Laur. 70.6, rather than another manuscript in its line of transmission.[11] Moreover, Fryde proposed that "insertions of missing Greek passages" at 122v, 125r, and 129r may have been made by Valla, along with the conversion into the western "1318" format of the Byzantine date given at the end by the

9 F. Pagani, "*Damnata verba:* Censure di Pletone in alcuni codici platonici," *BZ* 102 (2009): 201.

10 The text of his subscription is in Turyn, *Byzantine Manuscript Tradition*, 230 n. 212a; idem, *Dated Greek Manuscripts*, 1:132; for a translation, see the fourth section of chap. 2.

11 G. B. Alberti, "Il codice Laurenziano Greco LXX,6 e la traduzione latina di Erodoto di Lorenzo Valla," *Maia* 11 (1959): 315–19, based on the fact that it was in Rome in 1480 (see below) and that traces of the "Florentine" transmission can be detected in Valla's translation; for the other mss. he used, see idem, "Autografi greci di Lorenzo Valla nel codice Vaticano greco 122," *Italia medioevale e umanistica* 3 (1960): 287–90. S. Pagliaroli, *L'Erodoto del Valla* (Messina, 2006), 107 n. 1, regards Alberti's thesis about Laur. 70.6 as only a hypothesis. For Valla as a translator, focusing on his Thucydides, see M. Pade, "Valla's Thucydides: Theory and Practice in a Renaissance Translation," *ClMed* 36 (1985): 275–301.

copyist Nikolaos Triklines (at 341r., facing Triklines's own sub-scription).[12] I have not found further discussion of these alleged "insertions." It is not clear whether Fryde means the marginal notations on those folio pages. Paleographical analysis should be able to clarify this, as we know the hands of almost everyone involved in the history of this manuscript.

1480 (ROME): Laur. 70.6 was the original from which Demetrios Raoul Kabakes copied Vat. gr. 1359 (containing only Herodotos); his subscription specifies both the date and the place.[13] We do not know how Laur. 70.6 ended up at Florence after that.

12   Fryde, *Humanism and Renaissance Historiography*, 91.

13   Alberti, "Codice Laurenziano Greco LXX,6"; for the subscription, see Stein, *Herodoti Historiae*, 1:xvii.

Abbreviations

ArchOtt	*Archivum Ottomanicum*
AVen	*Archivio veneto*
BAcBelg	*Bulletin de la Classe des lettres et des sciences morales et politiques,* Académie royale de Belgique
BBulg	*Byzantinobulgarica*
BMGS	*Byzantine and Modern Greek Studies*
BollClass	*Bollettino dei classici*
BSl	*Byzantinoslavica*
BSOAS	*Bulletin of the School of Oriental and African Studies*
ByzF	*Byzantinische Forschungen*
BZ	*Byzantinische Zeitschrift*
ClMed	*Classica et mediaevalia*
DOP	*Dumbarton Oaks Papers*
EI²	*Encyclopaedia of Islam,* 2nd ed. (Leiden–London, 1960–)
GRBS	*Greek, Roman, and Byzantine Studies*
JEChrSt	*Journal of Early Christian Studies*
JHS	*Journal of Hellenic Studies*
JÖB	*Jahrbuch der Österreichischen Byzantinistik*
LXX	Septuagint
Νέος Ἑλλ.	*Νέος Ἑλληνομνήμων*
PG	Patrologiae cursus completus, Series graeca, ed. J.-P. Migne (Paris, 1857–66)
REG	*Revue des études grecques*
RQ	*Römische Quartalschrift für christliche Altertumskunde und für Kirchengeschichte*
StVen	*Studi veneziani*

Bibliography

Primary Sources Cited

The following section includes only post-classical sources cited in the notes or those not found in standard collections. "Edited by" means only that the publication contains the original text, not necessarily a critical edition (though that may be the case). Byzantine authors are listed by last name, unless they are known by their first name. The bibliography aims to explain my citations, not to give a comprehensive or up-to-date list of editions and translations. Texts that are cited from the PG in only one footnote are not included here. Translations are listed only for texts cited often.

Ahmedi. *İskendername*. Partially edited and translated by K. Sılay. "Ahmedi's History of the Ottoman Dynasty." *Journal of Turkish Studies* 16 (1992): 129–200.

Akropolites, Georgios. *Against the Latins*. Edited by A. Heisenberg. Revised by P. Wirth. *Georgii Acropolitae opera*. Vol. 2. Stuttgart, 1978.

Anonymous Bulgarian Chronicle. Edited and translated by D. Nastase. "La version slave de la Chronique byzantine perdue de Jean Chortasmenos (début du XVᵉ siècle)." *Études byzantines et post-byzantines* 5 (2006): 321–63; translation by K. Petkov. In *The Voices of Medieval Bulgaria, Seventh-Fifteenth Century: The Records of a Bygone Culture*, 456–64 (no. 211). Leiden, 2008.

Anonymous. *Address to the Council of Florence*. Edited by S. P. Lambros. In *Παλαιολόγεια καὶ Πελοποννησιακά*, 1:3–14. Athens, 1912–23.

Apostoles, Michael. *Letters*. Edited by E. Legrand. In *Bibliographie hellénique*, 2:233–59. Paris, 1885; and edited by H. Noiret. *Lettres inédits de Michel Apostolis*. Paris, 1889.

———. *Menexenos*. Edited by B. Laourdas. "Κρητικά Παλαιογραφικά 17: Μιχαήλ Αποστόλη, *Μενέξενος*." *Κρητικά Χρονικά* 6 (1952): 51–58.

Argyropoulos, Ioannes. *Monodia for Ioannes VIII Palaiologos*, and other works. Edited by S. Lambros. Ἀργυροπούλεια. Athens, 1910.

Aşıkpaşazade. German translation by R. F. Kreutel. *Vom Hirtenzelt zur hohen Pforte: Frühzeit und Aufstieg des Osmanenreiches nach der Chronik "Denkwürdigkeiten und Zeitläufte des Hauses Osman" vom Derwisch Ahmed, genannt 'Asik-Pasa-Sohn*. Graz, 1959; translation of the sections down to Murad I by E. A. Zachariadou. Ἱστορία καὶ θρύλοι τῶν παλαιῶν σουλτάνων, *1300–1400*. Athens, 1991.

Bessarion. *Address to the despot Konstantinos*. Edited by S. P. Lambros. In Παλαιολόγεια καὶ Πελοποννησιακά, 4:32–45. Athens, 1930.

———. *Encomium for Trebizond*. Edited by O. Lampsides. "Ὁ «εἰς Τραπεζοῦντα» λόγος τοῦ Βησσαρίωνος." *Ἀρχεῖον Πόντου* 39 (1984): 3–75.

Bruni, Leonardo. *Constitution of the Florentines*. Edited by A. Moulakis. "Leonardo Bruni's Constitution of Florence." *Rinascimento* 26 (1986): 141–90; translation by G. Griffiths, J. Hankins, and D. Thompson. In *The Humanism of Leonardo Bruni*, 171–74. New York, 1987; edited and translated by P. Viti. In *Leonardo Bruni: Opere letterarie e politiche*, 771–87. Turin, 1996.

Chalkokondyles, Laonikos. *Histories*. Edited by E. Darkó. *Laonici Chalcocandylae Historiarum demonstrationes*. 2 vols. Budapest, 1922–23; English translation by A. Kaldellis. *Laonikos Chalkokondyles: The Histories*. 2 vols. Washington, D.C., 2014.

Chrysoloras, Manuel. *Address to Manuel II*. Edited by C. G. Patrinelis and D. Z. Sofianos. Μανουὴλ Χρυσολωρᾶ Λόγος πρὸς τὸν αὐτοκράτορα Μανουὴλ Βʹ Παλαιολόγο. Athens, 2001.

Daphnopates, Theodoros. *Letters*. Edited by J. Darrouzès and L. G. Westerink. *Théodore Daphnopatès: Correspondance*. Paris, 1978.

Doukas. *History*. Edited and translated by V. Grecu. *Istoria Turco-Bizantina*. Bucharest, 1958; translation by H. Magoulias. *Decline and Fall of Byzantium to the Ottoman Turks, by Doukas*. Detroit, 1975.

Enveri. *Düsturname* (section on Umur Beg). Edited and translated by
   I. Mélikoff-Sayar. *Le Destan d'Umur Pacha*. Paris, 1954.

Eustathios of Thessalonike. *Commentary on Dionysios Periegetes*. Edited by
   C. Müller. In *Geographi Graeci Minores*, 2:201–407. Paris, 1861.

Ioannes VIII Palaiologos. *Chrysoboulla regarding the Florentines*. Edited by
   S. P. Lambros. In Παλαιολόγεια καὶ Πελοποννησιακά, 3:334–52. Athens,
   1926.

Isidoros of Kiev. *Panegyric for Manuel II and Ioannes VIII*. Edited by S. P.
   Lambros. In Παλαιολόγεια καὶ Πελοποννησιακά, 3:132–99. Athens, 1926.

Kanaboutzes, Ioannes. *Commentary on Dionysios of Halikarnassos*. Edited
   by M. Lehnerdt. *Ioannis Canabutzae magistri ad principem Aeni et
   Samothraces in Dionysium Halicarnasensem Commentarius*. Leipzig, 1890.

Khwandamir. Translated by W. M. Thackston. *Habibu's-siyar, Tome three:
   The Reign of the Mongol and the Turk*. 2 vols. Cambridge, MA, 1994.

Kinnamos, Ioannes. *History*. PG 133.

Komnene, Anna. *Alexiad*. Edited by D. R. Reinsch and A. Kambylis. *Annae
   Comnenae Alexias*. Berlin, 2001.

Kritoboulos. *History*. Edited by D. R. Reinsch. *Critobuli Imbriotae Historiae*.
   Berlin and New York, 1983; translation by C. T. Riggs. *History of Mehmed
   the Conqueror*. Princeton, 1954.

Kydones, Demetrios. *Apologia for His Faith*. Edited by G. Mercati. In *Notizie
   di Procoro e Demetrio Cidone, Manuele Caleca e Teodoro Meliteniota*, 359–
   437. Vatican City, 1931.

———. *Letters*. Edited by R.-J. Loenertz. *Démétrius Cydonès: Correspondance*.
   2 vols. Vatican City, 1956–60.

Kyriacus of Ancona. *Later Travels*. Edited and translated by E. D. Bodnar
   (with C. Foss). *Cyriac of Ancona: Later Travels*. Cambridge, MA, 2003.

———. *On the Order of the Months of the Year*. Edited by S. P. Lampros. In
   Παλαιολόγεια καὶ Πελοποννησιακά, 4:96–98. Athens, 1930.

Manuel II Palaiologos. *Dialogue with a Persian*. Edited by E. Trapp. *Manuel
   II. Palaiologos: Dialoge mit einem "Perser."* Vienna, 1966.

———. *Funeral Oration for his Brother Theodoros*. Edited and translated by
   J. Chrysostomides. *Manuel II Palaeologus: Funeral Oration on his Brother
   Theodore*. Thessalonike, 1985.

Melissourgos (Melissenos), Makarios. *Chronicle of Pseudo-Sphrantzes*. Edited
   by I. Bekker. *Georgius Phrantzes: Chronicon Maius*. Bonn, 1828.

Menandros Rhetor. *Discourses*. Edited and translated by D. A. Russell and N. G. Wilson. *Menander Rhetor*. Oxford, 1981.

Metochites, Theodoros. *On Character or on High Culture*. Edited and translated by I. Polemis. Θεόδωρος Μετοχίτης: Ἠθικὸς ἢ περὶ παιδείας. Athens, 1995.

———. *Moral Essays*. Edited by M. C. G. Müller and M. T. Kiessling. *Theodori Metochitae Miscellanea philosophica et historica*. Leipzig, 1821.

———. *On Ancient Authors and Philosophy*, ed. and trans. K. Hult Göteborg, 2002.

———. *Second Imperial Oration*. Edited and and translated by I. Polemis. Θεόδωρος Μετοχίτης: Οἱ δύο βασιλικοὶ λόγοι. Athens, 2007.

Nikandros. *Journeys*. Edited by J.-A. de Foucault. *Nicandre de Corcyre: Voyages*. Paris, 1962.

Philotheos Kokkinos. *On the Fall of Herakleia*. Edited by V. Pseftogas. Φιλοθέου Κοκκίνου λόγοι καὶ ὁμιλίαι. Thessalonike, 1981.

Pius II. *Commentaries*: Books 1–4. Edited and translated by M. Meserve and M. Simonetta. *Pius II: Commentaries*. 2 vols. Cambridge, MA, 2003–7; all books translated by F. A. Gragg. *The Commentaries of Pius II* = Smith College Studies in History 22.1–2 (1936–37); 25.1–4 (1939–40); 30 (1947); 35 (1951); 43 (1957).

Plethon, Georgios Gemistos. *Address to Demetrios Palaiologos*. Edited by S. P. Lambros. In Παλαιολόγεια καὶ Πελοποννησιακά, 4:207–10. Athens, 1930.

———. *Address to Ioannes VIII Palaiologos* [actually Manuel II]. Edited by S. P. Lambros. In Παλαιολόγεια καὶ Πελοποννησιακά, 3:309–12. Athens, 1926.

———. *Address to Manuel II*. Edited by S. P. Lambros. In Παλαιολόγεια καὶ Πελοποννησιακά, 3:246–65. Athens, 1926.

———. *Advice to Theodoros II regarding the Peloponnese*. Edited by S. P. Lambros. In Παλαιολόγεια καὶ Πελοποννησιακά, 4:113–15. Athens, 1930.

———. *Corrections to Some of the Mistakes in Strabo*. Edited by A. Diller. "A Geographical Treatise by Georgius Gemistus Pletho." *Isis* 27 (1937): 441–51.

———. *Historical Excerpts*. Edited by E. V. Maltese. *Georgii Gemisti Plethonis opuscula de historia graeca*. Leipzig, 1989.

———. *Laws*. Edited by C. Alexandre. *Pléthon: Traité des Lois*. Paris, 1858.

————. *Muhammad the Leader and Lawgiver of the Arabs.* Edited by F. Klein-Franke. "Die Geschichte des frühen Islam in einer Schrift des Georgios Gemistos Plethon." *BZ* 65 (1972): 1–8.

————. *Monodia for Helene Palaiologina.* Edited by S. P. Lambros. In Παλαιολόγεια καὶ Πελοποννησιακά, 3:266–80. Athens, 1926.

————. *Reply to Scholarios regarding Aristotle.* Edited by E. V. Maltese. *Georgii Gemisti Plethonis contra Scholarii pro Aristotele obiectiones.* Leipzig, 1988.

Poem of Almería. Edited by J. Gil. "Carmen de expugnatione Almariae urbis." *Habís* 5 (1974): 45–64; translation and commentary by G. E. Lipskey. "The Chronicle of Alfonso the Emperor: A Translation of the *Chronica Adefonsi imperatoris.*" Ph.D. diss., Northwestern University, 1972.

Souda. Edited by A. Adler. *Svidae Lexicon.* 5 vols. Leipzig, 1928–38.

Spandugnino, Teodoro. *Patritio Constantinopolitano de la origine deli imperatori Ottomani,* etc. Edited by C. N. Sathas. In *Documents inédits relatifs à l'histoire de la Grèce au Moyen Âge,* 9:133–261. Paris, 1890; translated by D. M. Nicol. *Theodore Spandounes: On the Origin of the Ottoman Emperors.* Cambridge, 1997.

Sphrantzes, Georgios. *Chronicle.* Edited by R. Maisano. *Giorgio Sfranze: Cronaca.* Rome, 1990; translation by M. Philippides. *The Fall of the Byzantine Empire: A Chronicle by George Sphrantzes, 1401–1477.* Amherst, 1980.

Theophylaktos. *History.* Edited by C. de Boor. Revised by P. Wirth. *Theophylakti Simocattae Historiae.* Stuttgart, 1972.

Zonaras, Ioannes. *Chronicle.* Edited by T. Büttner-Wobst. *Ioannis Zonarae Epitomae historiarum.* 3 vols. Bonn, 1841–97.

Modern Scholarship

Aerts, W. J. "*Imitatio* and *Aemulatio* in Byzantium with Classical Literature, Especially in Historical Writing." In *Constructions of Greek Past: Identity and Historical Consiousness from Antiquity to the Present,* ed. H. Hokwerda, 89–99. Groningen, 2003.

Akbari, S. C. *Idols in the East: European Representations of Islam and the Orient, 1100–1450.* Ithaca, 2009.

Akışık, A. "Self and Other in the Renaissance: Laonikos Chalkokondyles and Byzantine Intellectual Tradition." Ph.D. diss., Harvard University, 2013.

Alberti, G. B. "Il codice Laurenziano Greco LXX,6 e la traduzione latina di Erodoto di Lorenzo Valla." *Maia* 11 (1959): 315–19.

———. "Autografi greci di Lorenzo Valla nel codice Vaticano greco 122." *Italia medioevale e umanistica* 3 (1960): 287–90.

Alexander, P. *The Byzantine Apocalyptic Tradition.* Berkeley, 1985.

Alexandre, C. *Pléthon: Traité des lois.* Paris, 1858.

Anastos, M. V. "Pletho's Calendar and Liturgy." *DOP* 4 (1948): 183–305.

Angelou, A. D. "'Who am I?' Scholarios' Answers and the Hellenic Identity." In Φιλέλλην: *Studies in Honour of Robert Browning,* ed. C. N. Constantides, 1–19. Venice, 1996.

Angelov, D. G. *Imperial Ideology and Political Thought in Byzantium, 1204–1330.* Cambridge, 2007.

———. "The Donation of Constantine and the Church in Late Byzantium." In *Church and Society in Late Byzantium,* ed. D. G. Angelov, 91–157. Kalamazoo, 2009.

Angold, M. *Byzantium: The Bridge from Antiquity to the Middle Ages.* London, 2001.

Arbagi, M. G. "Byzantium in Latin Eyes, *800–1204.*" Ph.D. diss., Rutgers University, 1969.

Arnold, B. *Medieval Germany, 500–1300: A Political Interpretation.* Toronto, 1997.

Asakoy, A. "George Gemistos Pletho and Islam." In Benakis and Baloglou, eds., *Plethon and his Time,* 339–53.

Athanassiadi, P. "Byzantine Commentators on the Chaldaean Oracles: Psellos and Plethon." In *Byzantine Philosophy and Its Ancient Sources,* ed. K. Ierodiakonou, 237–52. Oxford, 2002.

Babinger, F. *Mehmed the Conqueror and his Time.* Edited by W. C. Hickman. Translated by R. Manheim. Princeton, 1992.

Bachrach, B. S. "Pirenne and Charlemagne." In *After Rome's Fall: Narrators and Sources of Early Medieval History,* ed. A. C. Murray, 214–31. Toronto, 1998.

Bakalopoulos, A. E. Ἱστορία τοῦ Νέου Ἑλληνισμοῦ, vol. 1, Ἀρχὲς καὶ διαμόρφωσή του. Revised edition. Thessalonike, 1974.

Balsamo, J. "Byzance à Paris: Chalcondyle, Vigenère, L'Angelier." In *Sauver Byzance de la barbarie du monde,* ed. L. Nissim and S. Riva, 197–212. Milan, 2004.

Baragwanath, E. *Motivation and Narrative in Herodotus*. Oxford, 2008.

Bargeliotis, L. "The Enlightenment and the Hellenic 'Genos': From Plethon to Vulgaris." *Skepsis* 20 (2009): 44–61.

Barker, J. W. *Manuel II Palaeologus (1391–1425): A Study in Late Byzantine Statesmanship*. New Brunswick, 1969.

Baron, H. *The Crisis of the Early Italian Renaissance: Civic Humanism and Republican Liberty in an Age of Classicism and Tyranny*. Princeton, 1966.

Bartlett, R. *The Natural and the Supernatural in the Middle Ages*. Cambridge, 2008.

Baştav, S. "Die türkische Quellen des Laonikos Chalkondylas." In *Akten des XI. internationalen Byzantinistenkongresses, München, 1958*, ed. F. Dölger and H.-G. Beck, 35–42. Munich, 1960.

Beck, H.-G. *Theodoros Metochites: Die Krise des byzantinischen Weltbildes im 14. Jahrhundert*. Munich, 1952.

———. *Res Publica Romana: Vom Staatsdenken der Byzantiner*. Munich, 1970.

Benakis, L., and C. Baloglou, eds. *Proceedings of the International Congress on Plethon and his Time, Mystras, 26–29 June 2002*. Mistras, 2003.

Benardete, S. *Herodotean Inquiries*. The Hague, 1969.

Ben-Tov, A. *Lutheran Humanists and Greek Antiquity: Melanchthonian Scholarship between Universal History and Pedagogy*. Leiden, 2009.

Bianconi, D. *Tessalonica nell'età dei Paleologi: Le pratiche intellettuali nel riflesso della cultura scritta*. Paris, 2005.

———. "La biblioteca di Cora tra Massimo Planude e Niceforo Gregora: Una questione di mani." *Segno e Testo* 3 (2005): 391–438.

Bisaha, N. *Creating East and West: Renaissance Humanists and the Ottoman Turks*. Philadelphia, 2004.

Black, J. *Absolutism in Renaissance Milan: Plenitude of Power under the Visconti and the Sforza 1329–1535*. Oxford, 2009.

Blancs, D. R., and M. Frassetto, eds. *Western Views of Islam in Medieval and Early Modern Europe: Perception of Other*. New York, 1999.

Botley, P. "Renaissance Scholarship and the Athenian Calendar." *GRBS* 46 (2006): 395–431.

Bourbouhakis, E. C. "Rhetoric and Performance." In *The Byzantine World*, ed. P. Stephenson, 175–87. London and New York, 2010.

Boureau, A. *The Myth of Pope Joan*. Translated by L. G. Cochrane. Chicago, 2001.

Breton, J.-F. *Arabia Felix from the Time of the Queen of Sheba (Eighth Century B.C. to First Century A.D.)*. Translated by A. LaFarge. Notre Dame, 1999.

Brown, T. S. "History as Myth: Medieval Perceptions of Venice's Roman and Byzantine Past." In *The Making of Byzantine History: Studies Dedicated to Donald M. Nicol*, ed. R. Beaton and C. Roueché, 145–57. Aldershot, 1993.

de Bruijn, J. T. P. "Musannifak." In *EI*² 7:663. Leiden, 1992.

Cammelli, G. *Demetrio Calcondila*. Vol. 2 of *I dotti bizantini e le origini dell'umanesimo*. Florence, 1954.

Christian, K. W. *Empire without End: Antiquities Collections in Renaissance Rome, c. 1350–1527*. New Haven, 2010.

Cochrane, E. *Historians and Historiography in the Italian Renaissance*. Chicago, 1981.

Connor, W. R. *Thucydides*. Princeton, 1984.

Croke, B. "Uncovering Byzantium's Historiographical Audience." In *History as Literature in Byzantium*, ed. R. Macrides, 25–53. Farnham, 2010.

Curry, A. *The Battle of Agincourt: Sources and Interpretations*. Woodbridge, 2000.

Curta, F. *The Making of the Slavs: History and Archaeology of the Lower Danube Region, c. 500–700*. Cambridge, 2001.

Daniel, N. *Islam and the West: The Making of an Image*. Edinburgh, 1960; 2nd ed. Oxford, 2009.

Darkó, E. "Zum Leben Laonikos Chalkondyles." *BZ* 24 (1923–24): 29–39.

———. "Neue Beiträge zur Biographie des Laonikos Chalkokandyles." *BZ* 27 (1927): 276–85.

Dedes, D. "Die Handschriften und das Werk des Georgios Gemistos (Plethon)." *Ἑλληνικά* 33 (1981): 66–81.

Demetriades, V. "The Tomb of Ghazi Evrenos Bey at Yenitsa and its Inscription." *BSOAS* 39 (1976): 328–32.

Dewald, C. "Form and Content: The Question of Tyranny in Herodotus." In *Popular Tyranny: Sovereignty and its Discontents in Ancient Greece*, ed. K. A. Morgan, 25–58. Austin, 2003.

Diller, A. "A Geographical Treatise by Georgius Gemistus Pletho." *Isis* 27 (1937): 441–51.

———. "The Autographs of G. Gemistus Pletho." *Scriptorium* 10 (1956): 27–41.

Ditten, H. "Laonikos Chalkokondyles und die Sprache der Rumänen." In *Aus der byzantinistischen Arbeit der Deutschen Demokratischen Republik*, ed. J. Irmscher, 1:93–105. Berlin, 1957.

———. "Ἡ περὶ Ρωσίας παρέκβασις τοῦ Λαονίκου Χαλκοκονδύλου." *Παρνασσός* 3 (1961): 89–99.

———. "Spanien und die Spanier im Spiegel der Geschichtsschreibung des byzantinischen Historikers Laonikos Chalkokondyles (15. Jahrhundert)." *Helikon* 3 (1963): 170–95.

———. "Βάρβαροι, Ἕλληνες und Ρωμαῖοι bei den letzten byzantinischen Geschichtsschreiber." In *Acts of the XIth International Congress of Byzantine Studies*, 2:273–99. Belgrade, 1964.

———. "Bemerkungen zu Laonikos Chalkokondyles' Nachrichten über die Länder und Völker an den europäischen Küsten des Schwarzen Meeres (15. Jahrhundert u. Z.)," *Klio* 43–45 (1965): 185–246.

———. "Bemerkungen zu Laonikos Chalkokondyles's Deutschland-Exkurs." *ByzF* 1 (1966): 49–75.

———. "Die Korruptel Χωρόβιον und die Unechtheit der Trapezunt und Georgien betreffenden Partien in Laonikos Chalkokondyles's Geschichtswerk." In *Studia Byzantina: Beiträge aus der byzantinischen Forschung der Deutschen Demokratischen Republik zum XII. Internationalen Byzantinistenkongress in Oxford*, ed. J. Irmscher, 57–70. Halle, 1966.

———. "Die Namen für Venedig und Genua bei den letzten byzantinischen Geschichtsschreiber (15. Jahrhundert)." *Helikon* 6 (1966): 51–70.

———. *Der Russland-Exkurs des Laonikos Chalkokondyles interpretiert und mit Erläuterungen versehen.* Berlin, 1968.

———. "Zwei verschiedene 'Wien' bei Laonikos Chalkokondyles." *BBulg* 5 (1978): 323–28.

Ducellier, A. "La France et les Îles Britanniques vues par un byzantin du XVe siècle: Laonikos Chalkokondylis." In *Économies et sociétés au Moyen Âge: Mélanges offerts à Edouard Perroy*, 439–45. Paris, 1973.

———. "La peninsule ibérique d'après Laonikos Chalkokondylis, chroniqueur byzantin du XVème siècle." *Norba* 5 (1984): 163–77.

———. "L'Europe occidentale vue par les historiens grecs des XIVème et XVème siècles." *ByzF* 22 (1996): 119–59.

———. *Chrétiens d'Orient et Islam au Moyen Age, VIIe–XVe siècle.* Paris, 1996.

Eckhardt, A. "Le cercueil flottant de Mahomet." In *Mélanges de philologie romane et de littérature médiévale offerts à Ernest Hoepffner*, 77–88. Paris, 1949.

Featherstone, J. M. "Theodore Metochites's *Semeioseis Gnomikai*: Personal Encyclopedism." In *Encyclopedic Trends in Byzantium?* ed. P. van Deun and C. Macé, 333–44. Leuven, 2011.

Feeney, D. *Caesar's Calendar: Ancient Time and the Beginnings of History*. Berkeley, 2007.

Fine, J. *The Late Medieval Balkans: A Critical Survey From the Late Twelfth Century to the Ottoman Conquest*. Ann Arbor, 1994.

———. *When Ethnicity Did Not Matter in the Balkans: A Study of Identity in Pre-Nationalist Croatia, Dalmatia, and Slavonia in the Medieval and Early-Modern Periods*. Ann Arbor, 2006.

Fleet, K., ed. *The Cambridge History of Turkey*, vol. 1, *Byzantium to Turkey, 1074–1453*. Cambridge, 2009.

Fleet, K. "The Turkish Economy, 1071–1453." In Fleet, *Cambridge History of Turkey*, 1:227–65.

Fleming, M. H. *The Late Medieval Pope Prophecies: The* Genus nequam *Group*. Tempe, 1999.

Fletcher, R. *The Barbarian Conversion from Paganism to Christianity*. Berkeley, 1997.

Fodor, P. "Ottoman Warfare, 1300–1453." In Fleet, *Cambridge History of Turkey*, 1:192–226.

Folz, R. *The Concept of Empire in Western Europe from the Fifth to the Fourteenth Century*. Translated by S. A. Ogilvie. London, 1969.

Förstel, K. *Niketas von Byzanz: Schriften zum Islam*. Würzburg, 2000.

———. *Schriften zum Islam von Arethas und Euthymios Zigabenos und Fragmente der griechischen Koranübersetzung*. Wiesbaden, 2009.

Frakes, J. C. *Vernacular and Latin Literary Discourses of the Muslim Other in Medieval Germany*. New York, 2011.

Frangedaki, A. "On Fifteenth-Century Cryptochristianity: A Letter to George Amoiroutzes from Michael Apostolis." *BMGS* 9 (1984–85): 221–24.

Frankfurter, D. *Religion in Roman Egypt: Assimilation and Resistance*. Princeton, 1998.

Freeman, C. *The Horses of St. Mark's: A Story of Triumph in Byzantium, Paris, and Venice*. New York, 2004.

Fryde, E. B. *Humanism and Renaissance Historiography*. London, 1983.

Fudge, T. A. *The Crusade against Heretics in Bohemia, 1418–1437*. Aldershot, 2002.

———. "Seduced by the Theologians: Aeneas Sylvius and Hussite Heretics." In *Heresy in Transition: Transforming Ideas of Heresy in Medieval and Early Modern Europe*, ed. I. Hunter et al., 89–101. Aldershot, 2005.

Gabba, E. *Dionysius and the History of Archaic Rome*. Berkeley, 1991.

Gallotta, A. "Il 'mito oguzo' e le origini dello stato Ottomano: una riconsiderazione." In Zachariadou, ed., *Ottoman Emirate*, 41–59.

Gamillscheg, E. "Der Kopist des Par. gr. 428 und das Ende der Grosskomnenen." *JÖB* 36 (1986): 287–300.

Ganchou, T. "Théodôra Kantakouzènè Komnènè de Trébizonde (°~1382/ †1426), ou la vertu calomniée." In *Geschehenes und Geschriebenes: Studien zu Ehren von Günther S. Heinrich und Klaus-Peter Matschke*, ed. S. Kolditz and R. C. Muller, 337–50. Leipzig, 2005.

Gaparis, Ch., ed. *Οι Αλβανοί στον Μεσαίωνα*. Athens, 1998.

Garzya, A. "Byzantium." In *Perceptions of the Ancient Greeks*, ed. K. J. Dover, 29–53. Cambridge, MA, 1992.

Geanakoplos, D. J. *Greek Scholars in Venice: Studies in the Dissemination of Greek Learning from Byzantium to Western Europe*. Cambridge, MA, 1962.

———. "The Discourse of Demetrius Chalcondyles on the Inauguration of Greek Studies at the University of Padua in 1463." *Studies in the Renaissance* 21 (1974): 118–44.

———. *Interaction of the "Sibling" Byzantine and Western Cultures in the Middle Ages and Italian Renaissance (330–1600)*. New Haven, 1976.

Giannakopoulos, D. K. "Η θεώρηση του πολιτικού συστήματος των ιταλικών κρατιδίων (α'μισό του 15ᵒᵘ αιώνα) από το Λαόνικο Χαλκοκονδύλη." *Έῷα καὶ Ἑσπερία* 5 (2001–2003): 69–88.

———. *Δουκάτο των Αθηνών: Η κυριαρχία των Acciaiuoli*. Thessalonike, 2006.

Gibbon, E. *The History of the Decline and Fall of the Roman Empire*. Edited by D. Womersley. 3 vols. London, 1994.

Gill, J. *The Council of Florence*. Cambridge, 1961.

Glaser, T. "The Remnants of the Hellenes: Problems of Greek Identity after the Fall of Constantinople." In Konstantinou, ed., *Beitrag der byzantinischen Gelehrten*, 109–209.

Glei, R., and A. T. Khoury. *Johannes Damaskenos und Theodor Abu Qurra: Schriften zum Islam.* Würzburg, 1995.

Göllner, C. *Turcica: Die europäischen Turkendrücke des XVI. Jahrhunderts.* 2 vols. Bucharest, 1961–68.

Gounaridis, P. "Η εξέλιξη της ταυτότητας των Ελλήνων στη Βυζαντινή αυτοκρατορία." *Études balkaniques* 6 (1991): 51–68.

Grabler, F. "Aus dem Geschichtswerk des Laonikos Chalkokondyles." In *Europa im XV. Jahrhundert von Byzantinern Gesehen,* ed. F. Grabler and G. Stökl, 11–97. Graz, 1954.

De Gregorio, G. "L'Erodoto di Palla Strozzi (cod. Vat. Urb. gr. 88)." *BollClass* 23 (2002): 31–130.

Güterbock, K. "Laonikos Chalkondyles." *Zeitschrift für Völkerrecht und Bundesstaatsrecht* 4 (1909): 72–102.

Hankins, J. *Plato in the Italian Renaissance.* Leiden, 1991.

———. "Renaissance Crusaders: Humanist Crusade Literature in the Age of Mehmed II." *DOP* 49 (1995): 111–207.

Harris, J. *Greek Emigres in the West, 1400–1520.* Camberley, 1995.

———. "Being a Byzantine after Byzantium: Hellenic Identity in Renaissance Italy." *Kambos: Cambridge Papers in Modern Greek* 8 (2000): 25–44.

———. "Laonikos Chalkokondyles and the Rise of the Ottoman Empire." *BMGS* 27 (2003): 153–70.

———. "The Influence of Plethon's Idea of Fate on the Historian Laonikos Chalkokondyles." In Benakis and Baloglou, eds., *Plethon and his Time,* 211–17.

———. *The End of Byzantium.* New Haven, 2010.

Harrison, T. *Divinity and History: The Religion of Herodotos.* Oxford, 2000.

———. *Writing Ancient Persia.* Bristol, 2011.

Hartog, F. *The Mirror of Herodotus: The Representation of the Other in the Writing of History.* Translated by J. Lloyd. Berkeley, 1988.

Heath, M. J. "Renaissance Scholars and the Origins of the Turks." *Bibliothèque d'humanisme et Renaissance* 41 (1979): 453–71.

Heather, P. *Empires and Barbarians: Migration, Development and the Birth of Europe.* London, 2009.

Hemmerdinger, B. *Les manuscrits d'Hérodote et la critique verbale.* Genoa, 1981.

Heywood, C. *Writing Ottoman History.* London, 2002.

Homeyer, H. "Zur Synkrysis des Manuel Chrysoloras, einem Vergleich zwischen Rom und Konstantinopel: Ein Beitrag zum italienischen Frühhumanismus." *Klio* 62 (1980): 525–34.

Hopf, C. *Chroniques gréco-romaines inédites ou peu connues.* Berlin, 1873.

Hoyland, R. G. *Seeing Islam as Others Saw It: A Survey and Evaluation of Christian, Jewish and Zoroastrian Writings on Early Islam.* Princeton, 1997.

Hunger, H. *Graeculus perfidus, Ἰταλὸς ἰταμός: Il senso dell'alterità nei rapporti Greco-Romani ed Italo-Bizantini.* Rome, 1987.

Imber, C. "The Ottoman Dynastic Myth." *Turcica* 19 (1987): 7–27.

———. "The Legend of Osman Gazi." In Zachariadou, ed., *Ottoman Emirate*, 67–75.

———. "Canon and Apocrypha in Early Ottoman History." In Imber and Heywood, eds., *Studies in Ottoman History*, 117–38.

Imber, C., and C. Heywood, eds. *Studies in Ottoman History in Honour of Professor E. L. Ménage.* Istanbul, 1994.

İnalcık, H. "The Rise of Ottoman Historiography." In Lewis and Holt, eds., *Historians of the Middle East*, 152–67.

———. "The Conquest of Edirne." *ArchOtt* 3 (1971): 185–210.

———. "How to Read Ashik Pasha Zade's History." In Imber and Heywood, eds., *Studies in Ottoman History*, 139–56.

Inglebert, H. *Interpretatio Christiana: Les mutations des savoirs (cosmographie, géographie, ethnographie, histoire) dans l'Antiquité chrétienne, 30–630 après J.-C.* Paris, 2001.

Innes, M. "Historical Writing, Ethnicity, and National Identity: Medieval Europe and Byzantium in Comparison." In *The Oxford History of Historical Writing*, vol. 2, *400–1400*, ed. S. Foot and C. F. Robinson, 539–75. Oxford, 2012.

Janssens, B., and P. Van Deun. "George Amiroutzes and his Poetical Oeuvre." In *Philomathestatos: Studies in Greek and Byzantine Texts Presented to Jacques Noret for his Sixty-Fifth Birthday*, ed. B. Janssens, P. Van Deun, and B. Roosen, 297–324. Leuven, 2004.

Jeffreys, E. M. "The Image of the Arabs in Byzantine Literature." In *The 17th International Byzantine Congress: Major Papers*, 305–23. New Rochelle, 1986.

Kafadar, C. *Between Two Worlds: The Construction of the Ottoman State.* Berkeley, 1995.

Kaldellis, A. "The Historical and Religious Views of Agathias: A Reinterpretation." *Byzantion* 69 (1999): 206–52.

———. *The Argument of Psellos' Chronographia.* Leiden, 1999.

———. *Procopius of Caesarea: Tyranny, History, and Philosophy at the End of Antiquity.* Philadelphia, 2004.

———. *Hellenism in Byzantium: The Transformations of Greek Identity and the Reception of the Classical Tradition.* Cambridge, 2007.

———. "From Rome to New Rome, From Empire to Nation-State: Reopening the Question of Byzantium's Roman Identity." In *Two Romes: Rome and Constantinople in Late Antiquity,* ed. L. Grig and G. Kelly, 387–404. Oxford, 2012.

———. *Le discours ethnographique à Byzance: continuités et ruptures.* Translated by C. Messis. Paris, 2012.

———. "The Date of Laonikos Chalkokondyles' *Histories.*" *GRBS* 52 (2012): 111–36.

———. "The Interpolations in the *Histories* of Laonikos Chalkokondyles." *GRBS* 52 (2012): 259–83.

———. "The Greek Sources of Laonikos Chalkokondyles." *GRBS* 52 (2012): 738–65.

Kampouroglous, D. *Οἱ Χαλκοκονδύλαι.* Athens, 1926.

Karabelias, G. *Το 1204 και η διαμόρφωση του νεώτερου Ελληνισμού.* 3rd ed. Athens, 2007.

Katsoni, P. *Μία επταετία κρίσιμων γεγονότων: Το Βυζάντιο στα έτη 1366–1373.* Thessalonike, 2002.

Khoury, A. T. *Polémique byzantine contre l'Islam: VIIIe–XIIIe s.* Leiden, 1972.

Kiousopoulou, T. "Η έννοια της πατρίδας κατά τον 15° αιώνα." In *1453: Η Άλωση της Κωνσταντινούπολης και η μετάβαση από τους μεσαιωνικούς στους νεώτερους χρόνους,* ed. T. Kiousopoulou, 147–60. Heraklion, 2005.

———. *Βασιλεύς ή οικονόμος: Πολιτική εξουσία και ιδεολογία πριν την άλωση.* Athens, 2007.

Kitromilides, P. M. "'Imagined Communities' and the Origins of the National Question in the Balkans." *European History Quarterly* 19 (1989): 149–94.

———. "On the Intellectual Content of Greek Nationalism: Paparrigopoulos, Byzantium and the Great Idea." In *Byzantium and the Modern Greek Identity,* ed. D. Ricks and P. Magdalino, 25–33. Aldershot, 1998.

Klein, H. A. "Refashioning Byzantium in Venice, ca. 1200–1400." In *San Marco, Byzantium, and the Myths of Venice*, ed. H. Maguire and R. S. Nelson, 193–225. Washington, DC, 2010.

Klein-Franke, F. "Die Geschichte des frühen Islam in einer Schrift des Georgios Gemistos Plethon." *BZ* 65 (1972): 1–8.

Konstantinou, E., ed. *Der Beitrag der byzantinischen Gelehrten zur abendländischen Renaissance des 14. und 15. Jahrhunderts*. Frankfurt am Main, 2006.

Koutrakou, N. A. "The Image of the Arabs in Middle-Byzantine Politics: A Study in the Enemy Principle (8th-10th Centuries)." *Graeco-Arabica* 5 (1993): 213–24.

Krallis, D. *Michael Attaleiates and the Politics of Imperial Decline in Eleventh-Century Byzantium*. Tempe, 2012.

Kreutel, R. F. *Vom Hirtenzelt zur hohen Pforte: Frühzeit und Aufstieg des Osmanenreiches nach der Chronik "Denkwürdigkeiten und Zeitläufte des Hauses Osman" vom Derwisch Ahmed, genannt 'Asik-Pasa-Sohn*. Graz, 1959. [Translation of Aşıkpaşazade sections down to Murad.]

Laiou, A. E. "Italy and the Italians in the Political Geography of the Byzantines (14th Century)." *DOP* 49 (1995): 74–98.

Lambros, S. P. "Ὑπόμνημα τοῦ καρδιναλίου Βησσαρίονως εἰς Κωνσταντῖνον τὸν Παλαιολόγον." *Νέος Ἑλλ.* 3 (1906): 12–50.

Lamers, H. "A Byzantine Poet in Italian Exile: Manilius Cabacius Rallus's Self-Presentation in the Context of Leo X's Philhellenism." In *Acta Conventus Neo-Latini Uppsaliensis: Proceedings of the Fourteenth International Congress of Neo-Latin Studies, Uppsala, 2–9 August 2009*, ed. A. Steiner-Weber, 593–604. Leiden, 2012.

———. "The Imperial Diadem of Greece: Giovanni Gemisto's Strategical Representation of 'Graecia' (1516)." In *Discourses of Power: Ideology and Politics in Neo-Latin Literature*, ed. K. Enenkel et al., 65–95. Hildesheim, 2012.

———. "Reinventing the Ancient Greeks: The Self-Representation of Byzantine Scholars in Renaissance Italy." Ph.D. diss., Leiden University, 2013.

Lateiner, D. *The Historical Method of Herodotus*. Toronto, 1989.

Lemerle, P. *L'émirat d'Aydin, Byzance et l'Occident: Recherches sur "La Geste d'Umur Pacha."* Paris, 1957.

Lewis, B., and P. Holt, eds. *Historians of the Middle East*. London, 1962.

Lieberich, H. *Studien zu den Proömien in der griechischen und byzantinischen Geschichtsschreibung*. 2 vols. Munich, 1898–1900.

Livanos, C. "The Conflict between Scholarios and Plethon: Religion and Communal Identity in Early Modern Greece." In *Modern Greek Literature: Critical Essays*, ed. G. Nagy and A. Stavrakopoulou, 23–41. New York, 2003.

———. *Greek Tradition and Latin Influence in the Work of George Scholarios: "Alone against All of Europe."* Piscataway, 2006.

Loenertz, R.-J. "Autour du *Chronicon maius* attribué à Georges Phrantzès." In *Byzantina et Franco-Graeca*, ed. R.-J. Loenertz and P. Schreiner, 3–44. Rome, 1970.

Lopez, R. "Il principio della guerra veneto-turca nel 1463." *AVen* ser. 5, 15 (1934): 45–131.

Lowry, H. W. *The Nature of the Early Ottoman State*. New York, 2003.

Magdalino, P. "The Beauty of Antiquity in Late Byzantine Praises of Constantinople." In Odorico and Messis, eds., *Villes de toute beauté*, 101–15.

Maisano, R. "Il problema della forma letteraria nei proemi storiografici bizantini." *BZ* 78 (1985): 329–43.

Maltezou, C. "Still More on the Political Views of Bessarion." In Konstantinou, ed., *Beitrag der byzantinischen Gelehrten*, 99–105.

Mango, C. "The Legend of Leo the Wise." *Zbornik Radova Vizantinološkog Instituta* 6 (1960): 59–93.

Mantouvalou, M. "Romaios—Romios—Romiossyni: La notion de 'Romain' avant et après la chute de Constantinople." Ἐπιστημονικὴ Ἐπετηρὶς τῆς Φιλοσοφικῆς Σχολῆς τοῦ Πανεπιστημίου Ἀθηνῶν 28 (1979–85): 169–98.

Manz, B. F. *The Rise and Rule of Tamerlane*. Cambridge, 1989.

Markopoulos, A. "Das Bild des Anderen bei Laonikos Chalkokondyles und das Vorbild Herodot." *JÖB* 50 (2000): 205–16.

Martin, D. B. *Inventing Superstition from the Hippocratics to the Christians*. Cambridge, MA, 2004.

Masai, F. *Pléthon et le platonisme de Mistra*. Paris, 1956.

Masai, R. and F. "L'oeuvre de Georges Gémiste Pléthon." *BAcBelg* (1954): 536–55.

Mastrodimitris, P. D. Νικόλαος Σεκουνδινὸς (1402–1464): Βίος καὶ ἔργον. Athens, 1970.

Mavrommatis, L. "ʻΡωμαϊκὴ ταυτότητα, Ἑλληνικὴ ταυτότητα (ΙΓ–ΙΔ αἰ.)." Σύμμεικτα 7 (1987): 183–91.

McGlew, J. F, *Tyranny and Political Culture in Ancient Greece.* Cornell, 1993.

Ménage, V. L. "The Beginnings of Ottoman Historiography." In Lewis and Holt, eds., *Historians of the Middle East,* 168–79.

———. "The *Menaqib* of Yakhshi Faqih." *BSOAS* 26 (1963): 50–54.

Meserve, M. *Empires of Islam in Renaissance Historical Thought.* Cambridge, MA, 2008.

Messis, C. "Lectures sexuées de l'altérité: Les Latins et identité romaine menacée pendant les derniers siècles de Byzance." *JÖB* 61 (2011): 151–70.

———. "De l'invisible au visible: Les éloges de Venise dans la littérature byzantine." In Odorico and Messis, eds., *Villes de toute beauté,* 149–79.

Meyendorff, J. "Byzantine Views of Islam." *DOP* 18 (1964): 113–32.

Miller, W. "The Last Athenian Historian." *JHS* 42 (1922): 36–49.

Mioni, E. "La formazione della biblioteca greca di Bessarione." In *Bessarione e l'umanesimo,* ed. G. Fiaccadori, 229–40. Naples, 1994.

Missiou, D. "The Importance of Macedonia during the Byzantine Era." In *Byzantine Macedonia: Identity, Image, and History,* ed. J. Burke and R. Scott, 102–10. Melbourne, 2000.

Mohler, L. "Bessarions Instruktion für die Kreuzzugspredigt in Venedig (1463)." *RQ* 35 (1927): 337–50.

Mondrain, B. "Les Éparque, une famille de médecins collectionneurs de manuscrits aux XVᵉ–XVIᵉ siècles." In *Η ελληνική γραφή κατά τους 15° και 16° αιώνες,* ed. S. Patoura, 145–63. Athens, 2000.

———. "Jean Argyropoulos professeur à Constantinople et ses auditeurs médicins, d'Andronic Éparque à Demétrios Angelos." In *ΠΟΛΥΠΛΕΥΡΟΣ ΝΟΥΣ: Miscellanea für Peter Schreiner zu seinem 60. Geburtstag,* ed. C. Scholz and G. Makris, 223–50. Munich, 2000.

———. "Démétrios Angelos et la médecine: contribution nouvelle au dossier." In *Storia della tradizione e edizione dei medici greci (Atti del VI Colloquio Internazionale, Paris, 12–14 Aprile 2008),* ed. V. Boudon-Millot et al., 293–322. Naples, 2010.

Monfasani, J. *George Amiroutzes: The Philosopher and his Tractates.* Leuven, 2011.

Moraitis, S. "Sur un passage de Chalcondyle relative aux Anglais." *REG* 1 (1888): 94–98.

Moravcsik, G. *Byzantinoturcica*, vol. 1, *Die byzantinischen Quellen der Geschichte der Türkvölker*. Berlin, 1958.

Morfakidis, M. "La península ibérica en la obra de Calcocondilas." *Erytheia* 6 (1985): 69–82.

Morfakidis, M., and E. Motos Guirao. "Un pasaje de Laonicos Calcocondylas relativo a la batalla de la Higueruela y a sus consecuencias inmediatas." In *Relaciones exteriores del Reino de Granada: IV Coloquio de Historia medieval Andaluza*, ed. C. Segura Graiño, 71–82. Almeria, 1988.

Moulakis, A. "Leonardo Bruni's Constitution of Florence." *Rinascimento* 26 (1986): 141–90.

Moustakas, K. "Byzantine 'Visions' of the Ottoman Empire: Theories of Ottoman Legitimacy by Byzantine Scholars after the Fall of Constantinople." In *Images of the Byzantine World: Visions, Messages and Meanings. Studies Presented to Leslie Brubaker*, ed. A. Lymberopoulou, 215–29. Farnham, 2011.

Mureşanu, C. *John Hunyadi: Defender of Christendom*. Iaşi, 2001.

Murray, O. "Herodotus and Oral History." In *Achaemenid History*, vol. 2, *The Greek Sources*, ed. H. Sancisi-Weerdenburg and A. Kuhrt, 93–115. Leiden, 1997.

Necipoğlu, N. *Byzantium between the Ottomans and the Latins: Politics and Society in the Late Empire*. Cambridge, 2009.

Nicol, D. M. *The Last Centuries of Byzantium 1261–1453*. Cambridge, 1993.

———. *Theodore Spandounes: On the Origin of the Ottoman Emperors*. Cambridge, 1997.

Nicoloudis, N. "Observations on the Possible Sources of Laonikos Chalkokondyles' *Demonstrations of Histories*." *Byzantina* 17 (1994): 75–82.

———. "Byzantine Historians on the Wars of Timur." *Journal of Oriental and African Studies* 8 (1996): 83–94.

———. *Laonikos Chalkokondyles: A Translation and Commentary of the Demonstrations of Histories*. Athens, 1996.

———. *Μεσαιωνική Μακεδονία, Θράκη και Μικρά Ασία: Προσεγγίσεις και αντιπαραθέσεις Βυζαντινών, Σλάβων και Τούρκων*. Thessalonike, 2006.

Nikolaou, Th. S. *Αἱ περὶ πολιτείας καὶ δικαίου ἰδέαι τοῦ Γ. Πλήθωνος Γεμιστοῦ*. Thessalonike, 1989.

Nimet, A. *Die türkische Prosopographie bei Laonikos Chalkokandyles*. Hamburg, 1933.

Ocak, A. Y. "Social, Cultural and Intellectual Life, 1071–1453." In Fleet, *Cambridge History of Turkey*, 1:353–422.

Odorico, P., and C. Messis, eds. *Villes de toute beauté: L'ekphrasis des cités dans les littératures byzantine et byzantino-slaves.* Paris, 2012.

Orwin, C. *The Humanity of Thucydides.* Princeton, 1994.

Pade, M. "Valla's Thucydides: Theory and Practice in a Renaissance Translation." *ClMed* 36 (1985): 275–301.

Pagani, F. "*Damnata verba*: censure di Pletone in alcuni codici platonici." *BZ* 102 (2009): 167–202.

Page, G. *Being Byzantine: Greek Identity before the Ottomans.* Cambridge, 2008.

Pagliaroli, S. *L'Erodoto del Valla.* Messina, 2006.

Paparrigopoulos, K. Ἱστορία τοῦ Ἑλληνικοῦ Ἔθνους, vol. 3. Athens, 1902.

Parker, R. *On Greek Religion.* Ithaca, 2011.

Paschoud, F. "Influences et échos des conceptions historiographiques de Polybe dans l'antiquité tardive." In *Polybe*, ed. F. W. Walbank, 305–44. Fondation Hardt pour l'étude de l'antiquité classique, Entretiens 20. Geneva, 1974.

Patrinelis, C. G. "Mehmed II the Conqueror and his Presumed Knowledge of Greek and Latin." *Viator* 2 (1971): 349–54.

Philippides, M. "Early Post-Byzantine Historiography." In *The Classics in the Middle Ages*, ed. A. S. Bernardo and S. Levin, 253–65. Binghamton, 1990.

———. *Byzantium, Europe, and the Early Ottoman Sultans, 1373–1513: An Anonymous Greek Chronicle of the Seventeenth Century (Codex Barberinus Graecus 111).* New York, 1990.

———. *Mehmed II the Conqueror and the Fall of the Franco-Byzantine Levant to the Ottoman Turks: Some Western Views and Testimonies.* Tempe, 2007.

Philippides, M., and W. Hanak. *The Siege and the Fall of Constantinople in 1453: Historiography, Topography, and Military Studies.* Farnham, 2011.

Pippidi, A. *Visions of the Ottoman World in Renaissance Europe.* New York, 2013.

Pitsakis, G. "Universalité et nationalisme: La Nouvelle Rome. Quelques points de repère à travers les textes grecs." In *Umanità e Nazioni nel Diritto e nella Spiritualità da Roma a Costantinopoli a Mosca (Rendiconti del XII Seminario Internazionale di Studi Storici "Da Roma alla terza Roma")*, 25–42. Rome, 1995.

Raby, J. "Mehmed the Conqueror's Greek Scriptorium." *DOP* 38 (1983): 15–34 (plus plates).

Rajna, P. "Contributi alla storia dell' epopea e del romanzo medievale, VII: L'onomastica italiana e l'epopea carolingia." *Romania* 18 (1889): 1–69.

———. *Le fonti dell'Orlando furioso: Ricerche e studii.* 2nd ed. Florence, 1900.

Rapp, C. "Hellenic Identity, *Romanitas*, and Christianity in Byzantium." In *Hellenisms: Culture, Identity, and Ethnicity from Antiquity to Modernity*, ed. K. Zacharia, 127–47. Aldershot, 2008.

Reeves, M. *The Influence of Prophecy in the Later Middle Ages: A Study in Joachism.* Oxford, 1969.

———. "Some Popular Prophecies from the Fourteenth to the Seventeenth Centuries." In *Popular Belief and Practice*, ed. G. J. Cuming and D. Baker, 107–34. Cambridge, 1972.

———. *Joachim of Fiore and the Prophetic Future: A Medieval Study in Historical Thinking.* 2nd ed. Sutton, 1999.

Reinsch, D. R. "Η θεώρηση της πολιτικής και πολιτιστικής φυσιογνωμίας των Ελλήνων στους ιστορικούς της Άλωσης." *Études balkaniques* 6 (*Byzance et l'hellénisme: L'identité grecque au Moyen-Âge*) (1991): 69–86.

von Richthofen, E. "Problemas rolandinos, almerienses y cidianos." *Anuario de estudios medievales* 5 (1968): 437–44.

Rödel, F. "Zur Sprache des Laonikos Chalkondyles und des Kritobulos aus Imbros." *Programm des königlichen humanistischen Gymnasiums Ingolstadt 1904–1905* (Munich, 1905): 12–34.

Romm, J. S. *The Edges of the Earth in Ancient Thought.* Princeton, 1992.

Runciman, S. *The Emperor Romanus Lecapenus and his Reign.* Cambridge, 1929.

———. *The Last Byzantine Renaissance.* Cambridge, 1970.

Sakel, D. "A Probable Solution to the Problem of the Chronicle of the Turkish Sultans." In *Byzantine Narrative: Papers in Honour of Roger Scott*, ed. J. Burke et al., 204–20. Melbourne, 2006.

Saradi-Mendelovici, H. "Christian Attitudes toward Pagan Monuments in Late Antiquity and their Legacy in Later Byzantine Centuries." *DOP* 44 (1990): 47–61.

Saradi, H. "The Monuments in the Late Byzantine Ekphraseis of Cities: Searching for Identities." *BSl* 69 (2011): 179–92.

Schott, J. M. "Porphyry on Christians and Others: 'Barbarian Wisdom,' Identity Politics, and Anti-Christian Polemics on the Eve of the Great Persecution." *JEChrSt* 13 (2005): 277–314.

Scialuga, M. "Un'inedita grammatica greca alle soglie dell'età moderna: il περὶ παιδείας di Giorgio Gemisto Pletone." *Atti della Accademia delle Scienze di Torino. Classe di scienze morali, storiche e filologiche* 129 (1995): 12–29.

Setton, K. M. *Athens in the Middle Ages.* London, 1975.

———. *The Papacy and the Levant, 1204–1571.* 4 vols. Philadelphia, 1976–84.

Ševčenko, I. "The Decline of Byzantium Seen through the Eyes of its Intellectuals." *DOP* 15 (1961): 169–86.

———. *La vie intellectuelle et politique à Byzance sous les premiers Paléologues: Études sur la polémique entre Théodore Métochite et Nicéphore Choumnos.* Brussels, 1962.

———. "Levels of Style in Byzantine Prose." *JÖB* 31 (1981): 289–312.

Shawcross, T. "Re-Inventing the Homeland in the Historiography of Frankish Greece: The Fourth Crusade and the Legend of the Trojan War." *BMGS* 27 (2003): 120–52.

———. "'Do Thou Nothing without Counsel': Political Assemblies and the Ideal of Good Government in the Thought of Theodore Palaeologus and Theodore Metochites." *Al-Masaq* 20 (2008): 89–118.

Sılay, K. "Ahmedi's History of the Ottoman Dynasty." *Journal of Turkish Studies* 16 (1992): 129–200.

Simelides, C. T. "The Byzantine Understanding of the Qur'anic Term *al-Samad* and the Greek Translation of the Qur'an." *Speculum* 86 (2011): 887–913.

Siniossoglou, N. *Radical Platonism in Byzantium: Illumination and Utopia in Gemistos Plethon.* Cambridge, 2011.

Smarnakes, G. "Ἀρχαία ιστορία και ερμηνευτικές στρατηγικές στον Πλήθωνα." In *1453: Η Άλωση της Κωνσταντινούπολης και η μετάβαση από τους μεσαιωνικούς στους νεώτερους χρόνους*, ed. T. Kiousopoulou, 173–81. Heraklion, 2005.

Smith, J. M. H. *Europe after Rome: A New Cultural History, 500–1000.* Oxford, 2005.

Smith, O. "Tricliniana II." *ClMed* 43 (1992): 187–229.

Smith, R. *Julian's Gods: Religion and Philosophy in the Thought and Action of Julian the Apostate*. London, 1995.

Southern, R. W. *Western Views of Islam in the Middle Ages*. Cambridge, MA, 1962.

Stavrides, T. *The Sultan of Vezirs: The Life and Times of the Ottoman Grand Vezir Mahmud Pasha Angelović*. Leiden, 2001.

Stefec, R. "Aus der literarischen Werkstatt des Michael Apostoles." *JÖB* 60 (2010): 129–48.

Syros, V. "Between Chimera and Charybdis: Byzantine and Post-Byzantine Views on the Political Organization of the Italian City-States." *Journal of Early Modern History* 14 (2010): 451–504.

Taeschner, F., and P. Wittek. "Die Vezirfamilie der Gandarlyzade (14./15. Jhdt.) und ihre Denkmäler." *Der Islam* 18 (1929): 60–115.

Tambrun, B. *Pléthon: Le Retour de Platon*. Paris, 2006.

Thomas, R. *Herodotus in Context: Ethnography, Science and the Art of Persuasion*. Cambridge, 2000.

Thomson, R. W. "Armenian Variations on the Bahira Legend." *Harvard Ukrainian Studies* 3–4 (1979–80): 884–95.

Thorn, L. "Das Briefcorpus des Manuel Chrysoloras: eine Blütenlese." In Konstantinou, ed., *Beitrag der byzantinischen Gelehrten*, 17–28.

Tolan, J. V. *Saracens: Islam in the Medieval European Imagination*. New York, 2002.

Treadgold, W. *The Early Byzantine Historians*. New York, 2007.

Trizio, M. "A Neoplatonic Refutation of Islam from the Time of the Komneni." In *Knotenpunkt Byzanz: Wissensformen und kulturelle Wechselbeziehungen*, ed. A. Speer and D. Wirmer, 145–66. Berlin, 2012.

Turner, C. J. G. "Pages from the Late Byzantine Philosophy of History." *BZ* 57 (1964): 346–73.

Turyn, A. *The Byzantine Manuscript Tradition of the Tragedies of Euripides*. Urbana, 1957.

———. *Dated Greek Manuscripts of the Thirteenth and Fourteenth Centuries in the Libraries of Italy*. 2 vols. Urbana, 1972.

Van Dam, R. *Remembering Constantine at the Milvian Bridge*. Cambridge, 2011.

Vasiliev, A. A. "La guerre de Cent Ans et Jeanne d'Arc dans la tradition byzantine." *Byzantion* 3 (1927): 241–50.

Vereecken, J., and L. Hadermann-Misguich. *Les Oracles de Léon le Sage illus-trés par Georges Klontzas: La version Barozzi dans le Codex Bute.* Venice, 2000.

de Vigenère, B. *L'Histoire de la décadence de l'empire grec, et establissement de celuy des Turcs, par Chalcondile Athenien.* Paris, 1577.

de Vries-van der Velden, E. *Théodore Métochite: Un réévaluation.* Amsterdam, 1987.

Vryonis, S. "Byzantine Attitudes towards Islam during the Late Middle Ages." *GRBS* 12 (1971): 263–86.

———. "Evidence on Human Sacrifice among the Early Ottoman Turks." *Journal of Asian History* 5 (1971): 140–46.

———. *The Decline of Medieval Hellenism in Asia Minor.* Berkeley, 1971.

———. "Laonikos Chalkokondyles and the Ottoman Budget." *International Journal of Middle East Studies* 7 (1976): 423–32.

———. "Crises and Anxieties in Fifteenth-Century Byzantium: And the Reassertion of Old, and the Emergence of New, Cultural Forms." In *Islamic and Middle Eastern Societies: A Festschrift in Honor of Professor Wadie Jwaideh,* ed. R. Olson, 100–125. Brattleboro, 1987.

———. "Byzantine Cultural Self-Consciousness in the Fifteenth Century." In *The Twilight of Byzantium: Aspects of Cultural and Religious History in the Late Byzantine Empire,* ed. S. Ćurčić and D. Mouriki, 5–14. Princeton, 1991.

———. "Introductory Remarks on Byzantine Intellectuals and Humanism." *Skepsis* 2 (1991): 104–40.

———. "Greek Identity in the Middle Ages." *Études balkaniques* 6 (1991): 19–36.

Webb, R. "Describing Rome in Greek: Manuel Chrysoloras' Comparison of Old and New Rome." In Odorico and Messis, eds., *Villes de toute beauté,* 123–33.

Wickham, C. *The Inheritance of Rome: Illuminating the Dark Ages, 400–1000.* New York, 2009.

Wilkes, J. *The Illyrians.* Oxford, 1995.

Wilson, N. *Scholars of Byzantium.* London, 1983.

Witt, R. G. "The *De Tyranno* and Coluccio Salutati's View of Politics and Roman History." *Nuova Rivista Storica* 53 (1969): 434–74.

Woodhouse, C. M. *Gemistos Plethon: The Last of the Hellenes.* Oxford, 1986.

Wurm, H., and E. Gamillscheg. "Bemerkungen zu Laonikos Chalkokondyles." *JÖB* 42 (1992): 213–19.

Wurm, H. "Der Codex Monacensis gr. 307a: Ein Beitrag zur Überlieferungsgeschichte des Laonikos Chalkokondyles." *JÖB* 44 (1994): 455–62.

———. "Die handschriftliche Überlieferung der ΑΠΟΔΕΙΞΕΙΣ
ΙΣΤΟΡΙΩΝ des Laonikos Chalkokondyles." *JÖB* 45 (1995): 223–32.

Yildiz, S. N. "Historiography XIV: The Ottoman Empire." In *Encyclopædia
Iranica*, ed. E. Yarshater. Online resource: www.iranicaonline.org/
articles/historiography-xiv.

Zachariadou, E. A. Ἱστορία καὶ θρύλοι τῶν παλαιῶν σουλτάνων, 1300–1400.
Athens, 1991.

———. Τὸ χρονικὸ τῶν τούρκων Σουλτάνων καὶ τὸ Ἰταλικό του πρότυπο.
Thessalonike, 1960.

———. "The Conquest of Adrianople by the Turks." *StVen* 12 (1970): 211–17.

———, ed. *The Ottoman Emirate (1300–1389)*. Rethymnon, 1993.

Ziff, B., and P. V. Rao, eds. *Borrowed Power: Essays on Cultural Appropriation*.
New Brunswick, 1997.

Zographopoulos, K. *Ο Λαόνικος Χαλκοκονδύλης και οι απόψεις του για τους
Οθωμανούς Τούρκους*. Xanthi, 2002.

Index locorum

The format of this index is the following: DOML book and section number (= Darkó edition volume and page number): page number of this book.

General Index